Give
Me
One
Wish

GIVE
ME
ONE
WISH

Jacquie Gordon

W.W. NORTON & COMPANY
New York · London

The text of this book is composed in Gael, with display type set in Novarese Medium. Composition and manufacturing by The Haddon Craftsmen, Inc. Book design by Charlotte Staub.

First Edition

ISBN 0-393-02518-7

W. W. Norton & Company, Inc.,
  500 Fifth Avenue, New York, N. Y. 10110
W. W. Norton & Company Ltd.,
  37 Great Russell Street, London WC1B 3NU

1 2 3 4 5 6 7 8 9 0

Acknowledgments

★
★ ★

This book contains many scenes I never witnessed. It was written with the patient cooperation and openness of Christine's family of friends. In dozens of interviews and re-interviews, teachers and classmates supplied me with a rich source of information, including the reconstruction of dialogue. With the help of these private recollections and Christine's nine journals, the story is told. Some of the names of people and places have been changed.

Among Christine's classmates at Rye Country Day School, I would like to thank particularly Mark Read, John Egan, Andy Gibson, Claudia Blank, Jamie Allen, Amy Segal, Andrea Homolac, Jim Thomas, Phebe Straus, Jill Oppenheimer, Mark Brummitt, and Donald Gries. They gave their recollections generously, then read the manuscript to make sure I had it right.

Among the teachers, Dr. Lee Pierson, headmaster, Sylvia Hoag, dean of girls, Dick Brown, Karen Brilliant, Glen Robertson, Madame Amsellem, and Priscilla Funck.

Special thanks to Amy Segal, for her creative criticism of three drafts of the manuscript, and to Bruce McDaniel, for describing his many escapades with Christine.

Most of all, thanks to Mark Read, who led me through Book II. He offered editorial suggestions and unfailing encouragement whenever my momentum flagged over three years of writing.

Dr. Celia Ores gave me her records, when Christine's voluminous file at the Columbia Presbyterian Medical Center mysteriously vanished. She gave me a deeper understanding of my daughter's courage as well.

My dear friends Nancy and Joe Conte put me in touch with Angus Cameron, sportsman, writer, and editor nonpareil, who became my mentor. He in turn helped me find Molly Friedrich, my agent, whose care for the book matched his own.

Thanks to Christine's father, Jerry, whose importance in Christine's life was far greater than his role in the story this book tells.

Loving thanks to my family, my extended family, and the friends who read and offered advice, especially my daughter Jenny, who was nine when Christine died and remembered all kinds of things that no one else did because of her special point of view, and my husband Jim, who read the first draft of every chapter and never complained about the many nights I spent writing.

And finally, thanks to Hilary Hinzmann, my editor at Norton, for his encouragement, his sensitivity, and his belief in the story I had to tell.

Contents

For Christine

*Book II is dedicated
to Christine's family
of friends at Rye
Country Day School*

Introduction

Christine died of cystic fibrosis in 1982 when she was twenty-one. The average life expectancy of a child with cystic fibrosis was five years when she was born in 1961. When she died, the average life expectancy was nineteen.

I brought Christine's things home from the hospital the day after she died, and looked fondly at the entries in her last journal. She'd told me it wasn't a journal because she was too tired to write, and she'd titled it,

> *doodles*
> *scribbles*
> *important ideas*
> *and other loose ends.*

She filled only a few of the pages. There were sketches, a self-portrait, some lighthearted notations about fashion and films. Among the drawings I found some quotations from Dostoevsky's short story "What Men Live By." She'd read a volume of great Russian short stories during the summer, sitting on her bed like an Indian, her elbows on her knees, her head resting on her hands, and her black cat, Max, sound asleep, draped around the back of her neck like a limp scarf.

The quotations struck a familiar chord but I didn't understand their significance to Christine. Then I read the story.

In "What Men Live By," a poor Russian cobbler finds a man sitting naked in the snow. The cobbler is himself so poor that he has no winter coat. Yet he shares his clothing with the stranger and takes him home to work as his apprentice. Although the stranger never speaks, because of his fine work the cobbler's business flourishes.

After five years, the stranger seems to err in filling a customer's order. He makes funeral slippers instead of boots. When it's time for the customer to pick up his boots, his valet comes to say that his master has died and now needs funeral slippers. At last the stranger tells the cobbler his story.

The stranger was an angel who had disobeyed God. In punishment, he had been sent to earth to learn three truths. God said to him,

> Go and thou shalt learn three lessons: Thou shalt learn *what is in men,* and *what is not given unto men* and *what men live by.* When thou shalt have learned these three lessons, then return to heaven.

Christine had copied the lessons in her journal.

> *1. "Thou shalt learn what is in Men . . ."*
> *Love is in men.*
> *2. "Thou shalt learn what is not given to men . . ."*
> *that is the foresight to see what they will need to live   to know what is needed for their bodies . . .*
> *3. "Thou shalt learn what people live by . . ."*
> *I have learned that every man lives, not through care of himself, but by love.*

And she had also written the angel's testament:

> *"I was . . . kept alive through love . . .*
> *because there is Love in men."*

The angel in the story had learned what Christine knew and lived by. Her life was a love story.

BOOK I

SKIPPING
STONES

1 ★ Thumps

Andy Gibson was a senior at Rye Country Day School when he first saw her. His locker was across from hers and he noticed how pretty she was when she laughed. From the bits of conversation he overheard, she sounded English, like John Cleese from Monty Python. He asked a friend who the new girl was and learned she was a junior and her name was Christine.

Everyone knew Andy. Tall and lanky, with flirtatious brown eyes and unruly straight brown hair, he had a quick mind and was poised for a seventeen-year-old. He was the starting goalie on the ice hockey team, an important sport at Rye Country Day. This morning, Andy was preoccupied with Monty Python's Flying Circus, the English comedians whose zany antics on the "telly" had captured his imagination.

"Michael," Andy yelled to his best friend across the bustling hall. "Did you see the Mr. Gumby routine on 'Monty Python' last night?"

"It was a riot," Michael yelled back.

On "Monty Python," Mr. Gumby was not the little green rubber man of American television but a dimwitted fellow with a Hitler mustache who wore a white handkerchief rolled up on his head, round glasses, and lederhosen. Mr. Gumby moved stiffly like a horror movie zombie. His lisp turned *r*'s into *w*'s, and made him sound like a cockney Red Skelton.

"Doctuh, Doctuh," Andy called loudly, his mouth hanging open, his eyes unblinking. Several students looked over in Andy's direction and Christine turned around, watching him closely.

"Whad . . . is . . . it?" responded Michael.

"I . . . wanna . . . see . . . a . . . bwain . . . speciawist," Andy bellowed back, pointing to his head dumbly.

Michael wasn't the impromptu actor Andy was and he shrugged cheerfully. Chris smiled and trundled over, in fine Gumby fashion.

"Whad . . . da . . . ya . . . wanna . . . see . . . a . . . bwain . . . speciawist for?" she asked.

Andy turned to her and bellowed, "My bwain hurts!"

Chris reached up and hit him on the top of the head.

"Uhhhh . . . it's . . . got to come out!" She snapped the suspenders of his imaginary lederhosen, turned her back, and waddled across the hall to her locker. Everyone laughed. Then the class bell rang, lockers banged shut, and people started off in all directions. Andy looked over at Chris, who was burrowing into her locker.

What on earth was she wearing? It looked like a paper warm-up suit. She pulled books out of her locker. It couldn't be paper. It must be a new sort of rip-stop nylon. He walked over and touched her jacket sleeve, saying, "Hi, I'm Andy Gibson."

She straightened up, surprised he'd think anyone didn't know him. "I know. I'm Chris Nelson," she said, with her English accent. Andy rubbed the odd white fabric between his fingers.

"Is this paper?"

Chris looked at him boldly. "Why, yes, it is. How did you know?" She was English all right, he thought with delight. She sounded like she'd just walked in off the streets of Mayfair, with wispy blond hair, a fair complexion, and a long English chin.

"It looks like paper, and sounds like paper. Do you always wear paper clothes?"

"Now and then," she said, not taking her eyes off him.

"Uh, what happens when it gets wet?" he asked.

"Oh, nothing much really, it just disintegrates, and I throw it away."

Andy continued deadpan. "Oh, I see. And when it rains, you just run for cover?"

"No, I just wear my best underwear if it looks like rain."

Andy leaned against the lockers, trying not to smile.

"Where'd you get it, London?"

Chris watched his face intently, deciding to be serious.

"No. My mom's in the fashion business. She brought it back from Paris for a new fabric idea."

"I see. Well, I like the idea." He smiled broadly and looked her up and down.

Chris couldn't suppress a laugh and she closed her locker carefully, eyes down, blushing and loving it. "I've got to go to English. Nice meeting you." She walked away.

Andy waited to see if she'd turn around, and she did, smiling before she disappeared around the corner. He suddenly realized her English accent had disappeared.

I had thought of Christine as shy and tongue-tied with boys. Little did I know.

When Christine was born, Jerry and I were living the precarious, ever-hopeful lives of out-of-work actors in New York. Jerry's hero was Jack Kerouac, and my hero was Jerry, and we saw ourselves as part of the beat generation. We'd been married a year and hadn't thought about children when I discovered I was pregnant. We lived in a four-room, $85-a-month walk-up on East 89th Street. In my eighth month, I couldn't manage the five flights of stairs so we went to Ithaca, where my family lived, to wait for the baby.

I'd chosen natural childbirth—initially because I liked the sound of it. And then, too, it was less traumatic for the child and supposedly painless. I went to prenatal classes and learned all the breathing exercises. When my labor began, I was swimming in Buttermilk Falls, and by 10 P.M. I felt cheated—natural childbirth was anything but painless.

The doctor assured me it was always like this. At 9 A.M. on August 14th, Chris entered the world quietly, like a perfect lady, and started breathing on her own without the traditional smack on the bottom or the sudden lusty cry. When she was put in my arms a moment later, I forgot my distress as she quietly explored her face with her tiny fingers. She seemed deliberate—as if she was thinking, This is my mouth, and here is my chin, and this is my nose.

We named her Christine Elizabeth—Elizabeth for my maternal grandmother and Christine because we liked it. We talked happily about the future and wondered out loud to each other, "What will she be when she grows up?" and "Who does she look like?"

Back in New York, I didn't mind the four small rooms of our apartment. I still saw it through the eyes of a struggling artist. We'd come to the city to make it in the theater. A scrapbook bulging with theater and film credits would be the measure of our success—not material things. Surely Jerry would find a part soon.

It was too soon to go back to work, so I burlapped the walls in our bedroom and living room, covering the cracked and bumpy plaster. Then came full-length pinch-pleated drapes for our bedroom. I was busy dragging thirty feet of half-sewn yellow burlap drapes around the apartment the first time Christine smiled at me. Her little bare feet were kicking the air like an upside-down ladybug, when she looked right at me and smiled. She was six weeks old. Even though I had been with her every day, that smile of recognition was our first real contact.

When you drag yellow burlap around your "pad" day in and day out, everything glows with mustard yellow fuzz. I didn't vacuum until I'd finished the drapes. The fuzz looked like the last light of summer lingering, and I wrote in it with my finger, "I love Christine."

Before long Chris was sitting in her high chair like a hungry little bird, mouth open, eager for the next spoonful. She was always hungry. I was too inexperienced to know that her wonderful appetite was not normal. Mothers feel secure when they see their children eat, and that's how I felt.

Chris had recurring diarrhea. I'd refer to Dr. Spock's book, *Baby and Child Care,* and adjust her diet. The diarrhea would clear up for a while, then return. I wondered about it, but our doctor saw no cause for alarm. Surely she'd outgrow it soon.

Some children go through the "terrible twos," as they say, but for Chris it was the "wonderful twos." She never threw fits. If she was upset, her mouth would turn slowly down and stay that way,

like a tiny crescent moon that had fallen over. That little pout
before she cried, that one-minute warning as she tried to fight
back the tears, won my heart everytime—and I would run to hug
her.

Just as adorable was her little smile when she was happy. I
called her Pilot Small. He was the little person in a children's book
by Lois Lenski who always had a secret smile, just like Christine's,
a comma resting on its side.

I took care of her during the day while Jerry looked for theater
work and waited on tables. When I went back to work, singing at
the Gaslight Club, he stayed home nights. We lived in shifts, not
seeing much of each other, and as time went on tension and
silence grew between us.

We were both learning that talent was not enough. With a
child to raise, Jack Kerouac's beat life-style lost its appeal for me.
I turned from the theater to more everyday concerns. Jerry was
not so willing to give up his dream. As his acting prospects failed
to improve, he withdrew into himself. At heart he remained a
free spirit who followed his own rules, not society's. He seemed
content to carry on catch-as-catch-can with the occasional performing job. Now that I was a mother, I needed the security of
a more ordered life, and I too withdrew. I wasn't the free spirit
I had tried to be for him, but a very middle-class young woman,
though I did have a highly developed streak of rebellion. We
decided to separate for a while. Christine and I moved into a large
apartment on MacDougal and Eighth streets in Greenwich Village with two other girls who were separated, each with a child
near Christine's age.

Then Christine's diarrhea worsened. She began to cry with
pain from stomachaches and her belly was always bloated, like a
soccerball.

After Thanksgiving, when she was two and a half, Christine
had a series of tests and was diagnosed as a celiac child. Celiac
disease is an intolerance of gluten that interferes with digestion.
The children eat and eat but they are starving and have chronic
diarrhea. They usually improve after a few years and then outgrow it.

Chris went on a strict gluten-free diet of rice, rice cereals, milk, and bananas. She became quiet and watchful at meals. She drew her bowl of cereal and her glass of milk across the table close to her chest, extending her little arms in a circle around her meal. Everything she loved to eat had been taken away for reasons she couldn't understand. It frightened her. What else might disappear: the rest of her food, her toys, me.

I tried not to make a fuss about meals. I reassured her many times that she had to eat these special things only because of her stomachaches. After several weeks, she stopped trying to protect her food. She guarded her toys fiercely for a while longer, but I hoped she'd continue to adjust when she saw that nothing else was being taken away. Every day we went to Washington Square Park where she played in the big fountain—filling a paper cup, over and over, and offering a drink of water to strangers. Washington Square Park was a safe, happy place in 1963. A block away, Bob Dylan and Joan Baez were singing at Gerde's Folk City and the Bitter End Cafe, and a new generation was finding its voice. There were always young people on the benches or the grass, singing along to guitars, recorders, and autoharps. Chris ventured into the sandbox and learned to share her toys again.

That spring, the World's Fair was under construction in Flushing Meadows. Bil Baird had developed a revolving puppet show on four stages for the Chrysler exhibit, with puppets made out of car parts. He hired Jerry, who'd been working at his puppet theater in the village, and I went to work for him too, animating carburetors, pistons, nuts and bolts.

Jerry and I reconciled and rented a house near the fairgrounds on Queens Boulevard. We still loved each other and wanted to save the marriage if we could. We didn't fit in blue-collar Elmhurst, me with my silver rings and Indian wedding boots and Jerry with his guitar and his beard, but we focused on our work, our marriage, and Christine and didn't think about it. If we had, we wouldn't have changed.

Chris always had a cold, but so did many youngsters in the neighborhood. Her persistent cough seemed part of the colds and didn't worry me. But her stomachaches weren't getting better. The doctor was baffled.

I went to visit my family in the winter of 1965, before the second year of the World's Fair. My mother invited an English professor from Ithaca College, Mr. Taylor for dinner. Chris had supper at the table with us and Mr. Taylor noticed that she didn't eat what we did. I explained Christine was allergic to gluten.

"Oh, is it celiac?" Mr. Taylor asked. His knowledge surprised me. Most people had never heard of it.

While my mother and Mr. Taylor sat over a cup of tea, I went upstairs with Chris to run her bath. Her stomach was tied up in knots again.

"Oh, Mommy," she said, "I feel sick." She had diarrhea and sat on the toilet a long time, bent over in discomfort. When Chris had this diarrhea, it smelled sickly sweet and pungent like rotting oranges.

Mr. Taylor had young children and he'd found Chris very sweet. He came upstairs to say good-night to her before she got in the tub. Later, my mother and I were doing the dishes and she said, "Dear, you know how we've been talking about Christine's diarrhea, the smell of oranges?"

"Yes, she has it again."

"Well, I know. Mr. Taylor was very quiet after he said good-night to Chris. He sat down and I poured him some more tea, but he didn't drink any. Then he said he was very concerned about Christine."

"What?"

"He said his son had the same problems, and they thought he had celiac disease, just the way Chris does. But shortly after, they were told he had cystic fibrosis."

I stopped rinsing plates and looked at my mother. So that was how he'd heard of celiac.

"What's cystic fibrosis?"

"It's a lung disease, I think—inherited."

"But who in our family had it?"

"No one that I know."

I didn't say any more. At first I was angry with my mother. She always noticed everything. How could she even suggest Chris had such a problem? But I felt a terrible closing feeling, like I was trapped in a dark room with something fearful that I couldn't see. I kept thinking about the celiac. Mr. Taylor wouldn't have dared question Chris's diagnosis unless he had good reason. He was too polite. His son's being diagnosed as a celiac child, like Chris, scared me. Celiac itself was not common. And, so far, the special diet hadn't helped much.

The next afternoon, I went to the library at Cornell. Two hours later, I found three damning sentences in an encyclopedia. Cystic fibrosis was an inherited childhood disease of the exocrine glands (I didn't know what those were). It had been discovered in 1938. It was fatal.

Sitting on the floor in the stacks, I did some quick figuring. If the disease was discovered in 1938, how would my mother know if anyone in her family or Daddy's family had ever had it? They grew up in the 1920s. The symptoms would never have been diagnosed as cystic fibrosis. The encyclopedia said the average life expectancy was five years. A knot formed in my stomach that didn't leave for days.

Back in New York, I asked our pediatrician about cystic fibrosis.

"I don't think so," she said, "but it's something to consider. We could have a sweat test done at New York Hospital—to rule it out."

"What's a sweat test?"

"Children with cystic fibrosis lose too much salt in their sweat. It's the way we diagnose it."

"I thought it was a lung disease."

"Not exactly. It starts with the exocrine glands, in the pancreas, which produce mucus and sweat. A genetic flaw makes the glands produce a thick mucus, which clogs up the lungs and the digestive processes. The salt in the sweat is the easiest thing to measure and it's reliable."

"Is that why she might have diarrhea, because of the clogged-up digestion?" It certainly didn't sound fatal.

"It's possible." The doctor made an appointment for the sweat test at New York Hospital and readjusted Christine's diet, eliminating all fat: no more butter, cheese, bacon, or chocolate. But she added bread.

When Chris had two pieces of toast and jam without butter the next morning she piped up happily, "Mommy, I'm not allergic to bread anymore?"

"We're not sure, but we're going to try eating it again. We'll see what happens."

Looking back over that year is like trying to peer through a dark, densely woven shroud. The first sweat test settled nothing. I wrote my mother:

Jan 11th 1965

Dear Mom,

Much to my disgust, Christine has to have the test repeated. Blast! They didn't get enough sweat. Inexcusable to me. They must know how much they need. The doctor apologized profusely. Poor Christine. January 29th is the next and we hope the last.

I had to go to unemployment, but Jerry said they put two electrodes on the inside of her forearm, taped underneath a rubber patch about three inches square. The electrodes are charged with electricity and get hot, and make that patch of her arm sweat for six minutes. She cried continuously for the whole six minutes. The nurse said from discomfort and fear. But I've learned already about the euphemisms they use when it comes to pain. When a doctor says to you, "This isn't going to hurt a bit," what he means is "This is going to hurt." When they say "You may feel some discomfort," they mean you're going to feel a hell of a lot of pain.

They were burning her arm with electricity I think, because there are now two scabs where the electrodes were. Six minutes can be a long time.

Jerry and I are beside ourselves and we both feel as if time has been suspended till we know. And of course, I'm a wreck. But at least I've found a good nursery school for Christine for $10.00 a week.

love
jacquie

The second test didn't work either and so a third test was done. The doctor told us the third test was negative. I wrote my mother:

Feb 20th, 1965

Dear Mom,

Little news *except* Christine does *not* have cystic fibrosis. Siggggghhhhhh. . . . our prayers were answered.

Nessie [my sister] is working on Puppets too, and will probably work for Bil Baird for the second season of the Fair. All is well as can be, for the first time in a long time.

love,
jacquie

After the negative test, however, Christine still had digestive problems. How many times she would say to me in the middle of some activity, "Mommy, I don't feel very good." We'd stop what we were doing until her awful stomachache went away. We'd been adding different foods to her diet to see how she'd tolerate them, and I thought maybe that was the problem.

But she should have outgrown her susceptibility to colds by now and they were getting worse—not better. She caught the flu that winter and she was much sicker than I thought she should be. Her nights were terrible and frightening. She exploded awake into coughing spasms, choking and crying out, "Mommy, Mommy!" as I ran into her room. I'd find her sobbing and gasping for air, her fragile little shoulders wracked and shaking with the struggle. Three times her cough was so violent and reached so deep that she threw up her supper. I'd pick her up, wet, shivering, and miserable, and put her on my lap while I changed her into warm things. Her breath would tremble and catch as the agony of the cough subsided. Then I'd curl up in the canvas batwing chair with her. She'd fall back to sleep but cough all night, and I'd lie there with terror in my heart. She woke in the morning the same way, one breath and then a violent coughing spasm.

I was adamant with the doctor that this flu should not just "run its course." The doctor put her on antibiotics and cough syrup with codeine. Christine recovered dramatically and her cough disappeared for a couple of months, as if she'd never been sick. She seemed so well, I forgot about cystic fibrosis. Jerry and I thought the worst was past. She was four.

Then she caught the flu again, and this developed into bronchitis and then into bacterial pneumonia. She was admitted to Babies Hospital at Columbia Presbyterian and put on a course of antibiotics again. She responded quickly, but I was fed up. I hadn't lost confidence in my pediatrician; her credentials were impeccable. But maybe she was overlooking something.

"Something's not right," I said carefully. "Are you sure the last sweat test was negative? They made a mistake on the first two, maybe they made a mistake on the third."

The doctor thought it unlikely, but worth looking into. She called me the next day, and said quietly that the test had read positive-negative. In light of Christine's failure to thrive, we should do another one. So like some recurring nightmare, we went through it all again. And then again. Christine was four and a half.

March 25th, 1966

Dear Mom,

Here begineth the saddest letter I shall ever write. The fifth test was positive. Christine has cystic fibrosis.

Jerry and I can't believe it. He is almost catatonic and says her life is over. I have this carved out feeling in my middle, like now the wind could blow right through me. I'm not solid anymore. And Christine is innocent and knows nothing.

What can I do? Nothing's changed. The sun goes down as always, and CBS News comes on at 6 o'clock. The grass is growing too tall to cut in the backyard and cars pass and truck brakes screech on Queens Boulevard. What's different? Nothing, but nothing is the same either.

What I'm holding on to is that Christine's life is *not* over and I'm not ready to let her be a "sick" child, even though she is. She looks normal, sounds normal. She's not deformed, not crippled, not blind. There's just this invisible thing inside her and the doctors don't know how fast it will do its terrible work . . . this microscopic abnormality in her genes that makes the mucus in her body thick instead of thin like the rest of us, and it's going to kill her. Such a little thing. Why can't they fix it?

My instinct is to go on as if nothing's happened and raise her like a normal child; I mean a healthy one. I mustn't make her different, or she'll lose her place. I have to hold it open for her and let her live a real life. That's what I'll fight for. If I try to make things special for her, she'll notice she's different and so will others and no one will understand because she doesn't look sick. It's going to be hard.

But, Mom, in quiet moments when I have time to think, I'll ask—Why Chris, dear God, why Chris? and I'll never accept it and I know there'll never be any answers.

love,
jacquie

There was one more test. This one would tell if mucus was blocking the digestive enzymes produced by the pancreas. I grilled the doctor: How long would it take, and what was going to happen? Did it hurt? I didn't want any surprises.

It wouldn't hurt Chris, I was told, but it would frighten her. A tube is put down the esophagus, through the stomach, into the small intestine and duodenum. Bile is drawn out to be analyzed. It sounded easy but there was a problem—a small flap at the stomach exit that opens like a trap door, allowing food to pass out of the stomach. If there is a foreign substance in the stomach or if a patient is nervous or anxious, the flap locks shut. The doctor said this always happened, because the tube is a foreign object and the children are anxious. The test took hours because they had to wait for the stomach to relax so the tubing could get through.

I decided to describe the process to Chris even though she was only four and a half. Using simple words, maybe I could relieve the tension and fear that closed the little flap. If it worked, the test would be over sooner. I waited till the morning of the test.

"Christine, we're going back to the hospital for a test today." There was fear in her eyes. "It's for your stomachaches. It doesn't hurt." I drew a picture. "This is your stomach. You have tubes going down your throat: one where you breathe, and one where you swallow. In your stomach is some yellow liquid, bright as sunshine. The doctors have to get some out so they can see if it's giving you stomachaches.

"The doctor's tube will go down your throat into your stomach, not down your breathing tube—so it won't choke you. But it will feel icky and you may want to cough it out. But if you relax your throat and think as hard as you can, the tube will lie there and not bother you." She looked down at my drawing. "Do you know what I mean by relaxed?"

"I don't know."

"Well, you see how my hand is hanging floppy?" I let my hand go limp. "That's relaxed. When I clench it, like this, it's *not* relaxed. People can relax their stomachs by thinking about it. If you can too, the test will be over quickly."

When we got to the hospital, she wanted me to stay by her side and hold her hand. The nurse gave me a footstool, so my head just reached up to hers on the table.

"Mommy, can I lie on my side so I can look at you?" she asked.

The nurse said kindly, "If you're more comfortable, I don't see why not."

So Christine lay on her side, and held my hand. They began inserting the tube, pushing it gently down. She watched me with quiet dark eyes.

"Let's pretend it's a rainy day," I said. "The doctors are looking for sunshine and you've got it." She lay quietly with her jaw slack as she thought about going limp. Her gag reflex spasmed slightly a couple of times, but that was all. I told her to look for the bright yellow liquid in the tube and in about twenty minutes we saw it coming down into a beaker.

Christine smiled and so did I. As soon as they had enough, they drew out the tube, and the nurse said, "That was terrific." She looked at her watch. "It's a record. It wasn't even half an hour."

I hugged Christine proudly. She had done it.

The test result showed that Christine's digestive enzymes were being blocked by the thick mucus. She began to take an artificial enzyme called Cotazyme with every meal, and this ended her stomachaches.

Four months later, Jerry and I separated again, this time for good. There was too wide a gulf between my need for stability and order for Christine, and Jerry's anarchic approach to life. We went to a lawyer together and spent an afternoon drawing up an agreement. We had no animosity. I waived alimony, and child support was set at $15 a week. The figure seems ludicrous today, but we had no money and Jerry wasn't working now that the World's Fair was over. What we did do was write an escalation clause based on his earnings, rather than a cost-of-living increase. The lawyer knew that an actor's fortunes might change suddenly.

The beat generation had disappeared and the hippies had moved in. Timothy Leary was telling his followers to "turn on, tune in, and drop out." Bob Dylan went electric and the Beatles wrote a song called "Lucy in the Sky with Diamonds"—

supposedly about LSD. Jerry took his guitars and went to San Francisco to live in Haight-Ashbury with the hippies and the flower children. I lost track of him, but I didn't tell Christine.

Maybe Jerry took it harder when we learned about her illness. I can't imagine him feeling any bleaker than I did, but I was always a fighter and not afraid of anything life presented. Perhaps I was better equipped to raise Christine.

Six months after the final diagnosis, I consulted Dr. Agnes Wilson, who specialized in cystic fibrosis at the Columbia Presbyterian Medical Center. She arranged for us to go to the Vanderbilt Clinic, where for the next seven years Chris would be treated by many different physicians. We could not afford private care. Our first experience at the clinic was learning how to do postural drainage. Chris and I were taught by a young physical therapist named Arlene Olson, who was so cheerful you would have thought she was showing us how to make a chocolate cake. What we learned was nothing so nice.

Since the real danger in cystic fibrosis comes from the thick mucus, an attempt is made to keep the lungs clear. It's a losing battle, of course—you can't. But if you don't at least try, the child will die sooner. So postural drainage was developed to pound out the thick secretions. We called it "thumps."

First the child inhales a dispersant agent called Mucomyst through an oxygen mask to loosen and moisten the mucus in the lungs. The child then lies tilted downward, on a stack of pillows. Using carefully cupped, firm hands, the therapist or parent pounds on different parts of the child's chest, shoulders, sides, and back in a rapid alternating motion, like beating a drum. Each lung has nine lobes and each lobe must be pounded. After two minutes of firm pounding, the therapist says, "Breathe," and the child expels a long slow breath, while the therapist vibrates his hands on the child's chest, pressing down hard on the area that has just been pounded. When each lobe has been thumped and vibrated, the child sits up, coughs as hard as possible to bring up secretions, and spits them into a cup.

After the thumping and coughing of secretions, a second aerosol mask is done with antibiotics. The theory is that, inhaled directly after drainage, the antibiotics may reach newly cleared areas in the lungs and suppress infections that cause pneumonias.

If it seems endless, mask, thumps, mask again, it is. The whole process takes an hour and is repeated two, three, or four times a day, forever. All of the treatments of cystic fibrosis take aim at the same deadly enemy—lung infections. That is why the children die. Christine and I hated the whole process of thumps, but we had no choice. Thumps would keep her alive.

That same year, Mr. Taylor's son died. He was seven years old.

2 · Into the Circle

The next two years were hard. Depressed and immobilized, I lived alone with Christine in Elmhurst. Suppressing anger had always been easy for me when I was growing up, but now I buried it. I was afraid of anger, afraid it would poison me, and Christine. I didn't know yet that anger can make you strong if you learn how to use it.

At first I drew strength from my family. My father lived in Manhattan and was encouraging me to start my own dress business. My sisters, Roberta, Francie, and Vanessa, came down from Ithaca to visit and we pored over the lyrics of every new Beatles song, analyzing every line. I often drove up to Ithaca with Christine, horrifying my mother when I insisted the best way to make the long drive toward Cornell was to leave at 10 P.M. and drive through the night, making one stop at the Roscoe Diner, a famous truckstop an hour outside Ithaca.

"Don't you ever consider doing something the way other people do, dear?" she asked. She should have known better. One magical night in the deep of winter, I set off when heavy snow was forecast. There were chains and a shovel in the trunk, new batteries in my flashlight, hot cider in a thermos for Chris. I took extra blankets and sandwiches, my AAA card, and drove north. The first flakes fell before we crossed the Tappan Zee Bridge.

The snowstorm turned into a blizzard but nothing was going to stop us. At about two o'clock, I pulled over, got the chains out, then slid in the snow under the back wheels of my Valiant. It took half an hour of frozen fingers to put the chains on. Back on the road, Chris was too excited to sleep and knelt next to me looking out the window at the snow piling deeper and deeper on the roadside. We watched the headlights pierce the dense flurries of white before us and we saw fewer and fewer cars. We sang songs we knew when I found a stretch of smooth driving and then we made up songs.

I knew I was pushing the limit that night, but it was an adventure and we felt very brave together. When we pulled into my mother's unplowed driveway at 4:30 in the morning, I let out a long YAAYY and Christine laughed and cheered with me.

When Christine started nursery school, I didn't connect with other mothers and she didn't have anyone to play with at home. But Christine had enormous creative energy. Because she was lonely she invented two imaginary friends, Talky and Star. She enacted wonderful make-believe adventures, playing all the roles with distinctive voices. When I heard her telling Talky and Star about the yellow brick road, I made her a blue plaid pinafore and she called it her Dorothy dress. She wore it for weeks and went to Oz with Talky and Star. She loved to dress up.

At night, I played the guitar and sang folk songs for her, sitting on her bed till she fell asleep. The songs I chose were not the lowdown blues from the thirties that I'd sung at the Gaslight, like "Why Don't You Do Right," and "You Gotta See Your Mama Every Night." I sang folk songs with interesting minor chord progressions, like the ones Joan Baez sang. I wondered why Christine liked these songs from Appalachia and the West and England, songs like "Silver Dagger," "Lily of the West," "Barbara Allen," and "Mary Hamilton"—all songs of lost love, murder, misery, and mayhem. Maybe it was the comfort of my voice singing her to sleep.

Our life was offbeat, but we were happy with each other. For the most part cystic fibrosis remained in the background.

When Chris was five, I noticed that she glanced at me everytime she coughed. If I ran over or reacted at all, her cough would become a way of getting my attention and like any child she'd use it. Her cough had to be as natural as a hiccup or we were in trouble. It was easy in those early days to train myself not to react unless it was serious, to use my peripheral vision, and within a few weeks her quick looks at me disappeared.

Later I learned a more important reason not to react than just my worry about spoiling her. I read in Dr. Spock's *Baby and Child Care* that when I left her with a sitter to go to work, and she cried and clung to me as if she'd never see me again, I should give her a happy hug and go out the door cheerfully like nothing was wrong. Then she'd get over it. If I acted worried and torn and took too long, she'd think, I don't want my mother to leave me, and I can see she doesn't want to leave me either. There must be something terrible that could happen. And then she'd really be afraid. It was the same with her cough. If I let her see my concern, she'd think, Mommy is worried about my cough—it must be something terrible. To treat her cough with nonchalance would help her grow into a fearless, well-adjusted child. In both cases, Dr. Spock was right.

That summer, as the hippie revolution graced the covers of establishment magazines, Christine and I discovered the beauty of Robert Moses State Park and the pristine fields of Jones Beach. Too grown up to be a flower child, still I empathized and wore the emblems of the movement: little granny glasses like John Lennon's, handcrafted jewelry, and rolled-thin bandannas tied round my hair. I enjoyed the stares, both approving and disapproving, as our old Valiant joined the cars streaming into Jones Beach. My unemployment had run out; for a while we could live on the money I'd saved from the World's Fair. I began making dress samples for my first line, sewing in the attic after Christine fell asleep.

In 1967, when she was six, it was time for her to start first grade. Still living in the Elmhurst house, now we shared it with a silent but gentle nineteen-year-old French girl named Marie Jean who was working for me as an au pair. She lived with us for a year and I don't think I ever saw her use the bathroom or leave a sign of herself anywhere, except for the beautiful things she knitted for Christine.

Somehow, the day of registration for first grade passed unnoticed. School began, but Chris couldn't go because she wasn't registered. The next day, I took her to the doctor for a physical and filled out health and registration forms at the Board of Education. She started school on the third day. I was thoroughly disgusted with myself for being so careless. Offbeat was okay—irresponsible was not.

But all seemed to go well and she said she liked it, though not with much enthusiasm. One morning in the middle of the third week, as I was braiding her hair into wispy little pigtails, she said, "Mommy, I don't want to go to school today."

"Everybody has to go to school, Chris. Isn't it fun?"

She didn't say anything for a second and then said, "I guess so."

"Are you wishing you'd made friends already?" She shrugged and didn't answer. It wasn't like her.

"You'll make friends soon, Chris, it just takes a little time."

The next morning she said the same thing. She didn't want to go to school. I paused and sat on her bed. Maybe there was some problem she couldn't articulate. I leaned over and tickled her cheek with the end of her pigtail.

"How would you like it if I took you to school this morning? If we get there early, I can meet your teacher." She looked relieved.

We weren't early. When we walked up to the school, children were already yelling and clattering in the playground. We went inside and stopped at the door to her empty classroom. I leaned in to look at the arrangement of little desks running from the teacher's desk to the end of the room, around, and back in a large, upside-down horseshoe.

"Which is your desk, Chris?"

She pointed to the back of the room. At the far wall, one forlorn desk sat outside the horseshoe.

"Your desk is the one all by itself?"

She looked up at me, eyes waiting. A cold fury uncoiled inside me. Her desk was outside the circle. I knelt down to her.

"Oh Christine, no wonder you don't like school. I wouldn't either. What's wrong with your teacher? Come on. We're going to find her. She'd better change it today."

Chris was quiet and frightened but as I took her hand she said, "I think she's on the playground."

"C'mon." I was proud of her for not shrinking back as we hurried down the hall toward the sound of the children. I thought I was going to cry but then my anger pushed past the tears and I took a deep breath, keeping control. I didn't want to make things worse. I pushed the door hard out to the blacktop playground and paused, bending down.

"Do you see her?"

Chris nodded and said, "She's standing over there."

An older woman, ready to retire, with a bored face. Not even lipstick brightened her look. How could she be a first-grade teacher? A child's first teacher. Poor Chris. I walked over, hand in hand with Christine.

"Are you Christine's teacher?" She turned to say yes, and my fury returned.

"I'm Christine's mother. How dare you isolate one child from all the others the way you have Christine—with her desk separate." She stiffened. "Have you lost your senses? I've never seen such a thing." She opened her mouth to protest but I wasn't finished. "I want it changed today."

Her face flushed and she said, "Well, I'm sorry, but that's just the way it is. I had thirty-one kids in this class . . . already too many." I shuddered. She went on, "And then they told me there was one more coming. Well, there's no room for one more and I can't move the desks."

"Are they bolted to the floor?" I snapped.

"They won't fit any other way. I've—" I interrupted her.

"You listen to me. It's not Christine's fault if you have to teach thirty-two children. I'll have you before the school principal before you know it and I'll have you *and* the principal before the Board of Education tomorrow morning if you don't do something right away!" I don't know what I expected, but she just stared at me, as if nothing could reach me. I was trembling. If I kept pushing, her position would harden, but holding Christine's hand tightly and trusting my instincts, I hissed my last words so she wouldn't miss one. "Move . . . her . . . desk . . . today."

I turned abruptly, and stormed back into the school with Chris. This was no time to cry. I stopped at the bottom of a staircase and held on to the bannister, breathing hard, trying to calm down. But I kept seeing Chris, alone all day, pushed out, separate. It was going to be hard enough for her to be like the other kids. This was my fault. I had to calm down. I looked at Christine and smoothed her hair. Touching her made me feel better. "Are you okay?" I asked.

Another little nod.

"Good. Come on, I'm going to talk to the principal now and I have to try not to be so mad this time. It's not his fault."

In the office, I asked for the principal and got his assistant. I introduced myself and explained the situation. He made no attempt to excuse the teacher, or condemn her or agree with me.

"I'll look into it today and see what can be done."

"I must ask you to do better than that and assure me that the desk will be in place by the beginning of school tomorrow." Christine's eyes hadn't left the assistant's face.

"Very well, Mrs. Nelson, but I can't promise." He wasn't rude but he wasn't very nice.

"There's something else."

"Yes?"

"I was quite angry with Christine's teacher on the playground just now. How can I be sure that she won't take it out on Christine?" I felt Chris look up at me. He lifted his eyebrows.

"She is an experienced teacher and would *never* do such a thing."

"I hope you're right." I was glad I raised it just the same.

Christine and I walked home slowly. I felt awful. I could never make it up to her. We spent the afternoon carving pumpkins with Marie Jean and that cheered us up a little. The next day, her desk was in with all the others. But the children picked up the teacher's feelings and never really befriended her. In January, with the financial help of my best friends Nancy and Joe, Christine was accepted at a small private school in Long Island City. Then we moved to Jackson Heights.

In second grade, Chris told me one day, "Mommy, I don't like to cough in front of people. They don't like it."

"But your cough isn't contagious, dear."

"But how do they know?" She had a point.

"Well, I guess they don't. That's why you have to remember to cover your mouth and turn your head away."

Instead she taught herself not to cough in public. There were times when she couldn't help it, but, in general, she suppressed her cough and made the world think she was perfectly healthy.

3 · The Mist Tent

In 1968, when she was seven, the Vanderbilt Clinic said that Christine should start sleeping in a mist tent. The moisture would help keep viscous secretions in her lungs from getting stuck in the tiny passageways and solidifying.

It made sense. Doing Christine's thumps was like pounding ketchup out of a bottle. My father had shown me as a youngster that when ketchup was stuck in the bottom of the bottle, adding a tiny drop of water and shaking would loosen the ketchup and let it out. Maybe the mist tent would work on the same principle.

We'd never seen a mist tent, so the staff showed us one in Babies Hospital. There was no mist, since the front flap of the tent had been rolled up out of the way and the bed was empty. It looked awful just the same, a plastic prison, no place for a child to rest.

On an icy January morning, my breath making its own mist, I drove to the Inhalational Equipment Company on Second Avenue and 92nd Street. I drove back with the equipment and three pages of instructions. That afternoon, while Chris was at school, I set up the tent.

It took an hour to assemble the frame, then fit it under Chris's mattress, up behind and back over the bed, like a giant paper clip folded in half. When I draped the clear plastic over the frame, a cube-shaped tent was formed, just like the one in the hospital. I ran white corrugated tubing from the blue plastic water container into an opening at the top of the tent. An electric pump drove propylene glycol and water through the blue container, converting the water into a fine mist. When I dropped the front flap and turned on the pump, mist hissed into the tent. Instantly I hated it all. I left the room with the pump humming, the mist hissing.

An hour later, the tent had filled with mist so thick and white it would enshroud Christine. Her room would look like a hospital room: every night she'd be stuck in there alone. I put my arm through the flaps for a minute, feeling the dampness settle on my skin and then I threw the front flap up over the top.

The mist flooded into the room and vanished. I turned off the pump, relieved to hear the quiet.

When Christine came home from school, she stopped at the door to her room and looked at the mist tent. Her face still, her eyes unblinking, she said, "Oh, Mommy, do I have to sleep in there?"

She didn't look up at me. She knew the answer and I said quietly, "I think so, Christine."

She turned toward me and buried her head in my stomach. I hugged her and said lamely, "Maybe it won't be so bad." Who was I kidding? It was bad.

That night she ran away.

All week we'd had clear cold nights, the kind that make you thankful for a cozy warm kitchen. I put supper on the table and called Christine. There was no answer, so I walked to her room and found the TV on. I looked around the apartment and out in the hall, puzzled, calling her. Nothing. Was she hiding? I checked all the closets. No Christine.

Could she have gone downstairs to her friend Heather's without asking? She never had, but I called. She wasn't there. I went to the front door. The kneehole desk in my entrance hall was clear except for some unopened mail. I was terrible about opening the mail. I pulled open the center drawer and there was a folded piece of paper. I knew right away it was a note from Chris.

Dear Mommy,
    I don't like the tent. I don't want to sleep in it. I am running away. I have taken the mony in my piggy bank. I'm not mad at you. I love you.

                                    OO XX Christine

My God, she's so little, I thought. It's cold out and pitch dark. I could feel my heart speeding up. Her coat was gone. I grabbed mine and ran out of the house.

The cold bit my lungs and my breath puffed out white like a steam engine. Which way would she go? Jackson Heights was a grid, with predictable blocks. I always parked the car on the side street to the left. She knew that block, that's how she'd go. I started running, turning left and calling for Christine. Apartment lights were on everywhere, and the streets were empty. Everyone was inside at supper. There were no stores for three blocks. I hurried along not even noticing my panic; it felt natural. I passed a lady and was suddenly embarrassed. I stopped calling for Christine while she went by. Then I thought, What am I doing! So what if this woman wonders why I'm running and calling—who cares what she thinks? Maybe she's seen Chris. I ran back to her.

"Excuse me, ma'am, did you see a little blond girl walking alone?"

The woman looked surprised and shook her head no.

I fled back down the block and at the end I turned left again. No one. I kept running. How long had she been gone? At the end of the block, I looked in all directions: green lights down one block, red lights down another, car lights, but no little girl anywhere.

I turned left again, back to our street. I should call the police and then go out looking myself in the car. This was too slow. But there, at the corner under a streetlight, about to turn onto our block, there was Christine. I stopped myself from calling out, and raced after her on my toes. What if she was startled and ran into the street?

I was about thirty feet away when she heard my steps and turned around. I called "Chris!" and ran to pick her up and hug her. She was subdued, not crying. She couldn't hug me back because I had clasped her arms to her sides when I picked her up. I buried my face in her little shoulder and set her down.

She looked up at me now and burst into tears.

"Oh Mommy, I'm sorry, I'm really sorry. I was coming back. It's so dark, and I was so scared. Oh, I'm sorry." The words choked out between sobs. Her nose was running and her face was wet with tears, she must have been holding in the whole time. Nothing I could do would make the tent disappear. I crouched down to her level.

"I don't blame you for being scared, Christine. It's dark and cold and lonely out here." Home would seem wonderful after this. "I can't believe you went out alone."

I stopped for a minute and hugged her again. "Were you really on the way home?" She nodded and I took her hand. We walked into the lobby, I didn't want to rush either of us.

"Whew, I'm really out of breath," I said. "Let's sit down here for a minute, okay?"

We sat on the three low steps that led to the elevator. I put my arm around her and held her close, waiting for my heart to slow down. I was beginning to understand that her life was going to be burdened with troubles unlike anything I'd known, and there would be no sharing. The things I had to do to help her stay alive would seem more like things to punish her. What if she began to hate me for them? Already she was grumpy when I had to do her thumps twice a day. Although I wasn't grumpy back, at least not on the surface, sometimes I thought she knew how grumpy I felt inside.

As we sat together quietly, Chris asked, "Mommy, could we wait till next week? I don't like it."

"I don't either, Chris. I think a week's too much, but we can certainly wait a day or two. Then we'll try it. The doctor said it would be good for your coughing in the morning, and that once you got used to it you'd be glad. If all the secretions stay moist, they won't choke you in the morning and we'll be able to get more stuff out when we do thumps." She stared ahead. "If it's really awful, I'll call the doctor and tell her we want to stop."

She sat very still. She'd never been a complainer, but her eyes were tired and sad. I took off her ski jacket gently and balled it up in my arm, careful not to let the coins fall out of the pocket. One of her favorite books, *B is for Betsy,* had already slipped out onto the floor.

There had to be a way to make this a little better. I knew she could distract herself. She'd managed to have fun times in the hospital when she had pneumonia. I had one idea, and I didn't care if Dr. Spock would approve or not. I'd been sleeping in a single bed, giving her the big bedroom and the bed that had been her father's and mine, so she could play with her friends and have overnights when she was a little older.

"Christine, would it help if I slept in the big bed with you? There's not room for me in the tent, but I could be right next to you and I could hold your hand under the edge of the tent."

She looked up quickly, hardly believing her ears. "But Mommy, children sleep in *their* beds, and grown-ups sleep in *theirs.*"

"I know I always say that, Chris, but this is special. Besides, I've always loved that great big bed."

"Oh, that would be so much better."

"Good, then that's what we'll do, starting tomorrow. Let's go eat. I'm hungry." We went back up to our apartment, and that's how we managed to accept the mist tent. I slept next to her the following night and she held my hand under the plastic for about twenty minutes after the hissing started. Then she let go and curled up on her side in the thickening mist. After a week or two, she didn't hold my hand anymore.

We never got used to it, not one bit. She hated the damn thing and so did I. Instead of cozy mornings, warm and snug in her bed, she woke up clammy and shivering, her hair matted to her cheeks and neck. We washed her hair a lot because the propylene glycol was sticky and made her hair stringy.

If she woke up in the middle of the night, which she often did when her cough was bad, she couldn't go back to sleep until we dried her off, put warm pajamas on her, and cleared out the mist. Then we'd drop the front flap and start all over. Once in a while, I'd say, "Oh, it's almost morning, let's just forget it," and she'd get a little taste of how it had been before.

Four years later, mist tents were discontinued. Doctors decided the psychological and emotional damage from sleeping in the tent canceled out the benefits. I could have told them after the first night, it wasn't worth it.

When Christine was eight, I'd been designing dresses for my new business for two years. With a friend from the World's Fair and the name of Frock by Jacques, we'd begun. From a loft on 37th Street—our tiny, new dress firm sold to better dress departments in Bloomingdale's, Saks, Bendel's, Franklin Simon, and I. Miller's Galleria.

Like many small ready-to-wear businesses we were under-capitalized. That's putting it mildly. My father started us off with a $5000 loan. Our credit was so limited, we had to pay for fabric before it was delivered, and we had to pay the contractors who made our dresses *on* delivery. At the end of each month, we'd sweat it out, hoping none of the stores would be late paying us, so we could make our loft rent and our payroll: $100 a week each for me and my partner, Louise.

I'd wake up early, get Chris ready for school, drop her off, and drive into the city. A woman picked her up from school and kept her at her house till six, when I arrived and we went home for supper. We read and watched TV, played and did thumps, till she went to bed. After she was asleep, I worked at my sewing machine past midnight. Though a lot of work and worry, it was creative and I was independent.

On Saturdays, I brought Chris to the loft and she entertained herself while I pinned and sewed and Louise cut dresses. Now and then she'd come to me, stand on tip-toe to peer over the table, and ask, "What are you making me?" I'd put together striped and polka-dot scraps, whatever was around that worked, and I'd make her a jumpsuit or a dress. She liked wearing clothes that were different from what the other kids wore.

That Halloween, I made Christine a medieval princess costume, with a tall cone-shaped hat and a tulle veil floating down from the tip—the kind little girls dream about when they read *Grimm's Fairy Tales.* The dress was pink velveteen with trumpet sleeves, but it was the hat that made it. Chris thought it was the most beautiful thing she'd ever seen.

Besides Heather, her best friend was a little black boy who was crippled and went to school in a wheelchair. Chris couldn't go trick-or-treating with him because of his wheelchair and Heather was going out with other friends, so we made the rounds in our building. The way it turned out, she was mostly alone.

She said, "Mommy, I don't want you to come to the door with me, okay? Just be a little bit away, so they don't think I'm a baby."

And I said, "Okay, I'll stay out of sight."

I stood at the end of the hall while she rang the bell and I peeked at her as she smiled back at me, waiting for the door to open. I watched as she stood alone with her runny nose and her medieval hat in the clean, spartan halls of our building, looking up at the peepholes. After she got her treat, she came over to show me her bag filling with goodies. She had a good time in her glamorous costume, but to me it seemed dismal and I was ashamed.

My own Halloweens had been filled with friends and family traipsing through piles of leaves on the sparsely lit country roads of Darien, Connecticut, laughing and running along with our Labrador retriever. I'd had so much as a child. With all the advantages and lessons and education I'd been given, was this the best I could do for Christine? I seemed to have lost my way, living alone like a recluse, struggling with my business, living close to poverty, counting pennies. She deserved better. I tried to tell myself one lonely Halloween wouldn't ruin her life, but after I tucked her in bed, and put her bowl of candy outside the mist tent, the trouble was clear. My life was going nowhere. It wasn't enough to do her thumps and get her to the doctor. Why hadn't I seen it before? To give Christine a better life, *my* life had to be better. I wrote my mother,

> Sometimes my courage fails me and I wonder how I'll face the next day. I worry deeply about Christine, about new signs of lung damage and her extreme thinness. She really needs a nurse now. The thumping takes me 40 minutes and my arms give out.
>
> She needs a country house and a dog. I want so much for her to have that. There is more than my love I want to give her. It's hard to do everything myself.

My father had nearly died when a plane he was flying crashed, and it was many years before he was able to work on Wall Street again. My mother was a lawyer, and, as the family fortunes reversed, she had battled to support a family of five. She knew what

I was talking about. Her struggle had exacted an emotional toll on all of us, too.

A few months later, my partner said orders were so good that we couldn't fill them because we didn't have enough cash to pay up front for the fabric we needed. Louise asked, "What do you think we should do?"

"We need an angel, someone to invest second money." We couldn't go back to my father.

"But who and how?" she said. I raised something else.

"I don't know if I can go on anymore, working so hard for so little . . . putting all our profits back into the business. I want to give Christine something better." I suggested what I'd been thinking about since Halloween—closing the business. Louise wasn't married but she loved Chris and understood the pressure. We both looked at the dresses hanging neatly tagged on our showroom rack, the best collection I'd done, and we talked it through, that day and several more days, before we decided reluctantly to close Frock by Jacque. My father gave me a small loan to tide me over.

My plan was to land a nine to five job, where I hoped I could earn three times what my business had paid me, to find an apartment in Manhattan, and to get my life moving. To start I did two things. I walked into Robert Kennedy's campaign headquarters on Madison Avenue and volunteered. I could put in a lot of hours while I was looking for work. It was a campaign I believed in, and a way to reconnect with the world. I began picking Chris up from school myself, letting all the baby sitters go. We went to movies together, and when we liked a movie we splurged and saw it twice. We saw Zefferelli's *Romeo and Juliet* three times and I was surprised Christine liked it. She was in third grade.

My first nine-to-five job in the fashion industry was a plum. Paul Young hired me to design for Paraphernalia, replacing Betsey Johnson, who had left the company. The pressure was so intense Christine spent the summer with my mother in Ithaca.

I was no Betsey Johnson. I had no training, no experience, and I couldn't run a design room. That meant keeping four expert seamstresses busy with new designs every day. Frock by Jacques was a peanut compared with this operation. After two months, Paul Young put me on notice. He said my clothes were too elegant. He wanted a carnal look. It was the days of the Youthquake and he wanted shock-your-mother clothes for Paraphernalia.

I tried to adapt but it wasn't me. I never thought he'd fire me because his wife, Susan Saltonstall, was a relative of mine, but a few weeks after I was instructed to design carnal clothes, I was fired. I took my severance pay, badly shaken, and went to Ithaca to get Christine. I'd always thought my creative drive and my determination were unbeatable. I was wrong. I filed for unemployment and started looking for work with another small loan, from my mother this time.

That November, Chris got the flu and in two days she was coughing all night, choking and suffocating. I brought her in to the Vanderbilt Clinic and she was admitted with viral pneumonia.

The second day, a resident came in to start intravenous antibiotics. Christine remembered the horrible needles from her first admission and looked at me in terror.

"Chris, it will be over in no time. I'll come and hold your hand."

But the resident said, "I'm afraid you can't come into the treatment room, it's against hospital policy."

"Well, couldn't you just overlook hospital policy this time and let me stay with her?" I asked nicely.

"I'm sorry. I can't do that." It was absurd, but I didn't argue.

I stood outside the closed door. Two minutes stretched into five and then ten and then fifteen minutes. I could hear Christine crying out.

"No, no, please don't," and then she'd scream and cry, long wrenching, hysterical cries. I cringed outside the door, praying for it to be over. Then it would stop and I'd hear mumbling and then more screams.

"No, no, don't! Stop! It hurts—" And then more crying. I was dumbstruck. What the hell were they doing? It went on and on, with screams every minute. While I was pacing back and forth, holding my hands over my ears and muttering to myself, one of the nurses came out and I started to go in, but she pulled the door closed.

"I'm sorry, you can't go in there."

I glimpsed the resident bending over Christine's feet and said, "What's going on? What's the problem?"

She said, "They can't get the needle in; her veins aren't good," and then disappeared down the hall.

There was nothing wrong with Christine's veins—not at age eight. She started to scream again and I heard the resident say, "Hold still . . . you have to hold *still,*" and Chris crying, "I can't, I can't. It hurts too much."

It was almost half an hour that she'd been under what I could only describe as a needle attack. I was alone in the hall and then Chris cried out and I turned the knob and burst into the room. Chris was lying on the table and she turned to me, her arms out, pleading, "Mommy, Mommy—" and I heard myself saying, "I won't permit this another minute! I'm sorry. Find another doctor. There must be someone else who can do this!"

They stared at me. I didn't move. Chris didn't move. What was going to happen? Then the resident turned to one of the nurses and said in a blasé tone, "Go get Dr. Whitcomb. He's good at this." And just like that, without a word to me, the nurse left to get him. I was furious and turned to the resident.

"Why didn't you do that before?"

"I'm sorry. Her veins are very difficult."

"Her veins are nothing of the kind." But suddenly I understood. I could have stopped him at any time. I could have insisted they let me in. This was a teaching hospital. He was a student. I could have refused to let him touch her. I hadn't known I had any rights at all, but I knew now. The resident left and Christine said, "Mommy, the nurses were holding me down, and they tried putting the needle in so many times. They said the next place they were going to try if they couldn't get the needle in my foot was my forehead."

I caught my breath in horror. "Oh, Christine, I'm so sorry. I promise I'll never let this happen again."

I taught Christine what I'd learned: that she had the right to refuse treatment, though it was years before she had the guts and know-how to do it, and that doctors are just people and no two are the same. Some have gentle, gifted hands. But some are nervous and clumsy, and no matter how hard they try, they always hurt you. She should remember the names of the doctors with good hands and always request them.

The next day Chris and I both wrote her father in San Francisco, care of a friend, asking him please to come back. In my letter, I told him how much she needed him.

Years later, Jerry told me, "Christine was my salvation. I was on a dead-end street, playing the guitar in folk clubs and passing the hat. When I got her letter, I had thirty dollars to my name. I sold my twelve-string guitar and borrowed the rest for a one-way plane ticket to New York. And I stayed for good. Before long, I was working—first for the Bil Baird Theater again, and then for the Muppets. She saved my life."

When Christine was admitted, I spoke to the admitting office of Babies Hospital, feeling like a charity case when I explained my predicament: no job, no insurance, and uncertain where Christine's father was. Columbia Presbyterian, the immense medical complex that always insisted on prepayments and guarantees, made an exception. When Christine was discharged, I was presented with no bill.

Until now, the antibiotic pills had been keeping her lung infections under control, and though we couldn't for a minute forget the mist tents and thumps, we didn't yet see that cystic fibrosis was life threatening. I had begun to think that she was luckier than most. But the disease was working silently.

The day after she got out of the hospital, I was offered a job in the fashion office of Celanese. Security, at last, and a good salary.

But the hard times weren't over yet. When I gained job security, I gave up flexibility. Celanese hadn't hired my problems and when Christine came down with the flu again, she had to stay home from school. I couldn't find a sitter. I had to leave her alone. I made her lunch, turned on "Sesame Street," told her not to answer the door, and went to work. She was eight and a half. Thank God she heard her father's voice on "Sesame Street."

I called every hour, sounding as cheery as an April robin, but feeling like I'd been through a shredder. At noon, we talked through lunch. She seemed chipper, but when I hung up and called my best friend, I burst into tears.

"Oh, Nancy, I had to leave her alone. I can't do a thing here, but I can't leave. All she has to talk to is her little hamster."

We had fun on weekends campaigning for Carter Burden, who was running for city council. Though the other volunteers probably wondered what a divorcée who lived in Jackson Heights was doing campaigning for Carter Burden, I knew. My establishment roots were strong and I was moving back where I belonged. I brought Christine with me when I collected signatures and handed out campaign buttons in Yorkville on weekends. At a campaign function, I met a man six years younger than I and an inch shorter. When I asked him what he did, he said he was a pudding king. It was the family business. He took me for a midnight breakfast at the Carlyle Hotel where Bobby Short played the piano. This seemed very sophisticated, but as we left, I couldn't help saying, "That was awfully nice, but goodness sixty dollars is a lot to pay for eggs."

He walked me back to my car near campaign headquarters. He watched as I got in, turned on the ignition, got back out, lifted up the hood, took a screwdriver out of my purse, reached in under the hood, and started the car with the screwdriver.

He said with concern, "When did your starter conk out, this morning?"

"Oh no," I said, "it happened two months ago." I closed the hood. He was staring at me.

"You've been starting your car with a screwdriver for two months?"

"Well, I couldn't afford to fix it so the mechanic at the garage showed me how to do it. I think it's kind of neat." He laughed.

"You shouldn't be driving home alone at this hour in a car like that. Why don't you let me drive the car? When we get back to

Queens, I'll call a cab to take me back to the city." I was amazed he'd go all the way out to Queens with me at that hour.

Shortly thereafter, I rented a two-bedroom apartment on East 82nd Street, sold my old Valiant (the starter had been fixed), and moved. Christine enrolled at P.S. 86 and at last found a friend, Claudia Harris, who was in her class and lived in the same building. Soon Chris and Claudia were inseparable.

Carter Burden was elected and I married the man who took me to the Carlyle. It wasn't a very likely match but I told myself opposites attract and I was madly in love. Slowly but surely, my life improved, and as we put down roots in a spacious apartment on East 73rd Street, so did Christine's.

4 · *Bleed*

★
★ ★

June 1973 was hot and muggy that year in New York—
not the best time to be seven months' pregnant. I knew from
experience. I'd gone to my mother's in Ithaca to escape the heat
before Christine was born. Twelve years older now, and more
mature, I was better equipped to handle the discomfort. Still,
sitting in the living room talking with our dinner guests over
coffee, I couldn't remember when I'd been so tired—not since
July twelve years ago.

I appeared to be listening, but my mind was elsewhere. I was
going to have to take a leave soon from Cotton, Inc., where I was becoming known in the industry for my color forecasts, predicting
the colors that would be fashionable in women's and men's wear
two years ahead. It was too much. Cotton, Inc. could do without
my color forecast for two months and I was certain we could
manage without my salary.

Christine called me, "Mom, could you come here?"

Something in her voice kept me from giving my usual "You
can come here, dear" answer. I excused myself and went to her
room. She was sitting on her bed, coughing gently.

"What is it, Chris?"

"I don't know. Something's wrong. I can't stop coughing." I
listened. The cough sounded odd, low and gravelly, not at all like
the times I heard her in the night, coughing dry, metallic coughs
every ten seconds or so for half an hour.

"It's not like your usual cough, is it?"

Her words slipped out in quick spurts. "No, it's so wet and just
keeps coming, in little waves." I stood a minute more, listening.
She could always stop her cough. Why not now?

"I feel sick to my stomach, too." I felt her forehead. No fever.

"Do you think you're going to throw up?" She nodded. "What are you swallowing?" She was gulping oddly.

"I don't know." She pushed straight wisps of blond hair out of her face, moaning softly as her stomach rolled and clenched.

"Let's go to the bathroom, Chris, just in case."

She was shaking. We walked slowly to the bathroom across the hall. Even though she was almost twelve, she was still afraid of throwing up. When she started to tremble it was about to happen. We sat on the edge of the tub. She was coughing more now—a little faster.

"Mom, I saw blood in the cup when I spit into it before."

I felt something change inside me but I said calmly, "You did? Blood?" What the devil could that be? My mind searched for an answer. "Maybe your throat's raw from the coughing."

"Maybe," she nodded, shivering.

I got up slowly and went back to the paper cup beside her bed. We always used eight-ounce wax cups. She hated the flimsy little cups they used in the hospital and preferred something sturdy between her hand and the mucus she had to spit up. There were little blobs of pinkish blood inside the cup. It didn't look serious. As I walked back across the hall, I thought that it was just something to tell one of the doctors at Columbia Presbyterian next time we went. Then Chris bent over the sink in a coughing spasm that sounded like a motor grinding over on a cold morning. She spit into the basin and a trickle of bright red blood ran down the side. Alarmed, I turned on the faucet, and rinsed it away.

"Chris, what's that? Where's it coming from?" I didn't expect her to answer and she couldn't anyway. She was coughing and spitting blood in the sink. I put my arms around her and moved close, supporting her. Her voice was small.

"Mommy, I'm scared."

"Chris, I don't like this at all." My heart was beating hard and I was scared too. Even while I said it, another wave of coughs came and more blood. Her hands gripped the sides of the sink as she bent over and shook with the coughing. And then it let up. I filled the bathroom glass with water and gave her a sip, but she wouldn't swallow.

"Mommy, I can't drink it. I'll throw up." She rinsed her mouth.

"Can I leave you a minute?" I asked. "I'll call the hospital." She nodded again, shivering still. In my room I dialed Columbia Presbyterian and asked who was on call on the eleventh floor for cystic fibrosis.

"Dr. Celia Ores. If you'll give me your number, I'll have her call you back."

"No, no. I need to talk to someone now. My daughter is coughing up blood. Is there a resident on the floor?"

"Just a minute—I'll page him."

The resident came on the line and I told him what was happening.

"Do you have any cough suppressant with codeine?" he asked.

"No, but I have Emperin with codeine."

"How strong?"

"Five milligrams."

"How old is she?"

"Twelve."

"Give her a tablet and then turn the shower on hot. You want to steam up the bathroom and keep her there until the coughing stops. Call me back if it doesn't. I'm on extension 2774."

I went to give her the codeine and told my husband and our friends that Christine needed me.

Chris sat on the toilet seat while we steamed the bathroom. But it didn't help.

"Mom, I hate this. It's making me cough more. Can we stop?"

"We sure can. This is stupid."

I brought her back to bed. There were more coughing spasms but no more blood. When the codeine took hold her cough stopped. I tucked her in and she asked me not to say anything to our guests. Within twenty minutes, she was asleep.

I rejoined our company in the living room. All I could think about was the blood in the sink. An hour must have passed when Chris called.

"Mommy, come here, quick!" I ran.

"What is it?"

She was sitting up in bed with a pan in front of her and she said, "I feel sick again, I think I'm going—" She didn't finish, because she threw up—effortlessly, as if in slow motion. A terrifying dark liquid projectile missed the pan she was holding, overshot the bed, and splattered on the floor. We both stared in horror at the huge pool of red and black blood spreading on the black and white tile. She started to cry and threw up again—a tiny bit in the pan. I froze for one beat and then said, "That's it. We're going to the hospital."

A rush of adrenalin drove me into action, hurried me into the bathroom for a glass of water. Christine shivered violently as she rinsed her mouth.

There was so much blood. The wet cough, that's why it wouldn't stop. Her eyes were dark with fear.

"Don't be frightened, dear. The blood is so dark. It's not fresh. It must have been in your stomach a long time. The bleeding's stopped." I sat down next to her and brushed her damp hair back. "We're going to Lenox Hill Hospital. It's only a few blocks. I'll call the doorman for a cab." Pretending to be calm helped.

There was a cab waiting when we got downstairs. Five minutes later we were all there—my husband, our guests, and Chris and I.

Then everything stopped. If the bleeding was serious, no one acted as if it was. I explained that she was followed at the Cystic Fibrosis Clinic at Columbia Presbyterian. We waited for half an hour in the empty emergency room. Groggy and weak, eyes closed, Chris leaned quietly against me. Finally, a resident appeared and asked us to come in.

He took a brief history, glancing over at me when Chris faltered. Experience had taught me to let her talk when the residents took histories because that way I learned what she was feeling. The resident said little, wrote quickly, and took her to X ray. I didn't ask why. In the hospital, I felt safer. She was gone forty-five minutes and returned exhausted. She coughed every now and then—little dry coughs, like hiccups. We waited another half hour in the examining room for the X rays.

When the resident returned he said nothing about the X rays—just gave us a small bottle of cough suppressant with codeine and said we could go. So I asked.

"What was it? Could you tell anything by the X ray?"

"No, we didn't see anything. Perhaps she just broke a capillary from violent coughing and it bled."

"But she never has a violent cough."

"I don't think it's serious."

"But something must be wrong."

"I'd call your doctor in the morning to be sure. Give her a teaspoon of cough suppressant at four o'clock this morning."

"So that's it?" I didn't believe him. I thought he was hiding something. I searched his face for some clue, but saw nothing. Maybe I was overreacting.

At home, I changed Christine's bed, noticing the tiny drops of blood on the sheet.

"Mommy, I'm sorry, your dinner party."

"Christine, I don't care a hoot about the dinner party. The Franks are good friends. They understand. We have too many dinner parties anyway." She looked at me gratefully and I hugged her good-night. She was asleep in minutes.

I cleaned up the blood on the floor and saw what I thought were large clots. Obviously, her body had tried to stop the bleeding, and something had kept the blood coming. I didn't like the size of the clots and the amount of blood—eight or nine ounces. How much more was in her stomach? I started to wring out the towels I'd used on the floor, but it was so awful I threw them in the garbage instead.

Dr. Ores called at 1:30. She was one of several doctors who treated children at the clinic but we hadn't seen her much. The resident had called her at home. I went over the events, and what the resident at Lenox Hill had said.

She asked, "Is Christine asleep now?"

"Yes."

"Don't wake her up for the 4 A.M. medicine. Let her sleep."

"Dr. Ores, have you ever heard of this before with cystic fibrosis? Is it related?"

"Yes. It comes from the lung infections."

"Oh," I said, as though that explained everything. I had no idea what she was talking about.

"Can you bring Christine in first thing tomorrow morning?"

"Of course."

"Very well. I'll meet you there at 8:30 on the fourth floor."
Eight-thirty on Sunday morning—I was impressed, then worried.

"Do you think it's over—the bleeding?"

"I don't know. Probably."

After I hung up I had a rush of questions, but it was too late.
She'd called me from home and I didn't have her home number.
I didn't even know where she lived.

I went back to bed and debated whether to call Jerry. He'd
probably be home. After years of struggling to find work as an
actor, he had joined the Muppets, where the many character
voices he'd developed over the years proved invaluable, and he
now performed daily on "Sesame Street." But still, to call at this
hour would scare him to death. The crisis was past. Better to call
tomorrow. How I could have slept the rest of the night, I don't
know, but I did.

I woke at 5:30 and sat alone in the kitchen for an hour, drinking coffee, thinking about the future, examining the past. Jerry
was living on the West Side with his girl. We were fond of each
other, but we didn't communicate often. He'd always had a surface calm that bordered on passivity and he kept his thoughts to
himself. Only people who knew him well saw his sense of humor.

Our outlooks had been so different. He was a cheerful pessi-
mist and I was a depressed optimist. He believed Christine's illness was his own bad karma returning to punish him. For what
I don't know. Maybe for that reason, he hated to talk about it and
preferred not to know about the day-to-day, minor crises. In the
old days it made me mad as hell, but I'd come to accept that Jerry
and I had different roles to play in Christine's life. Jerry was an
unstinting source of love and fun, always eager to distract Christine with odd voices, songs, and make-believe. He gave her a
talent for the ridiculous that sustained her at tough moments.
More than that, as I saw later, he gave her the gift of his own
performer's heart, the ability to enact some emotional truth for
others and to be nourished by their enjoyment. It was partly this
that brought Christine such wonderful friends.

My gifts to Christine were different. Never dwell on how bad
things are, or how much worse they would become. Keep your
eye fixed on the victories of learning and growing and friendship,

which seemed to come every day for Christine, as they do for all children. And, for the most part, Christine lived as other children did. She had her thumps every day, we knew we had to be watchful when she caught cold or had a sore throat. But she ran and played like her friends, who had no idea she was sick. Then along came something truly frightening, like this bleed. It was hard to think of victories now.

It was almost seven. I woke Chris and we made the long bumpy ride to the Vanderbilt Clinic at 168th Street and Broadway. I'd never noticed the bumpiness before. Every time the cab shuddered over a bump, I was afraid the bleeding might start. The streets of Spanish Harlem were quiet and dirty. It always shocked me to see how the poor had to live, the really poor. I'd gone through times when I had very little, but I always knew I had the power to change my life. I had an education, successful friends, connections to a better life. Poverty in Harlem was something else. On Park Avenue, flowers were planted along the median five times a year, but on Adam Clayton Powell Boulevard the median was bare. Nothing ever grew there. Usually, I felt so lucky. Today, I held Christine closer as the cab jolted over another pothole.

Dr. Ores met us on the fourth floor. She was an attractive middle-aged woman with blond hair and formal European manners. She examined Chris calmly and asked her if she felt well enough to have blood drawn. Chris nodded and an orderly took her off in a wheelchair.

"What happened?" I asked Dr. Ores.

"Occasionally, the lung infections will erode capillaries, veins, or arteries in the lung tissue. This may cause some bleeding."

"It seemed like a lot on the floor."

"Well, it always looks like more than it is that way, but the blood tests we're taking will probably show insufficient vitamin K as well, which is why it didn't stop more quickly."

"What's vitamin K?"

"The vitamin that helps the blood to clot."

"Oh." I waited outside the clinic office while she went to get Chris and see about the blood tests. She'd calmed Christine by saying everything so positively. "The bleeding's stopped now, that's a good sign," and "We're giving you a shot of vitamin K— that should fix you up." Her European accent was distinctive and reassuring, even elegant. With Chris, she sounded like a pediatrician treating a routine sore throat with a cherry lozenge. With me, her restraint and patience invited my questions—she gave me her time.

In the clinic waiting room a resident sat down beside me, wearing rumpled khakis and a blue oxford shirt—the same resident I'd talked to on the phone.

"How's she doing?"

"My daughter?"

"Yes."

"The bleeding's stopped, thank God. And she didn't need cough suppressant this morning." I asked him if he'd ever seen anything like this before.

"Oh yes. I might as well tell you, you're going to have to get used to this, you know."

"Used to it?"

He nodded diffidently. I stood up—I was furious.

"What the devil are you talking about? My daughter throws up a pint of blood, bleeds for hours internally—hemorrhaging— and you're telling me I have to get used to it? There's no way I'm going to get used to it."

I didn't give him a chance to say a word, but left the rows of empty seats and went back into the office. I put his words out of my mind, such stupidness. Later, I asked Dr. Ores.

"The resident who was here before told me that we'd better start getting used to this. How could he say that?" She was unperturbed.

"Don't pay him any mind. He's young. He has a lot to learn." Much later it occurred to me that she meant he had to learn not to frighten parents by telling them the truth when they weren't ready to hear it.

There was no more bleeding, and Chris liked Dr. Ores so much she asked, "Mommy, could she take care of me all the time?"

"We'll see." I asked Dr. Ores if she took private patients, and our days at the Vanderbilt Clinic were over. Dr. Ores admitted Chris to Babies Hospital that morning. Now that we had our own doctor, we found a new sense of security, of contact, of someone looking after us. I should have done it long ago. But before I'd remarried I couldn't afford it and later I'd never thought of it.

After Chris was settled, I asked Dr. Ores how long she would be in the hospital. "We're supposed to leave for Martha's Vineyard on the third of July for two weeks."

"You'll be able to go with luck. I won't make any promises."

While Christine was in the hospital, I worked for half a day and then went to the hospital. My boss said, "Jacquie, are you sure you don't want some time off?"

"Thank you, but I'd drive myself crazy with worry. And that would be terrible for Christine. I need to work." It was weird.

Jerry spent evenings in the hospital playing backgammon with Chris and I told him she was now a private patient of Dr. Ores. He was reticent and made no effort to talk to her. She finally introduced herself one afternoon when she was on rounds. She had noticed how attentive he was to Chris.

As it happened, Jerry had something on his mind. He asked Dr. Ores if he could talk to her.

"Of course. We can use the office on the tenth floor."

They went into the office around the corner when they got off the elevator. Jerry noticed how quiet the room was. He asked about the bleeding first.

"Jacquie told me Christine's bleeding was related to the lung infections, but I don't know what it is that happens, or if it means her condition is more serious than it was."

"The answer to the second question is yes, the bleeding represents a greater degree of lung infection, but that may have been present for some time. Bleeding episodes are erratic and difficult to predict."

"Does every c/f patient bleed like this?"

"Almost all at one time or another." Dr. Ores went on, "The answer to your first question is more complex. The lungs are a living organ made up of tissue, blood vessels, veins, and arteries that crisscross and branch out millions of times. The blood vessels subdivide into smaller and smaller branches, till you have a network of tiny microscopic capillaries where the oxygen exchange takes place. It's like the root system of a tree. The oxygen is exchanged in the alveoli, tiny balloon-like sacs at the end of each capillary. The problem is the abnormal mucus. It's so thick and tenacious, it blocks thousands and then tens of thousands of the tiny alveoli—and it sits there. Even when we pound it out and press and vibrate on her chest, two, three, even four times a day, most of it never moves. It keeps clogging up the works."

Jerry sat as still as he ever had in his study of Zen.

"You see, the thick mucus is an ideal breeding ground for opportunistic organisms and they're dangerous. There's chronic lung infection in Christine's lungs . . . sometimes bad, sometimes less bad. The infections cause erosion of the surrounding tissue. In time, it erodes into cavities and invades the walls of blood vessels. When this happens, bleeding occurs."

"Is there some warning?"

"No, it's invisible and silent, although some patients can identify the site of the bleeding."

"Can Chris do that?"

"Not yet, but she may learn."

Jerry hated that answer. "You mean it can happen again." Dr. Ores nodded but said nothing. "But how do you stop it?"

Dr. Ores never used words carelessly or quickly and she reflected, in no hurry. Many parents never asked these questions and she had no pat answers. "Well, we don't. It stops itself. We can give cough suppressant to quiet the lungs, but we have few ways to stop it."

"What if it doesn't stop?" Jerry didn't want to be a pest, but he seemed to have reached a blind corner.

"In extreme cases, we can try an embolization—a complex process that seals off the infected area. There's also the possibility of a surgical lung removal, but this is rare." She didn't say it was a last resort.

Jerry stopped a minute. He still had to ask his question. "What does the future hold for Christine then?"

"Do you mean in terms of activities, or treatment?"

"I mean in terms of expectancy. How long does she have?"
This was the question Dr. Ores hated.

"It's hard to say. Each child is different; each illness is too."
Jerry felt her reluctance to speak filling the room, telling him his
daughter would never grow up. He asked another way.

"But, based on your experience, what do you think?" Maybe
he was breaking some code of silence asking this.

Dr. Ores didn't answer at first. She'd just finished telling him
she didn't know, though she had a pretty good idea and he was
asking her again. But she didn't mind. She liked him.

"Mr. Nelson, I don't know these things—maybe two years,
maybe twelve—I just don't know. It also depends on the patient's
attitude. If you have someone very positive, they can eke out a
life from something that has very little to offer."

Jerry's stillness broke and he slumped the tiniest bit in the
chair. "Maybe Chris will surprise us," he said.

And this time he didn't run away. He stayed in New York that
summer and took Christine to Fire Island for six weeks. It wasn't
that he'd run away from Christine the first time. He'd run from
himself, because he thought he was to blame and he was so afraid
of what she was so brave about. And when he'd returned from San
Francisco, she'd taught him how to be strong.

Jerry never shared Dr. Ores's prediction with me. I had no
idea she might live only two years. We went to Martha's Vineyard
as planned and brought Claudia Harris. The girls rode their bikes
into Edgartown, laughed and swam, and looked for jingle shells
on South Beach. They bought ice-cream cones at the Dairy
Queen, played hide and seek in the Edgartown graveyard near
our house, and screamed when I dropped live lobsters into a pot
of boiling water. We caught rings on the carousel in Oak Bluffs,
fished for bluefish off Chappaquidick Island, and wore cutoffs and
sandals to the Homeport in Menemsha. After her ordeal, our two
weeks seemed like a gift of roses—thorns and all.

We had terrible fights over her physical therapy. She was so
resistant and rude and insulting I actually spanked her as she tried
to convince me we could forget about it for two weeks. She
needed a vacation from her illness, but after almost losing her, I
wouldn't permit it. Then she'd cheer up till the next time. We

went through it twice a day and I explained and apologized to Claudia.

"Claudia, we have to clear her lungs. We do it to keep the thick mucus in her lungs from getting clogged up."

I also learned to examine what she coughed up. The mucus was streaked with blood for weeks. Chris may not have understood it then, but the bleeding never did stop right away after a crisis. It was like a leak that kept sputtering after it had been fixed.

Chris got tan and gained weight. Toward the end of the two weeks, I realized how afraid I'd been that Chris was going to die. As if anesthesia was wearing off, my feelings returned and I cried and cried.

Back home, there was a television commercial to raise money for the Cystic Fibrosis Foundation—about children with cystic fibrosis dying young. I worried that Chris would see it. Maybe she did. She asked me one day when we were cleaning up her room.

"Mommy, can people die from cystic fibrosis?"

I had been dreading the question so long, the answer I'd worked out came with no chilling pause, no telltale stumble. "No, Christine, people don't die from cystic fibrosis, but they can sometimes die from the complications—like pneumonia. Pneumonia is a lung disease and anyone can die from it. That's why we try so hard to keep you strong and your lungs clear, so you won't get pneumonia." I'd left something out. "But people who get pneumonia go to the hospital and get medicine, and most of the time they get well." Done. "Here, could you hold the dustpan for me?"

I swept. I was sure she didn't know what pneumonia was, or a complication, but if she'd wanted to go further she would have asked. I fudged the answer, but I think it saved her pain.

Our life changed. Chris didn't see it for a while, but something unwelcome had arrived again, without warning—an uninvited stranger in my peripheral vision. Something we had no control over.

I'd felt the feeling before, in that library in Ithaca years ago, but it was different then. I realized that the young resident at the hospital was right when he said we'd have to get used to it. It would happen again and again. We never got used to it.

5 · The Muppet Connection

★
★ ★

Jenny was born that September in 1973 at Mt. Sinai Hospital where I spent five of the happiest days of my life. I knew Jenny was healthy, I just knew. Christine loved Jenny from the first and never showed any signs of the jealousy I'd been so afraid of, maybe because they were twelve years apart and Chris cared little if her stepfather favored Jenny. All she cared about was that I love them equally, and I did.

The problem was finding time to show it. Jenny's father and I were busy having it all: two high-profile careers, constant socializing and entertaining, and for me the pressure of always being impeccably turned out, running the house, and trying my best to be a good mother. Having it all really meant doing it all, and doing it all was doing me in. In a very different way from my experience with Jerry, I once again found myself at odds with my husband over our life-style. If my children suffered from the way we lived I would have to change it. Neither man could change.

Dr. Ores knew none of this, but in her private medical records she observed of Chris, "In the midst of plenty, she is neglected." When Chris was thirteen, in the eighth grade at the Dwight School, in the whirlwind life our family was leading she was sometimes treated like excess baggage. Chris heard the comment made one night at the dinner table, that her father's child-support payments were helping to pay for her private school and "defray her expenses." She said later in hurt protest, "What am I, Mom, a piece of office equipment?" I began to think about shifting the family priorities. I suggested to my husband that I should stop working. His income was good. But he said it was out of the question.

Chris's health was deteriorating slowly, so that she thought about it and fought hard to stay well. There were intermittent hospital admissions and cystic fibrosis remained an undercurrent, a sinister presence. It didn't dominate her life yet, as we'd feared it would. When she was fourteen, I wrote my mother:

> Chris came out of the hospital quite a bit better and as fate would have it—someone dropped out of her school production of *Arsenic and Old Lace* and she was given the part, a nice supporting role. She was very good, projected well (no coughing), etc. It did wonders for her morale. She has her father's talents—no doubt about it.
>
> When Christine has especially wonderful, normal, happy times, like being successful in a school play, etc., and all signs of her illness disappear for two hours or so, she glows with happiness. I see clearly for a moment how her day-to-day life is haunted every minute by her health.
>
> Dr. Ores tells me Chris is moving into the critical emotional stage—where 90% of the kids withdraw into themselves—living in unspoken fear and loneliness. I'm on top of this and don't forget it as I try to lead her down a different road . . . "the road less taken and that" will make "all the difference."

Chris started keeping a journal as part of an ongoing English assignment for Pam Motley, her English teacher at Dwight. She had to turn it in once a month, and Mrs. Motley made comments. Christine loved the assignment. The fall of her ninth grade year was the premiere season of "Saturday Night Live," and through Jerry and the Muppets Christine was part of it.

Journal Entry—

> *The Saturday Night Live show was fun. Paul Simon was the guest host. Art Garfunkel was his guest. After hearing all those good old songs of theirs, I want to get all their records.*
>
> *I think I may have a fever. It better not get worse 'cause I refuse to miss more school.*

It was strange watching Saturday Night Live on TV because it wasn't the exact same show that we saw (we saw the rehearsal of the show 'cause this show is live and not taped and it's on very late). I saw the rehearsal because my dad is on every week.

In adolescence, Christine's relationship with her stepfather soured, and she spent more time with Jerry on weekends and vacations. Jerry was a senior puppeteer now with the Muppets. On "Sesame Street" he played characters of The Count, Herry Monster, Biff, Snuffle-Upagus, and Sherlock Hemlock. He brought Chris to the Children's Television Workshop theater, where "Sesame Street" was taped. She got to know all the Muppet people. Jerry also played the role of Scred, the ghoulish little Muppet, in the early days of "Saturday Night Live." For the first time, Jerry received fan mail from grown-ups, and he took Chris into that world too. She went to rehearsals and hung out backstage in the greenroom, the actor's lounge, meeting the regulars and the guest stars, and she'd come home talking about Chevy and Gilda and John and Lily.

Journal Entry—

Saturday night I went to the Saturday Night Live rehearsal and show. Remember how I said that I sometimes felt out of place with the cast? Not anymore.

Oh, it was great. After rehearsal I went into the greenroom with the cast and sat and talked. I ate one of the sandwiches and listened and stuff. I even made a funny and everybody laughed. Oh, I felt so happy.

Journal Entry—

Sat. Night Live had me "rolling in the gutters" it was so funny. Ginny called me up and asked me if I would get her 3 tickets for her and some friends to see Sat. Nite Live. I don't know what to do. I mean it's a favor my Dad's doing when he gets me tickets and that (I'm family) kind of puts me on the spot to ask him to get me some for friends of friends. That's a "no-no," as Mom would say. I just don't think it's right. I mean I took Ginny once already. When a friend offers to make an order of some, let's say, pads with a monogram, and goes through special trouble to do so, you don't ask him to do it again no matter how much you want them. I don't know, I may be wrong . . . . am I??? You see tickets to Sat. Nite Live are not for sale, they're just complimentary.

It's kind of a hard thing for me to get across so I'm not sure if what I'm saying is making sense. I don't know how to say no to Ginny. I'll somehow get her the tickets but something is not right about it.

I'm scared. The doctor called me back and I told her how I felt. She said to call her in the morning and if I'm not better, I have to go in to see her. I don't want to go to the hospital . . . I just won't be sick tomorrow.

Jan 13, 1975

I'm in the hospital. I was admitted Friday. I didn't write much yesterday. I guess I was too upset. I cried a lot though nobody knows about it. Dad visited me last night.

When I saw him, I ran and hugged him and started crying. He started crying too. He's so sweet. I was just very lonesome last night. It was right after Mom left.

It's so boring being in the hospital. The hours just seem to run together. My IV hurts sometimes and I'm afraid to use my arm. The food is awful as always and it's so lonely on this floor.

The last few mornings when I wake up a cockroach is on the wall next to my bed staring at me. I scream for the nurses each time. (I'm absolutely terrified of bugs . . . especially a cockroach). That first morning I cried and cried and was shaking, I was so mortified and terrified. Sometimes I get so lonely that I cry. I miss home.

At night, even when the air conditioner is on full blast,

I sweat all over. Is it my fever spiking? In the morning at 5 A.M. during my first set of thumps, and when my Daddy leaves at night, I feel I just can't go on anymore.

Now I do 4 sets of therapy a day as if 3 weren't enough. The doctor said I just have to get my lungs cleared out. I was so angry and upset when she told me the news that I cried almost until I fell asleep. How could God do this to me, I thought. First, he took away my little dear hamster and then my health and happiness. I wish my Dad could stay all day. I miss him more when I'm sick.

I'd bought Chris a pet hamster and he'd somehow escaped from his cage and disappeared. She'd only had him for three days and hadn't even had a chance to name him. We never found him.

What will I write about for my essay in English? I'll have to sleep on it. Being in the hospital is a bit like being in prison. I was sentenced to two weeks for lung infection. The food is like prison food. Each patient, or prisoner as it were, has a cell or room, etc. Maybe I could write about that.

Her essay about hospital admissions was in her journal.

Journal Entry—

"Doing Time"
by Willy "the actor" Sutton

Many times I had thought of the fateful day that I had been sent here, and now my term was over. I was just now thinking of all that had happened here. I remembered I had just come up for a small claims hearing. Little did I know it would turn into a nightmare. It had been a cold day, thus I felt worse than usual. I took the doctor's stand and told the truth.

I was always tired and my coughing got out of hand during the course of the day. Unfortunately, I had a long medical record and the evidence was against me. The doctor thought it over but the prospects were grim. My sentence: two weeks in the hospital for harboring a lung infection.

This wasn't the first time that I had done time in the "jabber." I had been in 6 times before. I was considered an old-timer and therefore got seniority over my inmates. My cell no. was 1131. It was a small job with a bed, sink, night table, and air conditioner.

Nothing much happened the first night. My mom and dad visited till visiting hours were over. At 6:00, some horrible thing called "dinner" was set before me. I gathered that I was supposed to eat it and attempted to chisel away at the mashed potatoes. This was quite hard since the forks and knives were plastic (an extra precaution against hospital breaks). Of course, not all their food was bad. Breakfast in fact was pretty good. Two bowls of Captain Crunch, milk, juice, tea, and some soggy toast. (oh well)

At 9:00 I was sent to the treatment room for my first session. I was to go there every three days to have a new "I.V." stuck in my arm. The room was filled with needles, syringes, and blood-stained sheets. The doctor was finished with me at 9:30.

Since I had none of my belongings, I couldn't keep myself busy. Eventually, I got bored and fell asleep early. It was just as well, since they woke me at 5:30 A.M. I was awakened that morning and every morning at 5:30 by a therapist, whose job was to physically persuade my lungs to get better. I went back to sleep until 8:00.

That first day was a busy one. I had medicine. I had to get my hospital number tagged onto my wrist. I had to get into my hospital uniform. (striped pajamas)

At 9:30, I had to get my mug shots down at x-ray. Mugshots are no spring picnic. They make me take off most of my clothes. Then I have to lean against a frozen x-ray screen. But what's worse, is that I'm not allowed to *breathe or move for 45 seconds, while the mug shots are taken.*

I started making friends soon after the first few days. A new bunch of inmates came in. One of them said, "What are you in for?"

"Two weeks for harboring a lung infection," I replied.

I realize now the hospital was the best thing that could have happened to me. I feel better than I have in a long time, and for once I can take deep breaths of air without automatically coughing. I feel rested, but most important . . . I feel healthy. It's almost a new experience for me.

That was my essay. I got an A+.

But even with her troubles, she maintained an upbeat outlook about her life and the future. She spent carefree summers on Fire Island with her father. The first summer they lived on a houseboat in Fair Harbor and she told me she never had so much fun, loafing and gabbing and swimming and lying in the sun, spending all day with her dad. The next summer she fell in love.

She came back that August in a torn red T-shirt that said Fair Harbor Fire Department across the front and came down to her knees. I gave her a long hug and followed her into her room. I wanted to hear everything—all the details missing from the few short letters she'd written.

"How was your summer, dear? As good as last year?"

"Better. We had a beach house this time and it was even more fun than the houseboat. I wasn't sick once and I gained four pounds."

"That's great. Who gave you the T-shirt?"

"The fire chief." She was distant, as if she weren't home yet.

"Looks like it's ready for a car wash." It was stretched out and faded as well as torn.

"No, it's not. I wore it all summer and I love it. I slept in it too."

This was more relaxed living than I had imagined, and I said, "I can't imagine a life so unpressured that you don't even change your clothes."

"You wouldn't understand. You're too square."

I didn't answer. Was that what she thought? The way she said it, like a door closing, made me uneasy. I'd have to open that door in the next few days before she locked me out. She didn't seem glad to be home the way she had been last year. Or was it a message in code that meant, I need you?

I didn't have to wait to find out. The next day, she came into my room in tears, coughing and crying. She was so miserable she didn't think she could go on with her life. When I asked her what she was talking about she threw herself across my bed and said, "Oh Mom, I'm in love with the fire chief and he doesn't even know I exist. To him, I'm just a little girl." I relaxed.

"You *do* look young, but you're far from a little girl. A fourteen-year-old can feel love as deeply as any grown-up."

"I know," she said. "Romeo and Juliet were only twelve."

We talked for a while and I asked, "What's his name?"

"Matt Murphy."

"What does he look like?"

She showed me a picture. "That's him at the table on the left." I chuckled to myself. I'd never seen a fire chief like this. He was about thirty, wore swimming trunks and sandals, and had a light-brown beard and long hair. He was sitting at the end of a table next to her father, holding a mug of beer.

"He's nice looking." So because she needed a shoulder to cry on, we talked about love and how to survive without it. It was Chris and me again, together, working things out.

She begged for a dog, a golden retriever. I didn't think we should have a hunting dog cooped up in an apartment, so I got her a new hamster. Hardly the same thing, but she took all the love she would have heaped on a dog and gave it to the hamster.

Journal Entry—

I've got the cutest hamster in the world and his name is Paddington.

I think Paddington's beginning to like me. Hope so 'cause I like him.

If I like-a you and you like-a me . . . I went to the doctor's today—I'm not doing so good.

I love Paddington

Journal Entry—

My weight's down and my slight lung infection hasn't been affected by the antibiotics.

I get worried when I've had a bad checkup. I thought I had been eating a good 3 meals a day. I guess I better start recording and watching my eating habits.

Good Night Prayer

Now I lay me down to sleep,
I pray the Lord my soul to keep.
If I should die before I wake,
I pray the Lord my soul to take.

Dear God, God Bless: Mommy, Daddy, Padding, Jenny, my stepfather, Nipper, Paddy-paws . . . Nonnie, Papa, Martin, Janis, Jackie, Mike . . . Grandma, Grandpa, Nancy, Matthew, Nessie, Francie, Berta, Jeff, Tucky. . . .
Jean, Babe, Betty, Janie, Jim, David . . .
Matt, Mrs. Motley, Caroline, Cindy, Ginny, Mrs. Monohan, Claudia, Emily and all my other friends at school . . .
Chevy, John, Jane, Lorraine, Gilda, Garret, Herb, Michael, Elliot, Candice, Buck, Lily, Scred, and all my other friends from NBC Saturday Nite Live . . .
Jim, Frank, Richard, Rollie, Carroll, Fran, and all the rest of the gang at Muppets . . .
and God Bless all the people in the world that I know and love and care for . . . and protect them from any harm—physical or mental harm and don't let anything really bad happen. And please as I say everynite help us humans solve at least some of the problems in our world. P.S. include me in all that too, please. Now as for me . . . Please God, please make it so I zip through my Latin

term paper and let me get a B or better on it. Oh! please, please, please, please!!

Also, help me clear up my tiredness and frustration.

Last but not least, please give me a good long life and let my parents grow old and have a very long life with me.

(Give me a boyfriend also please. Hey! You could even let me get married to Matt Murphy and let us be happy together till we. . . . pass away (I don't like the word die).

But for the moment your main job is the Latin term paper. Please make it so that I start writing and don't stop practically until I'm finished.

Thank you, I love you and remember what I said. Please God, bless me also.

Good night, I love you and AMEN.

This is what I really say each night (except for some of the wishes which change). As a matter of fact that was actually for tonight. I thought it would turn out more correct and true and real that way.

Good night   (yawn)

I love Paddington

My idea was used for Saturday Night Live. I'm so proud. Well, I've got to hit the sack.

Good night
(Yeah!)

I love Paddington

Hee hee. Paddington's so cute. I love to watch him go about his work in such a serious business-like way. He's got such long claws—(make that nails—he's not a monster). I love it when his cheek pouches are stuffed with food. He looks so funny.

I love Paddington

I'm just so keyed up. I guess with my term paper coming up, and my health, and so on. But the thing is, I already can't find all that many things bothering me to make me so keyed up. I feel that something is terribly wrong like one would when they had a big problem, yet I can't think of anything that's big enough to be bothering me that much.

I don't have a fever, but I've got that awful feeling like I do. I've lost my will to do anything. What is that?

Journal Entry—

Dear Paddington,

I'm sorry I haven't been able to give you my undivided attention lately but I'm off balance with my schedule. I know how lonesome it must get when I'm not even present in the room and you have to make all the noise by yourself. But soon, as I have been saving money, I'll be getting you a nice female hamster for your companionship. Then, unless I miss my guess, there'll be lots of little Paddingtons around the place.

"We're happy as can be, doin' what comes naturally."

Just remember, I love you lots and . . . stop acting like a squirmy worm when I pick you up.

love Chris

I love Paddington

Tuesday night—My Dad looks good. Today I went to Sesame Street with him and watched him tape. Northern and Bob were telling me how beautiful I will be and . . . am. It was so embarrassing but nice anyway. I'm always embarrassed when complimented more than once. Oh God, Northern Calloway is so cute. He plays David on Sesame Street. I love hanging around my Dad at his work.

Good night

Oh, things don't seem to be going well. I'm angry when I wake up, angry during thumps, angry at my parents, angry at my friends, angry trying to get to school, angry about almost everyone and everything.

Arlene (my phys. therapist) asked me why I was angry this morning, and that's when I knew what is and has been wrong with me. I've said a few times that I felt strange and uncomfortable and that's what's wrong. I can't pinpoint why and what is causing my anger. This morning I got so fed up with my mother and stepfather talking quietly about my outlandish behavior, that I screamed. I mean really screamed. Not Ahhh but something like. . . . eeeeeaaaaaeeeeeaaaee!! (the kind of scream you hear in horror movies.) I heard my mother mumble, "Oh God, what is it now?" to herself. I yelled, "Maybe, I'm going crazy—alright?!"

Things that are making me emotionally unstable are:

a) My stepfather—when he has any tone of voice other than a happy one. Strange but it's true, his tired and annoyed voice kills me. Also, when he tells me to cool it or lower my tone of voice when his is just as bad. When he nags. When he is unfair. Also when he yells at me when Jenny is out of hand and I get upset.

b) My mother when she argues with me for anything and claims that I didn't tell her my plans or something and I know I did.

c) Stupidity—as in cab drivers and bus drivers etc., or even a friend.

d) Nastiness—as in people in buses, esp. nasty old ladies

calling me and my generation degenerate and people just violently pushing and shoving. I feel like scratching their faces off.

e) Any little thing that goes wrong.

f) Thumps and my sickness. I always go upstairs at school and then pant, gasp, and cough my guts out. I also (almost always) feel anger towards whoever does my thumps. Just cause they're doing it.

g) Of course, being around people I detest.

Good-bye for now.

Journal Entry—

Monday: Paddington's gone. Friday night while I was asleep he got out of his cage. I love him so much and now he's gone. I don't know where he is or what he's doing. My heart is broken.

People think I'm silly to be so upset, but I can't help it. I love all animals and I love him. I just feel dead or lost or something. I don't know. My stepfather got all angry with me cause I wouldn't tell him and Mom what was wrong. (They didn't realize how upset I was about Padd.) I just didn't want to discuss it cause it made me more upset, so I stayed in my room because otherwise they would have yelled at me for being so quiet and mopey. Instead I was yelled at for staying in my room and not being "one of the family."

Boy, what do they want from me? I only stayed in my room cause I was upset and didn't want them to get nasty with me. And finally my stepfather made me tell against my will. I felt I would get no peace until I told them, so I did at the top of my lungs and I said the reason I didn't was cause I didn't want to talk about it and besides it hurts to talk about Paddington being gone. I was crying and trembling and Mom ran and hugged me and you know what my stepfather did? Instead of saying he was sorry for *making me talk about it, he yelled, "What the fuck was so hard about that, blah, blah, blah." I could have slashed his face with a knife for that. Oh, I can't put it into words. Do you understand my getting mad? I wasn't ready to discuss it yet and he blamed me for it.*

Bye

Oh, I miss Paddington so much. I don't think I'll ever see him again. I always get cheated with animals. Either I have to give them away or they get lost or die. It's not fair. I take good care of my animals and I love them like I would my own child. It should happen to people who don't care for their animals. I say a prayer every night and still no hamster. Mom found a little space on the floor around my radiator pipe—big enough for him to get through. I think that's where he went. My other one too, I bet.

In the fall of 1976 when Chris was fifteen we moved to a Tudor house in White Plains. Maybe more room, and a change in surroundings and life-style, would cut through the tension that bound my husband and me in continual conflict. She entered the tenth grade at White Plains High.

A few months into our new arrangement Christine had a dreadful fight with her stepfather over the fact that an electric blanket had been purchased for the master bedroom, but when she requested one for her room, with a northern exposure the coldest in the house, he refused. I took her side and, later that week, I decided she was old enough (and unhappy enough) to know about my decision to initiate divorce proceedings sometime soon, confident she'd understand it had nothing to do with her. It was a dreadful, difficult decision, and I shared this with no one but Chris. She was then and remained my confidant. She used to call herself the dormouse.

Christine's hospital admissions came once or twice a year in those days. Though she wasn't very strong, and was alarmingly thin, she had only minor bleeding episodes. What she did have was a general and growing malaise of chronic, lesser symptoms. She told me she never felt healthy anymore but she still hoped to reverse the trend. She asked for a ten-speed bike for her sixteenth birthday. She only rode it once.

Colds, fevers, exhaustion, chills, dizzy spells, headaches, violent coughing spasms, interrupted sleep, the backaches and pains in the joints of her knees, which came from lack of oxygen and plagued her with no respite. Stairs were hard for her and at times she walked like an arthritic old woman.

In the hospital that winter, Dr. Ores walked into Christine's hospital room with a tiger-striped tabby kitten in her arms and said, "Christine, we really must find this kitten a home. Would you like to provide one?" Christine didn't even think twice.

"Oh yes, let me see." Dr. Ores had gently put the five-month-old kitten on Christine's lap. For the next five days the nurses helped hide the kitten, I got a traveling cat container, and she came home with a *real* pet. She named her cat Ivy, after the abbreviated form of intravenous. Ivy was a model cat, maybe a little shy, and Christine let Ivy sleep on her feet every night, which was not as warm as an electric blanket, but much nicer.

I'd begun an even more high-powered job that year as fashion director for Allied Stores. I loved the work in retailing, but no longer enjoyed my success. My disagreement with my husband about our pressurized life-style had worsened. The pressure grew and the demands grew. I left the house at seven and came home at seven and we went out several times a week. We entertained. Housekeepers came and went and my desire to be home with my children filled my thoughts. The theory that working mothers could make up for their absence by spending "quality time" with their children for an hour a day was nonsense to me. Jenny needed me now as much as Christine, and I was so overcommitted I didn't have enough time to give to anyone, myself included. Distracted and frenetic, I banged my legs black and blue walking into things as I rushed from here to there.

In August 1977, Chris was sixteen and my husband and I separated. With the children I moved to a three-bedroom apartment in White Plains. I regretted the break but I didn't feel any guilt this time. I had given everything but something was out of balance, and the marriage could not survive. As amicable as my first divorce had been, this one was ugly.

Over the course of the next year, I began seeing James Cordon, a brilliant, energetic man I'd worked for when I was a fashion director at a textile company. Recently separated from his wife, he had hazel eyes and hazel hair and saw himself as part Ernest Hemingway, part F. Scott Fitzgerald, part Baron Rothschild, part Mel Brooks (thank God for that), and a little Walter Mitty. We looked to each other for emotional support as we put our lives back together. We had a lot in common. He too was adjusting to a new life-style and had moved to a small apartment. His daughters were grown and he had custody of his son, Jimmy, a sophomore at Rye Country Day School.

In March 1978, Jim invited Chris and me to the student-faculty musical production of *Once Upon a Mattress*. Jimmy had a leading role. We went backstage after the curtain to say hi to Jimmy and Chris was very quiet. She stood and watched the chaotic scene, students hugging each other, teachers hugging students, parents calling congratulations and saying hello to teachers. The kids laughed and carried on—having a wonderful time, like a family reunion, and then went to the cast party.

When we got to the car, Chris climbed into the back seat and burst into tears.

"Oh God," she said, burying her head in her knees. I turned around.

"Chris, what is it?"

She kept crying. I gave Jim a bewildered look, and asked her again. She finally looked up and said, "Oh, Mom, that's what I want, what I saw backstage. Jimmy's so lucky to be part of it." She started to cry again.

I wasn't sure I understood and I said, "Chris, you're not just talking about the play, are you? You're talking about—well—the kids and the feeling backstage, the closeness. Is that what you mean?"

I handed her a Kleenex and she sat back with a long sigh, saying, "Sorry, Jim." She sounded very tired. "Yes, that's what I mean. They were having so much fun. I knew there had to be more than what I have at White Plains High."

How could I have missed it? Christine would never be happy in a huge public school of two thousand kids. She'd continue to be lost in the shuffle as she had been since she'd started the year before, in tenth grade. Without a second thought, I said, "Chris, would you like to apply to Rye Country Day for next year?"

"Oh, come on, Mom, it can't be that easy. It's March already. There isn't time. Besides, no one applies to a private school for one year. I'll be a senior next year."

"You'll apply for entry as a junior. It'll give you a chance to catch up." I looked over at Jim as I said it and he nodded just enough for me to see he agreed.

"No, they'll never go along with it. There's no chance."

"There's always a chance. How would you feel if I called tomorrow and talked to the director of admissions and tried to set up an appointment for you?"

She didn't respond at first and then she said, in the smallest voice, "Would you?"

Oh, how I loved her. The way she said it—as if she couldn't believe I was serious and as if she thought she wasn't good enough to want the best but she wanted it anyway. I couldn't afford it, but surely Jerry could. I was confident he'd agree with me and not be upset that I hadn't asked him first. I'd just explain that there wasn't time.

The next day I talked with the director of admissions. He hesitated; they really had no openings left in the eleventh grade. I explained the situation to him: Christine's illness and my new realization that she needed a different kind of school environment. He said we could apply even though it didn't look promising, and asked for the name of Christine's doctor. I gave him Dr.

Ores's name and all her phone numbers, and suggested that she might give him a clearer picture of Christine's health and her special needs.

Chris was so excited. I heard her discussing the idea with her physical therapists and with Jimmy and with Jim's daughters, Cindy and Lysa. It was all she talked about. Then a couple of days before her interview, she came into the kitchen while I was fixing supper, perched herself on the footstool and said, "Mom, maybe we shouldn't do this. I mean, it's going to be much tougher academically. Aren't we just fooling ourselves? My grades aren't as good as they used to be."

I looked at her in surprise. "Chris, what are you talking about? You don't usually quit before you start."

"Well, Jimmy says I'll never get in. He says it's too tough and we shouldn't bother. Play rehearsals are every night during productions, and you have to do all the homework anyway—and on time."

I looked at her, perturbed. "What does he know? He doesn't know what you can do. I wouldn't pay any attention."

"I don't know, Mom. He's possessive about his things. I mean, it's bad enough you may marry his father, but he made it pretty clear Rye Country Day is his territory."

I said slowly and deliberately, "Christine, Rye Country Day is *not* Jimmy's territory. It's the territory of anyone who's qualified to go there. *I* think you're going to get in." She didn't say anything. "Don't let him discourage you. You're an extraordinary girl and I'm sure the director of admissions will see it when he meets you. He's talked with Dr. Ores, you know."

She looked up with interest. "He has?"

"Yup. And I'm sure Dr. Ores was very complimentary and supportive. You know how effective she is when she uses her serious voice." Chris laughed. She hadn't heard that tone as often as I had, but enough to know what I meant. She brightened.

"Well, then he knows all the complications, like having to arrange physical therapy during one of my free classes, and all that stupidness?"

"Yes, dear, he knows everything."

She scrunched up her knees on the footstool, resting her chin on her hands, and said, "You think I'm going to get in?"

"Yes, I do."

She pondered silently—watching me clatter in the cupboard looking for the top to a saucepan that was heating on the stove. Out of the corner of my eye, I saw her foot start to jiggle restlessly, then stop.

"Well, maybe you're right." she said.

"Damn right I am," I muttered. And I was.

BOOK II

CLOUD NINE

"I want everyone to know me . . ."

—Christine, 1980

6 · Rye Country Day School

Chris made friends quickly at Rye Country Day. A master at camouflage by now, no one knew she was sick. Like a water skeeter finally pointed in the right direction, her course ran smooth. She talked about classmates and teachers and the names began to sound familiar even though I hadn't met them. There were no complaints.

I took a deep breath, but didn't react when she asked me to pick her up late one day because she was going to try out for cheerleading. She didn't make it, but she was fine. Then she told me she'd just wanted to meet people and get into the school spirit—which she did. She never actually did the cheers.

The day she wore her famous white paper jumpsuit and did the Mr. Gumby routine with Andy in the hall was the beginning of a long friendship. Whenever Andy threw out a line, Chris had the comeback and vice versa. They expanded "Monty Python" routines, added Steve Martin, Peter Cook and Dudley Moore, and "Saturday Night Live" skits. Chris had her father's gift with voices and could imitate any and all of the Muppets. Andy was fascinated to learn that Jerry had created the Muppet role of Scred in the early days of "Saturday Night Live." No one he knew had ever spent time on the set. Andy thought Chris was more English than American and should have an English name like Victoria or Stephanie or Elizabeth.

Rye Country Day's social life centered in the halls of the Pinkham Building where upper-school classes were held. In this respect, it was no different from White Plains High, but there the similarity ended.

The public high school was a typical, heterogeneous mix of two thousand teenagers with classes of thirty or more and free time loosely supervised. Rye Country Day was a homogeneous group of three hundred hand-picked students, who were closely watched and nurtured and of whom much was expected—a college preparatory school. Classes could be as small as half a dozen students.

The socializing of the upperclassmen here was more intimate and the carpeted halls were used as their common room. Friends were made and relationships begun as the students sprawled and relaxed between classes, watching each other come and go. When the aisles were clogged with students, rows of blue-jeaned legs and sneakered feet stretched across the floor from both sides as students cheerfully picked their way through a jagged pathway in the middle. Everyone knew everyone else. Chris loved it.

The school had done away with its dress code in the sixties and more than one parent had been taken aback by the students' ragged mix of apparel. But the relaxed appearance belied a demanding faculty, a rigorous and competitive attention to academics, and a proud, if understated, school spirit.

In October I asked Chris how things were going with Jimmy and she was noncommittal.

"We have English and history together, Mom, but he has his friends and I have mine."

When we went to Jim's for dinner that weekend, Jimmy invited two friends over from Rye Country Day, boys Christine knew. He ushered them into his room and shut the door—excluding her. I wondered why Jimmy's friends didn't object, but he was so overbearing I suppose they didn't dare—and neither did I. When I went to classes on Parents' Day, early in the first term, I understood why she wasn't bothered.

Chris and Jimmy were in the same American history class, and a planned debate about the Civil War pitted Chris and Jimmy against each other as captains of opposing teams. I was proud that she was captain of her team, but thought, Oh boy, Jimmy will wipe her out.

The debate began ten minutes after the class did, as the teams arranged themselves on opposite sides of the room and the parents watched from the back. It started simply enough, with standard rules and time limits, but there was considerable levity and, little by little, the debate got out of hand. Trying to keep order, the two captains took over—matched quips and insulted each other's positions, using their wits to win points. Both Chris and Jimmy were extremely funny and the teacher, who wasn't much older than the students, made the mistake of laughing at their jokes.

The others cheered, booed, and hissed, egging them both on, as voices kept rising and the amused parents looked back and forth. I kept my eyes on Chris. Then Jimmy started yelling at the top of his lungs, his two-hundred-pound baritone voice bouncing off the walls as everyone stared at him. The rules were ignored and he was in his glory.

But Chris was undaunted. Quoting Charles Laughton in *Witness for the Prosecution*, she accused him of "chronic and habitual yelling," and then she yowled a protest in her best punk-rock cockney. The teacher couldn't regain the authority she'd lost and, for sheer volume, there was no shouting down Jimmy. Chris walked saucily up to him and declared him out-of-line and overtime, in elegant Monty Python, then started to cough, collapsing in her seat as she laughed and choked. Her team booed Jimmy for his unfair tactics and his team cheered her sitting down, thinking it meant they'd won. But they hadn't and the class bell rang.

As she filed out, she grinned my way. It certainly hadn't been a wipeout. This was a Christine I'd never seen, though Jerry knew this side of her very well. For years they'd joked and clowned their way through long rehearsals on the Muppet set and she was no shy and tongue-tied teenager, but a self-assured, good-humored, clever, fearless charmer, who was very grown up and very, very funny.

Her instinct for holding center stage reminded me of her father, but her devastating wit was all her own. I never forgot that day and I knew why she loved the school and wasn't bothered by Jimmy. She belonged.

Her only disappointment was she didn't have a boyfriend and she talked about it all the time.

She said, "Lots of girls don't have boyfriends, so I'm not alone, but it doesn't help. And everybody seems to be in love with someone who doesn't love them." She had so many reasons why no boy would ever like her: She was too flat-chested, she had nothing to offer, they must know she was sick, her cough must be such a turnoff, she was too thin and they'd never take a chance with her.

We talked about love and infatuation and crushes and the difference between them, and how to get over boys who didn't know you existed and, even worse, boys who gave you signals in school, but didn't ever call. She'd say, "What's wrong with me, Mom, why don't I have a boyfriend? What am I lacking? I just can't stand it anymore."

Driving home with her classmate Phebe one night, as the evening star hung low in the sky, Chris had said,

> Star light, star bright,
> first star I see tonight,

and Phebe continued,

> wish I may, wish I might,
> get the wish I wish tonight.

And they both paused and then said in unison, "God, I wish I had a boyfriend." They laughed, amazed, amused, a friendship growing.

She kept looking for answers, while I tried to deflect her self-doubt, telling her it was the mischief of chemistry. I even suggested to her once, after Parents' Day, "You know, Chris, I wouldn't be surprised if some boys lacked confidence in their own appeal, just like you, and might feel they could never keep up with you. I mean how funny you are. They might rather be funny themselves and make you laugh."

But Christine dismissed it. She thought it was her illness. "Mom, everybody in school is funny . . . *almost* everyone. That has nothing to do with it." But I thought it could.

And then, as if to confirm her fears, in October, six weeks after she started school, she was back in the hospital, grumbling that now she'd never find a boyfriend. She told her friends she'd been

walking around with pneumonia and hadn't realized it. True—
but she said nothing about cystic fibrosis.

She had a bad time with needles at that admission. Her veins
kept "blowing" and her arms and ankles were punctured and
swollen and bruised. But two days before she got out, she changed
her tune about boyfriends. Jenny and I were visiting, and Jenny
and Chris were playing a game of Fish on the bed. Jenny was five
and her little hands couldn't hold the cards right.

"Mom, I know why I don't have a boyfriend—because I'm not
in the dating crowd." She almost sounded happy.

"Who told you that?" I bent over to adjust Jenny's cards.

"Claudia—on the phone last night." It was funny that again
her best friend was a girl named Claudia. "That's why Jay hasn't
noticed me."

Jenny and I looked up at her. "Who's Jay?" I asked.

"Jay Packer. You never heard of Jay Packer?" she said. Jenny's
mouth was open and she was shaking her head slightly as if the
question was for her. I could never think of clever comebacks,
only inane straight lines.

"How would I hear of him?"

She sat up high on the bed. "Jay Packer is *the* preeminent
soccer player at Rye Country Day and probably the most gorgeous blond-haired blue-eyed deity to touch the carpet on the
floor of the Pinkham Building. I'm not the only girl who has a
crush on him."

"It doesn't sound like you've made this easy for yourself," I
said.

Chris looked at Jenny. "That's me, Jen. I always go for the
best." And then she said, "Jacks."

Jenny handed her three jacks with a crestfallen look, and Chris
reached over and fixed Jenny's cards again.

"Let's face it, Chris," I said, "we're all of us part of a vast and
crowded cosmic dance—little molecules in the endless universe,
restlessly jostling each other."

"Yup," said Chris, "looking for mates and hoping for love.
Eventually I'll connect. It's just a matter of time. I have to find my
molecule."

Jenny looked back and forth at us, and said, "What are you talking about?" and then, accidentally, she leaned on Christine's IV tubing and Chris screamed as the needle started to pull loose. I yelled, yanked Jenny away, and cards scattered over the bed.

"Oh God . . . Oh God," Chris moaned. Jenny froze. She couldn't speak. Chris recovered quickly and said, "It's okay, Jenny, it's okay. It didn't come out. It's just that you have to be careful when you're sitting on the bed." Jenny's eyes filled with tears and she found her voice.

"I'm sorry, I'm sorry." She started to cry. Chris leaned over and took Jenny's hand.

"Jenny, it was an accident. It's okay. Don't cry. It's not the first time it's happened. Mom did the same thing once."

Jenny nodded in shame but it took her the rest of the day to forget what she'd almost done to her sister. It was odd. Chris was the one that was suffering, but Jenny seemed more fragile at times.

7 · Fitting In

Back at school, Chris made friends with John Egan.
John was a Falstaffian young man with golden red hair, a bubbling
laugh, and a surprising, turned-up nose. He towered over Chris
and they couldn't have a conversation that wasn't full of shrieks,
strange voices, and laughter. Like children, they could slip into
a world of fantasy. Chris said he was more of a media nut than she
was. He wanted to be an actor and they both tried out for all the
plays at school. Then John fell in love with her.

Journal Entry—

*It's so stupid. All my friends, practically, have a crush
on someone that doesn't know they exist. And at the same
time, someone who they don't like has a crush on them.
AGH! I have a crush on Jay. John Egan has a crush on me.
I like John . . . but not* that *way. I have to be careful.*

They'd been going to movies together and buying records and
rock magazines and suddenly Chris was afraid to let their friendship develop further, sure John would think she was leading him
on. She couldn't bear to hurt anyone, so slowly and carefully she
spent less time with him for a while, trying to let him know she
loved him dearly but didn't share his romantic feelings. But she
missed him and that was when her friendship with Claudia deep-
ened.

Claudia was a natural femme fatale with tawny chestnut hair.

She sent mixed messages of unattainability and availability, keeping the boys interested and off balance. Claudia knew what was going on with everyone and who had a crush on whom before anyone else did, and, because of her canny sense about people and relationships, she put great importance on loyalty to her friends. She counted John Egan as one of these friends and was sympathetic to his predicament, while at the same time becoming a close friend of Christine's. Claudia was the first person Chris told about cystic fibrosis.

Chris was back in the hospital again in December, the second time in three months. This time she was more frightened and depressed. She hated being conspicuous for the wrong reasons: for always having a cough, for being excused from sports, for landing back in the hospital. Most of her new friends had last seen the inside of a hospital at birth. At White Plains High the year before, she had been one of many students with unexplained absences. But Rye Country Day was so closely knit that everyone noticed. Andy, John, Claudia, and Phebe came to visit her.

While she focused on her friends, I focused on her grades. Now that she was at prep school, and talking about college, I diligently brought all her books and assignments to the hospital, noting with irony that, after at last being able to give my daughter the best, she might be too sick to take advantage of it.

Her books just sat there. She was cavalier and said, "I can't work in the hospital, Mom, you know that. I never could."

"But it's more important now, dear; maybe you could try a little harder. You have such a good mind and you have so much time on your hands."

"I can't."

Other kids in the hospital could do it. I saw them studying. Why couldn't she? I said abruptly after moments of silence, "You can't, or you won't?"

She didn't answer, but turned on the overhead TV, flipping through the channels idly, so I dropped it. There was no point in scolding her. Somehow she'd catch up.

When I spoke to Dr. Ores the next day she told me, "Christine is very depressed. She's not eating. She's not sleeping. She loves school and she's angry and resentful over what's happening to her. Don't expect her to do much homework in the hospital."

I nodded. "I suppose she has to have her way on something. Do you think a psychiatrist might help her deal with the anger?"

"I don't think so now. She's not neurotic. But if she was receptive, perhaps."

I tried talking to her, but didn't get far. She said, "I don't want to talk to some old German with a beard. How can you think he'll understand my problems?" She was munching pretzels.

"I'm not suggesting Sigmund Freud, you know—he's dead."

"Oh, you know what I mean, Mom. Me, with a shrink? Do you think I'm losing my marbles?" She was letting pretzels dribble out of her mouth as if she were demented.

"Chris, be serious. You're *not* losing your marbles—"

"No, I'm losing my pretzels"—and we both laughed.

I continued, "You have a real health problem that's doing a good job of ruining your happiness. It doesn't mean you're neurotic. It's what they call a reality conflict. Maybe a psychiatrist could help you deal with it?"

"Can he cure me?"

"I'm not going to answer that. You have nothing to lose."

"Nothing," she snapped, "except being forced to do one more thing I don't want to do. I can deal with it myself."

"It's your decision, Chris," I snapped right back. She could be such a know-it-all sometimes, and sometimes I was a nag.

When she got out of the hospital, she returned to drama club tryouts. She landed a small part in the school's production of *A Funny Thing Happened on the Way to the Forum,* and she also did props. Andy was in the chorus. She loved rehearsals and said it was a wonderful way to get to know people. Having a small part had certain advantages. She was almost never onstage—and that left her plenty of time to sit around and talk with her friends—her favorite pastime.

I was concerned about her schoolwork again. As the play progressed, she never seemed to study. And I was even more concerned about her health. She was the last one to turn out her lights every night. Her physical therapist came at six every morning, no matter how late she was up the night before. If she missed her morning thumps, she'd be congested and she'd cough all day, so she never did. She lost weight and she looked tired and drawn. Though she didn't usually wear makeup, the heliotrope shadows under her eyes were so noticeable that she started to use cosmetic whitener underneath, blending it artfully. The weekends were spent sleeping.

She refused to slow down and went to every rehearsal.

After dress rehearsal, she said, "Mom, I'm appalled at how much work the play still needs. Some kids still don't even know their cues, which is worse than not knowing their lines because the play just grinds to a halt." I was reading in bed and Jim was asleep. I put my book down.

"They don't take it seriously, Chris. It's a lark to them."

She was standing close to the bed and said in a low voice, "I don't mind doing less than my best in my studies, but to do less than my best onstage—it's unthinkable."

I sighed and smiled at her. She was watching to see if I disapproved. I could understand. Performing made her forget, and I said, "That's why you're so good, Chris." I didn't mention her studies.

Then on opening night, she fell in love again and I heard no more about the "dating crowd." A few minutes after the curtain fell, while the audience shuffled out, Chris went across the darkened stage, into the wings, to replace the props for the next performance. Andy stepped behind the curtain from out front and saw Chris there alone. Walking over to the prop table, he looked at her impishly, put down a makeshift sword, and said, "Chris, you wanna fool around?"

Chris looked up and said, "Yes."

If Andy was surprised, he never let it show. He put his arms around Christine, pulled her into the heavy velvet curtains, and kissed her passionately. She kissed him back and laughed at his sudden embrace.

Their "fooling around" ended as quickly as it had begun, for Andy at least. He had no way of knowing that Christine, for all her flirting and merriment at school, was too vulnerable for games. The kiss didn't mean anything to him but it was her first real kiss and she couldn't forget it. One kiss, and she was madly in love.

Journal Entry—

> *I wonder if it really meant anything to him. Sometimes I wish I could just cry on his shoulder and have him hold me and tell me it'll be alright—everything, I mean, my health, my loneliness, my schoolwork, my father, (sigh) my health.*

But Andy was going steady and Christine entertained no thoughts of winning him. Even if she'd had the confidence to try, which she didn't, the idea of stealing someone else's boyfriend was unthinkable. They kept on doing new "Monty Python" routines in front of their lockers, amusing their friends, and that just made Chris care even more.

A week after the play, Christine's lungs were filled up with secretions again. She increased her thumps to three times a day but it didn't help. She could hardly breathe and her violent coughing spasms were terrifying. She'd put it off too long. She refused to let her friends see her lose control of her coughing; on January 24th, she called Dr. Ores and made an appointment at Babies. She was admitted to the tenth floor again, having gotten out just a month before. Her mood blackened. But three days later, a new antibiotic from England took effect, her lungs began to clear, and when she could breathe she cheered up.

She hated the hospital, but she knew the antibiotics kept her going. And over the years, she managed to carve out a niche for herself. She knew everybody on the floor, the treating doctors, the interns, the residents, the orderlies who drew blood, the maids, the volunteers, the clinical-services staff. They liked her. Residents came and went—some gifted, some uninspired—and Chris had something to say about all of them. Her favorite was Dr. John Woods. He was a gentle, funny young man and a wonderful doctor, with rare compassion for the children.

He was the head pediatric resident now and Chris had known him since his internship. He had gifted hands. No matter how collapsed and scarred her veins were, he could slide the hated IV needle into her arm or wrist gently and painlessly the first time. He never let children scream while he probed. When Christine learned that starting an IV didn't have to be the the horrible ordeal it usually was, she refused to let anyone else do her IVs. And John Woods always found the time.

Chris was no prima donna, but she could be difficult. Experience had taught her that hospital policy was set for the benefit of the institution, not individual patients, and she was vehement when she felt she was being put through needless pain and aggravation simply to comply with a rule that didn't quite fit her situation.

She was in for two weeks this time and wrote in her journal:

I think I'll be getting out Friday. YAY!! I can't wait—it's been a long haul but I made it . . . . . Thank God!

I just can't take it anymore. The doctors who think they understand but they don't, the restless nights—it's no fun to spend the night in bed when you've been forced to spend the day in bed—the painful IVs, the endless hours alone, even the patients get on my nerves sometimes.

Now I have an IV in my left hand. All the veins in my arm are either thrombosed or collapsed.

Mr. Byrd's coming to the hospital today—any minute as a matter of fact. He's my homeroom teacher.

Mauricio came to visit yesterday. He brought a cold 6 of Mich . . . that was nice. We drank it all. I'll be a free bird soon!

I have so many feelings bottled up inside . . . many I need to tell to a guy who will listen and understand . . . or at least, try to.

Sometimes I wish there was a cloud 9 . . . and I could live there with fairies, elves, hobbits, wizards, and dwarfs. I think I kind of look like an elf . . . I think it's the hair and the nose. I almost wish I was.

Elves are so evasing and vaporlike . . . they have a magic quality to them that I wish I had. I wish I at least knew some elves. I'm such a dreamer. John says I am an elf with a magical mystical quality.

And guess what!! I'm 99 pounds. For me that's great.

That spring was full of good things. First, she stayed out of the hospital for four months. Then she got her driver's license and I bought her a yellow Toyota station wagon for $1000. It rattled and had rust spots on the fenders, but she didn't care. She was thrilled with her new independence. She discovered that the seniors socialized at a tavern called the Red Barn on a rural road near SUNY college, in the neighboring town of Purchase. It was a comfortable, informal bar and grill with tables and booths—a place where their parents wouldn't go, with no cover charge, no proof checks, and cheap pitchers of beer. Chris and her friends could go in jeans, without a date, and no one objected when they carved their initials into the wood tables in the booths. In fact the owner liked it, it was good for business. Claudia, Andy, John, Jay Packer, they all went.

When Chris told me, I was uneasy at first, thinking, My daughter is going to a bar? But she waived aside my questions about whether it was legal and if she was served liquor and who else was there and how late. She said all her friends went and she only drank Cokes.

I believed her because I wanted to and I had faith in her judgment, even though she was underage. And I told her so, thinking she'd be more likely to live up to my vote of confidence than my disapproval. It never occurred to me that she and Claudia had altered their driver's licenses. In 1979, New York driver's licenses were still made of thick paper stock, unlike the Connecticut license, which was laminated in clear plastic and couldn't be touched.

But there was another reason I was giving her such latitude. She was going to the hospital more often. Her disease was progressing faster. I knew what Chris wanted out of life—it was basic—to live. But I thought again about what I wanted for her—

the love she hadn't found. My feeling that a girl of seventeen was too young for a love affair no longer applied. There wasn't time. For years I'd buried the knowledge that she was going to die, but after three admissions to the hospital in six months, with her life moving in front of me like stop-motion photography, speeded up on the one hand and abbreviated on the other, I let her go to the Red Barn with her friends.

And then Jim and I decided to get married. We were very much in love and we'd been talking about it for some time, so it was anything but a whim. After seeing two marriages unravel, the first which I'd entered with joy, the second with confidence, I attributed my doubts and uncertainties this time to maturity and experience. Even the morning of our wedding, I still wasn't sure. When I told the girls Jim and I were getting married, Chris let out a shriek and gave me a big hug and Jenny looked at me with serious eyes—no hug.

We looked for a house to rent and found one in Connecticut, in Cos Cob. The house was in a clearing in the woods at the end of a long, rutted, unpaved driveway on Cat Rock Road. Jim and I both liked old houses, which this was not—and to my surprise Chris echoed my sentiments, noticing the cost-cutting details of modern construction, like hollow plywood doors with no moldings and Sheetrock walls that weren't soundproof. She was still easily influenced in matters of style. But we all liked the two glass walls in the living room and the kitchen as big as the living room, which also had a glass wall.

We moved on April 1st and were married in our new home—a simple, happy ceremony with the immediate family. Two weeks later, we were still climbing over boxes and I had to go to Europe to cover the ready-to-wear collections in Milan, Paris, and London. I hoped it would be the last time. Jenny went to visit her father and Jim, Chris, and Jimmy were on their own for two weeks.

When I got home, the boxes had disappeared and all seemed well with our new family, but Chris had been burning the candle at both ends. She was congested and breathless and white with exhaustion. She'd just gotten out of the hospital and it seemed she was in the same condition as before she'd gone in. What was happening to her? Jim thought Chris should be on a tighter rein.

"How can you let her keep such late hours? She starts to study when I go to bed at 10:30."

"How can I control her?" I said defensively. "I argue with her endlessly. Sometimes I walk into her room and turn out the lights on her, but all it does is infuriate her and make us both miserable and angry, so I let *her* manage that part of her life."

Jim shook his head in disapproval, saying, "Well, she doesn't manage it very well."

"I know. I used to keep after her, but I feel like I drive her crazy always fussing at her about school. She's so rude, sometimes, I think she hates me."

Jim looked at me in surprise. "Don't be ridiculous—she adores you. You're all she talked about while you were away. She missed you terribly."

The new house and family had a healing effect on Christine and she thrived on all the space—in the house and out where the land felt like ours. When we moved, I bought her a romantic double bed with a white eyelet canopy. It was a surprise I'd been planning from the day we started looking for houses and I decided to tell her why. I waited till I was comfortable with the reasons and had rehearsed in my mind what to say. If I was clumsy, I'd hurt her instead of help her because she'd figure out that I was reacting to her illness and her death—that I'd never do this for a healthy child.

Shortly after I got back from Europe, I found some courage. She'd been sleeping in the fairy-tale bed for a month. It was morning and she was on her way to school—an opportune time. She'd be busy and not have time to analyze and stumble onto the truth.

"Chris, there's something I've been wanting to talk about."

"Uh-oh," she rolled her eyes.

I laughed. "It's nothing bad, don't worry. I want to tell you why I bought you the beautiful bed." I paused but she said nothing. "Well, one of the problems most young people face when they're in love is that they have no place to call their own—no place to go." I was in trouble already. I tried another approach. "You have far more struggles than most teenagers, and maybe I can help balance things out and clear away one of the obstacles other teenagers face—and make it easier for you."

She was looking at me intently. Did she know what I meant? Did she know how hard it was to bring up this taboo subject? I walked over to her window. "I mean, a lot of kids first experience love in the back seat of their car. I shudder to think of it. I want you to know, if you fall in love, well, you have my permission. It's why I bought you the bed."

"I don't think you have to worry much about that happening. I don't even have a boyfriend." She sounded as natural as if I'd come in to give her a hand-me-down sweater.

"But you never know, dear. Of course I expect you to be discreet because of Jenny . . . and all of us. I wouldn't ever want a boy in your room when Jenny's here."

"God, I'd never do that. You know that."

"I know. I just wanted to tell you, it's okay."

"Thanks, Mom. I've got to hurry or I'll be late."

Good. The expected escape. We never spoke of it again and I prayed love wouldn't betray her good sense.

Greenwich was full of vest-pocket conservancies and we started taking nature walks. We saw beavers, hawks, pileated woodpeckers, a bluebird once, jack-in-the-pulpits. It was good exercise for Christine and she gamely kept up with us.

Jim had an amazing memory for Latin names and he would walk along pointing things out with his walking stick, spouting the Latin names of tiny little green plants and scampering creatures. It spoiled things for Jenny and Chris who never got to find any-thing. Chris teased him on the first walk and said, "Jim, stop showing off."

He protested, "I'm not."

The next time we went out together, I slowed him down and said quietly, "Dear, we don't want a tour guide and this is not a competition. Let Jenny and Chris find things. Let them show you."

"Oh, sorry," he mumbled and he was much better after that. All I heard was an occasional Latin word slip absently from his lips. And when he did start up, Chris would turn and give him the eye, saying, "Jiiiiimmmmm . . ." He was a good sport.

I decided to let Christine have her first party—not just because she wanted one, but because I knew it would be good for her and good for Jenny to see her sister having a wonderful time with her friends. Jenny was five and she didn't have a thought of how sick Chris was, and I didn't want her to. The more she saw Chris as a normal big sister, the better it would be for both of them.

Chris told Jenny she could join the party if she promised to observe quietly. Jenny was a wonderful dancer, like Chris, and she loved the New Wave rock music. As Chris filled bowls with pretzels and peanuts, Jenny followed behind, asking questions about what was going to happen.

"Oh, nothing much . . . nothing special."

Jenny pressed her, "Are you going to play some games?"

Chris said absently, as she flipped through her records, "Not that I know of . . ."

Jenny gave up and Chris lugged stacks of records downstairs, planning to keep a close watch over them—without being a total fusspot. She took fanatically good care of her records and she'd seen what could happen to them at a party if no one was paying attention.

Jenny said, "Could you tell me the records?" and Chris sighed and read the titles from the stack she had in her hand, flipping them against her chest—"Heart, Police, Devo, The Pretenders, The Stranglers, Sex Pistols, Siouxsie and the Banshees, Squeeze, Clash, AC/DC, David Bowie, Blondie, Lena Lovitch, Fleetwood Mac, The Human League, Talking Heads, Oingo Boingo, Bananarama, The B-52s . . ."

Jenny interrupted. "Could you play B-52s? I want to hear 'Rock Lobster,'" and Chris smiled.

"Cool choice."

She blew dust off the record and put it on. Jenny looked out the window and said, "Hey! What's that?"

Chris looked out. "It's the flares, Jenny. It must be the policeman."

Jenny's eyes got big. "A policeman? What's he doing here?"

"Moonlighting."

"What's that?"

And Chris explained. "It's an extra job. He's off duty. Mom thought it would be a good idea to have him here to help people park out on the road 'cause it's so narrow and winding."

That wasn't the only reason of course. Party crashers were a big problem in Greenwich. Jim and I planned to spend the evening in the kitchen, and from the sliding glass doors we could see the driveway. No one had arrived yet. We watched the flares, beacons of red light flickering in the darkness, and we could hear the music, floating out into the woods, content the sounds would be muffled.

The party was called for eight. When it was 8:30, and still no one had arrived, Jenny came running up the stairs to the kitchen, saying, "Mommy, Mommy, Christine is crying! She says no one is coming to her party and all her friends have deserted her. Do you think they have, Mommy?"

"Oh no, Jenny, of course not." Jenny looked over at Jim and he nodded in agreement.

I said to Jenny, "Jen, Chris must know that. She does the same thing. No one wants to be the first to arrive. Go tell Chris not to worry and I'll be down in a minute."

She nodded and went racing downstairs. She jumped the last three steps and landed with a thud, yelling, "Chris, Chris, it's okay. Mommy says you're wrong. They're coming."

All I could hear was a long coughing spasm, probably from the crying, and Jenny saying, "Chris, are you all right?" While Jenny tried to console her, the first three cars crunched slowly up the driveway. All was well.

The party was loud and lively, as expected. What Jim and I hadn't counted on was how well behaved Chris's friends were.

The girls came up to the kitchen to introduce themselves, and Andy and Michael sat down to talk with us about school and hockey while the party raged below.

Jim and I went downstairs at one point. There was Chris dancing the wildest dance I'd ever seen. She and John would crash into each other, dance apart laughing, and crash together again. How could she do that? But she wasn't coughing. She danced and crashed, and sang along with music about "pulling mussels from a shell."

Jenny was watching and I said, "Jenny, come here a sec." She backed over to me, her eyes on Christine and John.

"Jenny, what's Chris doing?"

"Slam dancing."

"Oh." I looked at Jim. I remembered reading about a violent new dance in *Rolling Stone*. This must be it.

The song ended. Chris and John hugged each other, and pulled up their shirts to look at each other's stomachs and backs.

"They must be looking for black-and-blue marks," Jim muttered. He was joking, but it turned out that that's just what they were doing.

By two, the party was over and the night was still. I heard the last footsteps on the gravel drive and voices fading as Christine's friends made their way in the dark. The flares had burned out long ago. I went downstairs to see if the house was locked. Chris wasn't in her room and the outside floodlights were on. I stepped onto the terrace, watching the black stillness of the woods and listening for night sounds. There was light coming from the downstairs den. She must be cleaning up. But I found Chris crying on one sofa and Claudia asleep on the other. I sat next to her.

"Chris, what is it?"

"Oh, Mom, the boy I like, who's one of the reasons I had this party in the first place, went home with another girl. He didn't even say good-night." She flopped down on the sofa again.

"You mean Andy?" I felt a rush of relief—such a normal problem.

"No, I've given up on Andy. Someone else."

I groped for words, knowing nothing I could say would help,

but I didn't want to make things worse. I said, "After all the effort you went to—all it brings you is misery. Life is so unfair."

She sighed and nodded, wiping her eyes. "Claudia's spending the night, okay?"

"Of course."

The party had started in tears and ended in tears, but I was so happy. She'd come a long way from the lonely isolation at White Plains High. She had friends and she was part of something she loved. I told Jim the next morning, "You know, the best thing that ever happened to Chris is Rye Country Day. It's you I have to thank for that—you and her father."

8 · Andy

After school got out in June Chris had to go back into Babies Hospital. The night before, we packed her bags in silence. Then she said, "Mom, what's happening? Why is God doing this to me? I was *in* last August, then *again* in October, then *again* in December, right up till Christmas. In *again* in January—and now this!" She was standing in her room, her fists clenched at her sides, her eyes shut tight and her cheeks wet.

"I don't know what's happening Chris . . . the drugs just don't seem to be working as well."

"Oh, Mom"—she flopped on the bed—"I'm going to miss everything . . . it's not fair." I sat beside her.

"I know, dear, but it's only for two weeks. There'll be lots of summer left."

But I was wrong. She was in the hospital for a month. When she got home, Andy called and asked her out. He'd broken up with his girl and suddenly her summer prospects looked better. The afternoon of their first date, I sat on the edge of the tub in her bathroom and watched her do her makeup. She never used a base, but lipsticks, lip gloss, eye shadows, and mascaras held magic for her.

I watched how gently she touched her skin, applying colors to her eyelids and brow, blending with quick strokes down to a suggestion of shadowy color.

"Mom, this is my real first date. Just me and Andy alone. He's picking me up and he's paying."

"I know." Even Jenny knew about the momentous event. She leaned back and appraised her image in the mirror.

"I'm very impressed," I said.

"Oh, I'm not finished yet."

"No, I mean about Andy."

Chris examined her mascara brush and slipped it in and out of the tube, wiping the globs off the little spiral brush.

"Mmmmmmm . . . all those looks he kept giving me meant something after all."

"Yes, but I mean, I'm impressed with *you*. You didn't chase him, you didn't make a fool of yourself or lie in wait on his doorstep . . . or do any of those things girls do."

Chris leaned forward, applying mascara to her top lashes. "It's only a date, Mom."

"I know." As usual, when the conversation took a serious turn, Chris cut it short. I was used to her double standard. She was allowed to have a serious conversation with me, but I couldn't initiate one with her. The bathroom was clinically silent except for the little clicks and taps of makeup applicators colliding in use.

Her bathroom was claustrophobic. The little window was under an eave and it was useless. I felt like talking.

"The yellow walls in here are much too strong a color, aren't they?"

"Yup! But what I really can't stand is the dark brown shag rug. I mean, who in their right mind decorates a bathroom brown and yellow—I mean really!"

I laughed. I'd never even thought of it. She picked up a doll-sized white comb and patiently combed her lashes. In all the years I'd been doing my makeup, even when I was an actress in New York, I'd never combed my lashes.

But I hadn't said what I wanted to say.

"Maybe you'll believe me now when I tell you how pretty you are."

She stopped combing her lashes and said happily, "Maybe."

My belief was finally made credible by Andy's interest, but my thought that her high humor was off-putting to boys was wrong.

Andy loved it and, as time went on, her sense of humor drew
more people to her than it pushed away.

So Christine started dating Andy before he went to college at
Hobart in upstate New York. She was quiet about their relationship and wrote instead in her journal. I never asked, I was so
happy for her.

July 1979

> *Guess what! Last night (Saturday, July 7th) I went out
> with Andy. First we went to dinner with his parents at
> Pepino's. That's a sort of not-too-fancy Italian restaurant
> in Glenville. We went to see the movie Meatballs, and
> then we sat and talked in the car for a while in the parking
> lot at Richard's. We went over to my house. We listened
> to the radio in the den and then went upstairs to watch
> TV and share our beer with Jimmy. Then Jimmy left and
> that's when the fun began.*
>
> *We watched TV in each other's arms for a while. Then
> he kissed me. That was nice. He's so romantic—almost
> poetic. He told me I tasted like roses (sigh) roses!*

She'd asked me once if cystic fibrosis affected the saliva glands,
because they, too, are exocrine glands, and I'd said I didn't think
so. How much it must have meant when Andy complimented her,
although he knew nothing of her worries.

Journal Entry—

> *I have more feelings for Andy than I ever had for
> anyone.*
>
> *We played with my cat Ivy for a while and Andy held
> her. Ivy likes Andy. That's a good sign. It just does no good
> if your cat doesn't like your close friend. We didn't hire a
> housekeeper once, because during the interview, Ivy
> started stalking her and she got so weird about it.*

I hope he thinks I kiss well. He does.

Good nite

Entry—

Two weeks later—and I'm going out with Andy Friday
night. He's caused me a lot of pain since that one night of
the play. He's not going out with Cathi anymore, but I
don't know if he'll want to get involved since he's going
to college in a month or so. I want to get involved. I want
to fall in love, but I'm afraid of being hurt.

And then there's Jeff, who likes me a lot but he's going
away to college and I don't want to hurt him with my
more intense feelings for Andy.

I know Andy knows I'm a virgin, but does he know
how inexperienced I am. They say it all comes naturally
but the nerve it takes to let yourself go—doesn't.

I'm fascinated by his mind. Mom said, "What you fall
in love with, Chris, is a man's mind." I didn't know what
she meant . . . but I do now.

Entry—

Things are going well I think. Tonite I'm going out
with Andy. My health, however, is bad and I've been
trying so hard during therapy and I've been taking my
pills everyday, GOD . . . .

please don't let me be sick—
help me—
help me pull through myself . . .
please!!

I'm going to try so much harder than I have been. I
know I can do it—but I think not just on 2 sets of therapy
a day. I'll have to increase to 3 sets a day for a while or
maybe even four.

I've been coughing so hard that I get nauseous and almost throw up.

Andy's here. We're going to the movies.

Entry—

Well, Amityville Horror was alright—but not great. I was pissed. Andy couldn't stay very long 'cause the movie got out at 12:00 and we couldn't go to an earlier one because of my stupid thumps. AARRRGH!

We could have gone to the Red Barn and everything. I still had a nice time. We came back here and ate some chicken. There was no beer so we had milk. I loved watching him eat. It did my heart good to see him eat. What an All-American boy.

He didn't touch me except for a couple of kisses goodnight.

Tomorrow I go to the Doctor's . . . . Yikes! Help! Help!. . . . Help!

Please, please, with all my heart, God I'm on my knees . . . . . . help me.

Entry—

I had lunch with Jeff today. I don't know about Andy at all. I want to always be something special to him. I wonder if he meant it when he told Claudia that he loved me. He's the first person I've ever wanted to be involved with, to go to bed with.

Dad's buying me a new car . . . a Datsun I think. I hope it'll be a red one. He and Mom say the old Toyota isn't safe. It fishtails on the highway. I agree with them.

Entry—

I got so drunk Thursday night—I made a scene with Jeff. We were at the Red Barn in a booth and started kissing and stuff. (aagghh!) I was really drunk or I wouldn't

have done it—not in the Red Barn and not so soon. It led
Jeff on and I feel bad—but he knows that I was really
drunk. Afterwards, I was sick to my stomach in front of
(sort of) everyone. I was under the table so no one actually
saw it. How embarrassing!

I don't like Jeff the same way—or actually now I know
that he's not the one for me. I felt uncomfortable—that
means it was the wrong thing to do; because I felt uncomfortable with Jeff.

Entry—

My new Datsun is brown, not red. Oh well, I still love
it.

I went to Leslie Sachs' party. Andy was at the party
with some 14-year-old girl—very pretty. He was basically
behaving like an asshole but I was above that and I talked
to them both.

I can't just not talk to him because of something like
that. It would be immature. Besides he's got good taste in
women. I like talking to the girls he goes out with. It must
make him feel uncomfortable though.

Entry—

I had a wonderful time at the Red Barn with Andy
Wednesday nite. We started talking and really had a great
conversation about friendship, he and Michael. He told
me the sweetest thing about Michael. He said that
Michael didn't like Jimmy because of the way he treats me
and Jenny.

Andy and I went out to dinner Friday night for my
birthday . . . and then we went to the Red Barn for a while.
It was nice to be there with him. Then we went to my
house. We sat in the living room and started to watch this
movie. It was so bad that I just got up and turned it off.

Then we sat back and just sat in the dark for a while—

uncomfortable at first. Then he got comfortable and put his head in my lap. He lay like that for a long time—we were just touching each other. Then he sat up and started kissing me and after awhile he picked me up saying, "Let's get this right" and put me in his lap.

We kissed some more. I told him that I didn't know what to do and I was afraid of doing the wrong thing. He said to do whatever I wanted and not "do" anything if I didn't want to or if I thought it was wrong.

But I just couldn't get up the courage to do anything.

Well, he's going to take me out to Maxwell's Plum, tomorrow. It's my birthday. So hopefully, that evening.

I really have big plans for that evening . . . and I hope they all work out and that my strongest wishes and desires come true that night. I want him to be my first.

P.S. He thinks my breathing sounds like a cat purring, (sigh). How wonderful.

(I have this strange sound all the time when I breathe, but you can only hear it if it is very quiet and you put your ear next to my mouth. It is sort of a staticky, crackly sound—it comes from the disease in my lungs—although I don't know if Andy knows that.)

Monday—August 22

Well, my health's not so great but that's not new. I'll be going into the hospital Wednesday. I knew it.

Tonight I'm going to the Red Barn in hopes of finding Andy there—alone. I want to say good-bye to him, again. We went to Maxwell's Plum on Friday nite.

It was special because it was something that we shared between the two of us and nobody from Rye was there or would be there or would ever be part of it. We were in our own world.

Afterward we went to the Red Barn for a while and

then he took me home. He didn't come in this time though, maybe he didn't want anything to happen between us and he knew it would if he came in.

We just kissed each other good-bye for a while and talked a little bit. He told me that he would write me—that next to Michael and Paul, I was his best friend. That makes me feel different—special from all the other girls. When I got out of the car to get his Prince Caspian book, I put my key on the dashboard and when I got back, it wasn't there. So we started looking for it—and he had it in his hand all the time. He just looked at me and smiled. We kissed good-bye again and I got out of the car. As soon as I got in the house I started crying. I'm glad everyone was asleep.

Tuesday—August 28, 1979

Last nite I went to the Red Barn and had a great time. Andy and Michael were sitting at the bar, so I stood and talked to them about politics for a while . . . that was great fun. Then Mauricio came over and sort of scolded me for going into the hospital again and said I could've done better. I couldn't have really though and it just reminded me of my therapists and how little they really understand even though they think they do.

Anyway, tears were in my eyes, and I must have looked very sad and upset, because Andy looked at me and gave me a questioning look and he came over. He asked me quietly, almost like no one else was there, if I wanted to talk. I said yes, so he said, "Well, talk."

I started to explain to him about Mauricio and the hospital and then the tears that I had been holding back just came like a tidal wave . . . and I started crying—hard, shaking crying.

Andy just put him arms around me and hugged me. I buried my face in his neck and hugged him back while he tried to calm me saying everything would be alright.

He told me that he wasn't worried about me because he knew that I would be fine and that he had more respect for me than anybody else he knew and that he was honored to know me . . . that I was strong and I'd succeed in life because I didn't let anything stop me. "I love you," he said.

Anyway—it was a nice evening.

The last two weeks before school, Christine's health took another turn for the worse. Dr. Ores admitted her quickly, hoping to get her out in time to start her senior year with her classmates. The only nice thing about the admission was that Claudia and Andy took her into the hospital.

Journal Entry—

I thought Andy was sort of cold on Wednesday when we said good-bye. Just a kiss on the cheek and an "Aslan be with you." I ran out of the hall to the elevator with tears in my eyes. Claudia knew why and grabbed Andy and told him to keep me company till the next elevator came. He did. I said "Thanks for bringing me in." I just hugged him good-bye and he left.

I hope he writes. I won't be able to for a few days. IV is going in my right hand. Let me just say what I haven't said yet.

I love Andy dearly and truly and I wish he loved me the same way. (sniff)

good-bye

It didn't occur to Chris that Andy might have been uncomfortable at the hospital—such a difficult thing. I said nothing but told her she was lucky to have such good friends. While she was in the hospital, Andy left for Hobart.

We employed a rotating team of five physical therapists now. Chris spent a lot of one-on-one time with them and a problem developed with two, Marcia and Lillian. I was slow to react, hoping the problem would resolve itself, but it didn't.

Marcia had gotten too involved in Christine's life. She had advice to give on the smallest matter, and told Chris how to run her life. She meant well, but she was a compulsive talker.

The other therapist, her friend, Lillian, had said, "Oh, I don't really mind treating Christine . . . I'd thump a dead cow for thirty dollars."

Marcia repeated the shocking comment to Chris. I probably should have fired them both, but they apologized to me and then to Chris. She told them outright she didn't accept their apology. She put up with the situation in silence for two more months, however, privately calling Lillian "the money monger" and Marcia "motor-mouth." Then Lillian hurt Chris again. Chris wrote in her journal,

> *Damn, I'm still fuming. Yesterday I had to do thumps with the money monger. I told her I was going into the hospital for two weeks and what do you think that bitch said—*
>
> *"Oh, good, I picked just the right time for my vacation."*
>
> *Can you imagine???*

Lillian's new comment was the last straw. When Chris told me about it, she started to cry.

"Mom, how can you make me do thumps with her? You've got to fire her. I can't stand her presence in my life another day."

I was disgusted too and said, "I should have done it before. I promise, the thump session you just went though will be her last."

And I called Lillian and told her that her services were no longer needed. To my relief, her friend Marcia quit as well, in support of Lillian. In fifteen years of hiring physical therapists from local hospitals, this was the only time we ever had a problem.

While Chris was in Babies, I called Priscilla Funck, the school nurse at Rye Country Day, and asked her if she'd consider treating Chris. She agreed to do her therapy on weekends and some evenings, replacing Marcia and Lillian. I wondered why I'd never thought of Priscilla before. It reassured Chris to know the school nurse was part of her routine treatment.

That fall, a new headmaster began at Rye Country Day, Dr. Lee Pierson. Priscilla asked for a private meeting to advise him of Christine's illness. In doing the physical therapy, she'd learned how much sicker Chris was than everybody thought. There was no guarantee that Chris would finish her senior year.

It was a disturbing thought on a beautiful warm September afternoon. The campus had an air of silent expectation. In a week, school would begin and the campus would explode into life. Chris had just gotten out of the hospital and seemed well at the moment, but Priscilla knew it wouldn't last. Dr. Pierson's secretary showed her into his office.

"Dr. Pierson, we have a student here who has cystic fibrosis. She's a senior named Christine Nelson. Her health is seriously impaired and I feel you should know emergency situations could arise." She spoke in a quiet monotone. "Do you know what cystic fibrosis is?"

"Yes, I think so, but I'm not familiar with the symptoms, just that it's a lung disease of children. My understanding is that it's limited to children because they don't live long enough to reach adulthood." Priscilla nodded. "But what kind of emergencies do you mean?"

"There would be two possibilities. Pneumothorax—which is a lung collapse. This can be life threatening, and it's very painful and very frightening. Many children with c/f experience it, often more than once."

"Has Christine?"

"No . . . not yet. Or, there might be hemoptysis—bleeding from the lungs. Christine's had hemoptysis several times. She hemorrhaged twice, but both times survived. This seems to be the greatest danger for her and there's no way of knowing when her lungs will bleed again or how much. If a major artery was to be involved, she could bleed to death in a matter of minutes." Dr. Pierson closed his eyes and turned his head away.

"In a matter of minutes . . . ," he said quietly. "What causes that?"

"The disease destroys lung tissue, possibly tissue that makes up the wall of an artery, in which case, it could rupture. This isn't common, but I did read of a c/f patient dying of a massive pulmonary hemorrhage."

"How long has she been a student here?"

"She came last year as a junior. The admissions director thought she was very special."

Dr. Pierson pondered. "I take it she wasn't this ill when she was admitted."

"No, her health has declined. It always does with c/f. But she's very determined. There's another possibility, a remote one. She could go into heart failure. That's the most common cause of death but there's no danger of this happening at school."

"Oh?"

"Well, heart failure has warning signs: exhaustion, edema, puffiness, blue lips and blue fingertips, chest pain. I see her everyday so I'd spot it."

Dr. Pierson shook his head. "How much does Christine know?"

"She doesn't talk about it . . . except for the bleeding, and she's terrified of that. The other day she thought she was bleeding in the middle of her therapy so we stopped. I've never seen her so frightened. She turned sheet white, trembling."

"Was she bleeding?"

"Yes, a small one. It stopped."

"What do you mean, a small one?"

"A tiny capillary. Nothing major."

Dr. Pierson was quiet. Priscilla waited. She'd told him the worst without minimizing or exaggerating. He had to know.

"I'd like to meet her. Could you arrange it?"

"When?"

"Anytime, just let me know—a brief introduction."

Priscilla said, "She'll be in the infirmary the first day, giving me her medications."

"Good . . . I'll come over as if I'm just stopping in."

So Priscilla knew about the extent of Christine's illness, as did the headmaster and the dean of girls, Sylvia Hoag. No one else. The teachers knew she had cystic fibrosis, no more. Chris didn't want special treatment and, to all appearances, she wasn't given any.

9 · Face-Time

School started the day after she got home from the hospital. I wanted to talk to Chris about college. We'd had so many confrontations the year before about her grades and poor study habits. They'd have to improve if she was going to get into college.

I went up to her room after supper. Her hair fell over her shoulders in the soft summer light like gold from Rapunzel's spinning wheel. She was trying on clothes. Her weight was so changeable, she had clothes in sizes 3, 5, and 7. I sat on the arm of her wooden deck chair. No one ever sat *in* the chair—it was always piled with clothes.

"Chris, I don't want to start fighting again when school starts. I can't stand it, so I have a thought."

"Sure, Mom, what is it?"

"Well, college applications have to be in this fall." I paused. No response. "Do you know what date they're due?"

"No." Did she do this on purpose?

"Chris, if there's a deadline, you have to know when it is."

"Okay, okay, I *will.*" She shut me off and turned around to see how the pants she was trying fit in the back. Too loose, I could see. I pushed on.

"I'd like you to take responsibility for filling out the applications, getting your transcript, without my nagging." I waited for an answer. Still nothing. "Do you think you can do that?"

"Yes, I can *do* it," she said rudely.

"Yes, you *can,* but *will* you? That means mailing the applications too, asking me for a check, writing the essays, and getting the essays typed."

"All right . . . all right! You want me to do it, right?" I wasn't using the word "procrastinate," but it was implied and aroused her hostility. I lowered my voice and she actually stopped what she was doing to listen.

"Dear, if you don't do it for yourself, how will I ever know if you want to go to college, or if I pushed you into it? It's not a punishment. It's the same thing other kids have to do."

She started putting on pants and pulling them off again— ignoring me and managing to have the last word without uttering a sound.

The silence was uncomfortable and I got up and left, wondering where I'd gone wrong.

School began and in her journal she wrote her constant prayer,

PLEASE GOD, don't let me down this year. I'm sick and tired of being sick and tired! Everytime I'm in the hospital, it's so hard to catch up and I'm always there . . . it seems.

I hate staying home . . . it's boring and I feel so guilty, even though my heart knows I have to stay home.

It drives me crazy . . . . AGGHHHH!

PLEASE GOD . . . . . I have a good year planned.

With luck, her health would hold for six months the way it used to.

Her friends knew she'd been dating Andy and her desire to be part of the "dating crowd" was long forgotten. When I asked her about it she said, "Oh, I've got my own crowd now, Mom."

"Oh. What's your crowd?"

She thought a minute. "We're all artistic, sort of creative."

She became the nucleus of her own circle and she and John, the two prime leaders of merriment, were never at a loss when it came to thinking of pranks and borderline things to do.

There was Phebe, pretty, energetic, rebellious, and unpredictable, as confused about her sex appeal as Claudia was certain of hers. The boys used to say she had the "deadliest hips on campus." There was Drea (short for Andrea), innocent, bubbling, willing to join John and Chris in any scheme, and a girl devoid of guile, always offering her friends a sympathetic shoulder. She had a beautiful complexion and her friends called her chubby cheeks. Jamie was tall and lean with brown hair like the boy on the Dutch Boy Paint can. More observer than instigator, he was a musician who wrote songs and played the guitar.

Seniors at Rye Country Day had privileges. They could leave campus and leave they did—usually to eat. They met at the Rye Feed Store, and ate in their cars or on the floor in front of their lockers.

Christine's locker was on the third floor—near the math room. Unlike the second-floor lockers adjacent to the dean's office and visible to the curious eyes of visitors, this corner of the building was remote. John's locker was around the corner and Phebe's, Andrea's, and Claudia's were next to Christine's. This corner was their turf.

Daily, they'd sit on the floor, trying to keep their voices down but always forgetting. The math teacher's head would appear from the classroom doors, swivel in their direction, and yell:

"No lounging!"

"Keep it down—keep it down!"

"Don't you have to get to class down there?"

"I hope you're going to clean up that mess."

"Put that food away—and spit out the gum."

"That's enough out there!"

Then his head would disappear as the bell rang and the door closed.

They'd stare at each other in stone-faced amusement, knowing if they kept quiet for a few minutes they could play till the next class bell. The school had a demanding academic curriculum, but for Chris and her artistic friends, studying wasn't the first priority. It wasn't even second or third. Drea said it was tenth. They were trying out their personalities. They already knew what their brains could do, so they concentrated on socializing and friendship, their success in the group, even giving it a name—"face-time." Were they interesting? Illuminating? Impressive? Could they tell jokes? Could they entertain? Were they sought after? Were they respected?

They sprawled on the floor, talked and did homework. They wrestled, picked each other up, climbed into pyramids. They practiced juggling, did yoga exercises, tap-danced on the rug, tried on each other's clothes, imitated the teachers, and most of all talked. Endless talking. Not certain of who they were, looking for themselves, it was show-and-tell every day, look-what-I-can-do, and, above all, laughter, an endless clown's dress rehearsal.

Chris taught her friends spoon-hanging, a tour de force she'd learned from her father—hanging a teaspoon on the tip of her nose. At first, none of them could get the spoon to hang on their nose at all. It dropped into their laps and they'd laugh and try again, without success. Drea, who wouldn't give up, leaned back against her locker and moaned. "I just can't get the hang of it"—which sent everyone into gales of laughter.

The secret was to breathe on the bowl of the spoon first. In the cafeteria, students and teachers would stop in their tracks and laugh at the sight of the seniors at Christine's table, with steel spoons jiggling on the tips of their noses. Chris was the best. She could talk, walk, laugh, giggle, and even run—as if she'd been born with a spoon on her nose.

Monday night . . .

I just got back from Phebe's with Mark Read. I gave him a ride home. I really like Mark—he's refreshing to talk to. We talked about sex mostly (on the way back). We were relating to each other our teenage hang-ups about sex.

I felt it was so hard on girls when they have desires . . . because they're considered sluts.

I meant it's too easy to lose another person's respect— and it's so hard to gain it. I don't want to lose Andy's.

It's hard though. He's up there and I'm here. I wish he

*could see how happy I could make him. I'm very loyal (as
Leos are) and devote myself to things I love.*

Journal Entry—

*It's been six weeks since Andy left and he's called me
several times.*

*I love being able to say to my friends "Oh, he's fine—I
talked to him just last nite."*

*He called tonight. He was pretty depressed. He's
having trouble making friends up there. Everybody just
walks away from him?????? That's what he said! I'm not
drunk.*

*Oh, by the way. I was clowning around at Phebe's
house, with Mark—he's the president of the senior class
and I think he and Phebe are going to start going together.
Anyway, he picked me up in the kitchen and threw me
over his shoulder in a fireman's carry, and somehow I just
didn't stop, and I continued right on over his shoulder and
down to the floor, on my head! On the way down, my head
hit the corner of the countertop!!*

*AArrgghhhh! AAiieeeee! I cracked my head open
and got 5 stitches in the emergency room at United Hospital. . . .*

*Lots and lots of blood—but no bandage—thank
God.*

*Andy sounded horrified! I'm not going to make a big
deal of it to Mom. I'll just tell her one little stitch.*

*She thinks I have pretty good judgment (and I agree
with her) and I wouldn't want her to start questioning my
judgment now. . . . I have too much important ahead of
me . . . heh . . . heh.*

Good-night . . . .

But even though she was having fun at school with her friends,
and felt as close to Claudia as a sister, she was lonely. As her
confidence grew, she expected more. Claudia was going steady

with a freshman at college and Chris couldn't say she was going steady with Andy.

Entry—

I've been feeling so terrible lately. I'm becoming obsessed with Andy. I'm so bored with everything— schoolwork, I mean. Nothing interests me.

It's scary. I don't want to live in a dream world . . . I want to be responsible. It's not too late.

I guess I feel alone and abandoned. Both my parents are away. My Dad is taping the Muppets shows in London, and my Mom is covering the collections in Paris. Everyone I love—somewhere else. My anchors pulled loose.

Maybe I'll be better when Mom gets home. But I can't just wait till then. I have to start now.

I'll try.

It's like having a thick mist in my brain. I can't concentrate on anything. AGH!

I tried to call Andy last night. He wasn't there. I was so low—sad. . . . lonely. . . . depressed. I needed him to talk to. I was there when he needed someone to talk to.

Maybe Mom will bring me something great to wear from Paris. She always does.

Funny how something new to wear can make you feel better—for a minute or two. . . . that is.

It was easy to buy Christine clothes now, because trendy clothes were oversize. I was dressing like Annie Hall. Whatever fit me would fit her, and she was learning how to make her body look chic-model-thin rather than poor-sick-thin. She was developing style.

Journal Entry—October 15th 1979

I talked to Andy last night. Some things he said pissed me off. Idealistic dreamer . . . . . Well, fuck him. He didn't have to say something that mean.

I don't understand him.

He's gonna be sorry when I don't love him anymore.

No . . . I'll always love him. Maybe I'll tell him about Mark Read.

Hhmmmm . . . .

No forget Mark. He still likes Phebe and Phebe likes him. . . . so I would never interfere.

Journal Entry—

I'm so upset about myself. I can't stand *it anymore.*

Fuck. . . . why does God put me through this anyway!! Boy, was I depressed today—Wednesday.

I've been sick all week, fevers, fevers . . . always fevers . . . I'm a Tylenol junkie.

Schoolwork . . . . I'm behind with a capital B. I'm scared and my health is just not holding up the way I prayed it would.

And today I was just crying and crying half the time. . . . for no reason.

Christine came home from school these days quiet and preoccupied, disappearing into her room until supper. She was tired and short-tempered at times, but she acted as if it was nothing a good-night's sleep or a boyfriend wouldn't cure. I thought it was her health, but when I asked her, she wouldn't talk about it. She wasn't lacking for friends. She was on the phone a lot and was busy on weekends with the group.

But the unbelievable was happening. Her health was failing again exactly like last year, and she'd only been out of the hospital for six weeks. There was nothing we could pin it on—like a bad cold, or exposure to the flu. We couldn't call this just bad luck. I wondered how she was able to keep her fears to herself. Did she just not listen to the inner voice that worried about her health? Did she just not hear it? Did she have no inner voice?

My own inner monologue never left me: Will she bleed tonight? Will she ever improve again? Will she live to be married?

Will they find a cure? How will she be tomorrow? Shouldn't she be in the hospital? Will there be a drug to help her? What if she catches a cold? Do the boys notice she's different? Do the girls? Is she afraid to die?

Surely Christine must have been thinking the same thoughts, but, if she was, our inner voices never met and we tried to live a normal life.

And then she'd leave a clue, her state of mind still more upbeat than mine. She asked, "Mom, do you think my illness is a turnoff to boys? It wasn't to Andy, I don't think, but I could never bring myself to ask him—am I acceptable, as a woman?"

"I don't know, Chris. You're so pretty and you have so much to offer . . . you're intelligent and funny. No, your illness is not a turnoff. But don't you think it depends on the boy? It's a tough question."

"Mmmmmm. Andy *did* notice my funny breathing . . . you know, that tiny sound in the back of my throat, like radio static."

She was thinking her health was keeping her from finding love and this wasn't something she could talk about with her friends or even with Dr. Ores. She was too embarrassed, and she only touched on it with me.

10 · Mark

Journal Entry—

There's no one to focus on to help me forget Andy.

I talked to Mom about it. She says not to blame Andy if he doesn't love me. He's never done anything to hurt me. She thinks I'm in love with the idea of Andy—and I'm making myself suffer. . . .

It's too bad Mark is so interested in Phebe. He's so much fun to be with. I drove him home today and he asked me to stay.

We talked for hours. It was like summer this afternoon . . . sooo nice to be alive. I can talk to him about anything . . . which means sex . . . of course.

I like his looks—blond, a prep, although he denies it, well built . . . confident . . . wooff.

It was Indian summer when Chris drove Mark home and he asked her to stay. She met his mother, and Mrs. Read remembered her from Parents' Day the year before as the zany girl who led the history debate.

Chris and Mark talked on the porch of the gray cottage overlooking an old stone wall. The only other house she could see was the back of a Georgian mansion on the hill.

They went for a walk and said little, watching the stillness of the afternoon. Fields stretched out before them and sleek crows, watching their progress, took flight and cawed rudely at being disturbed.

"It's beautiful here," she said softly.

"I know," said Mark, "I never get tired of it." He picked up a branch and snapped off the twigs to make a walking stick. They rambled on, and the heat of the late afternoon sun warmed Christine. She felt so good—like she wasn't sick. At the bottom of the hill along a ridge was a mountain of loosely piled leaves.

Chris took a step back and made a flying leap onto the top of the pile. Mark watched as leaves rippled and shuffled down the sides.

"Come on!" she yelled, and dug herself down till she vanished. Mark smiled. Years had passed since he'd jumped in the leaf pile. He flung his walking stick into the air and jumped in after her. Quiet returned. He heard rustling and Chris popped up. She sputtered, shook off leaves and spit leaf dust out of her mouth. She looked around slowly.

"What are all these leaves? The trees aren't anywhere near bare."

"This is just the beginning," Mark said.

"It looks like the end." She stuffed some into her blazer pocket and stared at the sugar maples still bright with leaves.

"How many trees do you have?"

"Forty acres."

"Forty acres of leaves . . ." Her voice faded as he lapsed into silence and then said, "That's what I said . . . this is nothing"—her voice drifted off—"just the beginning." She closed her mouth, held her nose, and dove back down.

Mark laughed. "Wait, you don't understand. The trees . . . they aren't mine!" He heard her voice wafting back.

"I know. They're your father's—same thing!"

"No," protested Mark, "my grandmother's!" Mark waited, but she didn't answer—quiet again—not a leaf stirred.

Suddenly, she popped up. "Whose?" she demanded.

"My grandmother's."

She stared at him slack-jawed. "Your grandmother's," she echoed. "You mean, all this isn't yours?"

Mark nodded, wondering what was coming next.

"That's it. I'm leaving." She tossed her head, turned, and started high-stepping and plunging her way out of the pile. Mark lurched forward and caught her wrist as it swept by, and pulled her back. They flopped down, laughing and pushing clumps of leaves at each other until they were buried and couldn't see each other at all. In the dark under the leaves Chris asked, "Who rakes them up?"

"The caretaker," Mark told her.

"Not you?" Chris asked.

"Sometimes me, he's getting old." There was a long silence.

"We don't rake leaves in Greenwich. They just fall into preppy little piles," she giggled happily.

Mark and Chris spent the afternoon hidden from the world, lying in the warm leaves, clearing little spaces around their faces, and enjoyed the soft cushion beneath them. Time stopped and the sun set and they talked and talked.

In her journal was the briefest entry.

> *Mark. I don't know. He turns me on . . . I'm attracted, but I couldn't fall in love with him.*

The feelings were indiscernible to her that day, but later, looking back, she knew she'd found the love she was looking for that unhurried afternoon in the leaf pile.

Journal Entry—

> *Today I got a bear hug from Mark. Gee . . . how nice. I'm so bean-thin his arms practically go around me twice. Siigghh . . . I felt loved.*
>
> *He asked me if I was gonna see Andy over Thanksgiving. I said maybe . . . casually.*
>
> *He said—good luck and if it didn't work out to call him. I wonder if he meant it. Maybe—you never know.*
>
> *p.s. John thinks Mark likes me.*
>
> *I wonder . . . .*

Chris found Mark handsome with straight blond hair, green eyes, gold rimless glasses on a little nose, and a square clean-cut jaw. His broad shoulders looked like they'd support the weight of the world.

Living in the gardener's cottage on his grandmother's estate in Purchase, Mark dressed with an air of studied poverty, wearing baggy wrinkled khakis and army fatigues with threadbare cargo pockets bulging at the thighs. Oxford button-down shirts inherited from his brothers were old and frayed, with the predictable wrinkles from being washed without ironing, not from being dirty. In the winter he wore dark turtlenecks with the neck up to his ears. Preferring beat-up hiking boots, his Top Siders lay coated with dust on his closet floor.

Christine loved the way he dressed and knew he was image conscious. She told me once he looked "like he'd just come down from Mt. Olympus—a closet Greek god in thrift shop clothes."

But I was thinking about other things, like her college applications. Since our talk before school, she'd done nothing. She knew I'd help once she got started; she just had to start. Her health was terrible again—but still I knew she wanted to go. The days were getting shorter and the weather was turning cold when I finally lost patience with her procrastination.

"Chris, did you find out when your college applications to Emerson and Ithaca have to be in?"

"Yes."

"And when is it?"

"November 15th."

"Do you know how many days away that is?" It was eight days.

"Yesss Mommmmmmm."

"Have you started your essay?"

"Nooo Mommmmmmmmm."

I stopped. I knew I shouldn't rescue her, but—how could I deal with this attitude? She was impossible. And I was angry.

"Chris, I know I told you I wasn't going to bug you about college, that you had to do it on your own. I'm sorry but I'm changing my mind. I'm not letting you pour your life down the drain. I want to see that essay finished, in whatever form, in three days! Do you understand?" Not a word from her, so I upped the stakes. "And if I don't see it done, I'm grounding you. I'll take your car keys and you won't go anywhere. *I'll* drive you to school and pick you up like a ninth-grader."

"Oh yeah?" she sneered. "I have another set of keys and you don't know where they are. You *can't* ground me."

"Nice try. Do you think I'd make a threat if I didn't know how to fix your car so that it won't start?"

No answer again. I was bluffing, but I knew Jim would know what to do. Remove a spark plug or something. "Just so it's perfectly clear, Chris, when I say grounded, I mean no dates, no phone calls—*nothing.* Do you get the picture?" I was furious. "I'd get busy if I were you," I snapped. Damn, when I got angry I never knew when to stop. I huffed out of her room and heard her chair scrape the floor as she got up, came to her door, and screamed after me, "You make me sick!"

I looked over my shoulder and yelled, "Ditto!" as she slammed the door in my face. My steps were heavy as I went downstairs. I was heartsick. Why did it have to be like this? Why couldn't she do what she was supposed to do? Why did I get so mad? I was such a hothead. Why couldn't I reason with her the way parents were supposed to? I knew why. Because it didn't work.

She spoke in icy monosyllables the next two days—when she spoke at all. Three nights after my edict, I was lying in bed reading *Newsweek* with Jim asleep next to me when Chris came in. Her deadline was midnight, but I'd decided to give her one more day of grace before I grounded her. Then I'd help her write it, though I hadn't told *her* that. She sat on the bed carefully so she wouldn't wake Jim.

"Here," she said grumpily, handing me a pad without meeting my look. I took it and read.

COLLEGE ESSAY
AUTOBIOGRAPHY

A written autobiography is required of all applicants seeking admission to Emerson College. Please use the following space to indicate why you want to attend college and why you selected Emerson. Also, please tell us something about your family, academic career, areas of interests, and

*any talents you feel you have. The autobiography should
be a minimum of 200 words in length and should be
printed legibly or typewritten.*

*I grew up in New York City. The last three years I've
lived in the suburbs of White Plains and now, Cos Cob,
Conn. My parents were divorced when I was quite young.
Although I live with my mother, my relationship with my
father is a very close one. My father is a puppeteer for the
Muppets. Consequently, I am frequently exposed to many
aspects of "show business"—some technical and some creative. My mother, too, spent some years as a puppeteer.
My main desire is to act. But I am also fascinated with
other areas of theater and the field of communications.
The career I wish to follow will most likely be a difficult
one, for besides my interest in such a competitive field, I
have cystic fibrosis.*

*I will not go into great detail. It's a genetic disease that
affects the production of mucus in the lungs. Instead of
normal mucus, which is helpful in cleaning and flushing
the lungs of bacteria and germs, it does the opposite—
attracts and retains bacteria. The lungs become chroni-
cally infected as well as congested. In order to keep ahead
of the infection and clear my lungs, I must have physical
therapy treatments twice a day. Sometimes this is not
enough and I must go into the hospital for intravenous
antibiotic treatments.*

*For me the hospital is always a nightmare. At times it
interrupts the momentum that I try to maintain at school
and sometimes I feel angry and bitter. But it is mostly the
loneliness and isolation that get to me. Since I face fighting
to stay healthy alone, it is loneliness I fear the most in life.
Perhaps fear of being alone is one reason that I enjoy
acting. Another smaller reason is that when I act, I can
become someone else—someone who is not sick. The
main reason is that I love it so. It's working with people,
it's expressing one's self, it's challenging, and it's fun. I
know it will be hard, but nothing could be much harder*

than the ordeals I've gone through with my health. It's very difficult to come to grips with oneself in a situation such as mine. The anger, bitterness, self-pity, and even lack of self-esteem must be overcome if one is to live a normal, fulfilled life. I have been learning this my whole life—especially the last couple of years.

Five years ago, I came close to death, although I didn't know it at the time. I can only imagine how my parents must have felt when my doctor told them afterwards that I had only two years left to live at the most. My doctor was wrong (fortunately) not because she was a bad doctor, but because she judged on the basis of how sick I was then and the damage to my lungs. What she didn't judge fully was my spirit and my will to fight back. But my physical and emotional health bounced back to a state that amazed her. Each time that I become sick in this way, I become more determined to fight even harder.

My physical and emotional health are so closely intertwined that my mental attitude contributes about fifty percent toward maintaining my health. Life has become very important to me because of this. So have people and my friends. I will want the community of other students and of teachers who share my interests.

I don't know what the future holds for me. Whatever it is it will be difficult. But I've become an extremely determined girl because of my illness, as well as a spirited fighter. That I feel is my best quality. Another is my ability to get along with people.

Emerson appeals to me because it is small and has a good reputation in the fields of Drama and Communications. A practical (although unusual) reason for my interest in Emerson is its proximity to Boston Children's Hospital which is famous for its work in cystic fibrosis. Even if Emerson were not near this hospital, however, I would still be applying and it would still be my first choice.

Christine Nelson

After I finished, I pretended to read for a few more minutes. It hurt so much. It was important to stay calm, and to let Chris know how fine an essay she'd written.

"It's good, Chris. There's some rough spots, but it's very good. You don't sound like a teenager, but an adult." She bit her cheek and said nothing. It was hard for her not to begrudge the compliment. Later, we went over the essay together, changing a few sentences and polishing it. But now I read it again and said, "I'm surprised though." She looked at me for the first time. "It's about your illness. I didn't think you'd write about that."

"What else is there?" She sounded bitter. "It's the biggest thing in my life."

"Yes, I guess it is." She sat quietly, and I went on. "I didn't think you knew." She looked puzzled. "That Dr. Ores told your dad the most you could live was two more years—when you were twelve."

"Yes, I knew," she said softly.

"How long?"

"A couple of years." She never ceased to amaze me.

"You've known all this time?" I asked. "I didn't even know until this summer." She watched me silently. "May I show this to Jim tomorrow?" I asked.

"Sure." That meant she felt good about the essay.

Dr. Ores read it that summer and said, "It's very nicely done, but where did Chris get the idea I predicted her demise in two years? I never would have said such a thing."

"Her father told her a couple of years ago, I think."

Dr. Ores thought in silence for some time. Then she said, "It's interesting. I remember a long talk we had one day. It was the only time Mr. Nelson sought me out. I recall telling him 'two to twelve years'—that the illness is impossible to predict."

"Really?"

"I think so. Parents rarely ask me how long. They don't want to know. I've learned that they hear selectively. Perhaps it isn't always the good news they select. Well, no matter, in her essay, it's fine and she got in."

So that fall, I threatened Chris into college, but I knew she wanted to go. When college applications were mailed, she came out of her funk. But it had nothing to do with college.

Entry . . . . . November 20th

Well . . . Mark definitely likes me. Saturday night I went to the AFS square dance by myself. I knew my friends would be there so I wasn't nervous. But I can't do that square dancing. I quickly found out (had a terrible coughing spasm) so I sat on the sidelines—feeling a little awkward because I was the only one sitting.

Mark came over and said, "Let's get out of here."

So we left the square dance and went to his house.

First we stopped at the Port Chester Package Store— what a funny name for a liquor store—and bought a six-pack of Molson's Red Label. We went up to his room and drank the beer and listened to records. I was cold and he got me a comforter to stay warm. We curled up together and looked at his Penthouse and Forum magazines.

We listened to Todd Rundgren and Utopia and his "Oops Wrong Plant" album. We played Love in Action over and over and listened to the radio too. They played Rock with You—that new Michael Jackson song—3 times that evening.

We mostly just lay around keeping each other warm. Then he nuzzled his face against mine and we started kissing.

Just a little at first—then more.

After awhile he started kissing my neck, my chest, and so on . . .

Mark's parents were away and Christine spent the night in Mark's room. The ceiling slanted down following the angle of the roof, into a small dormered window. Records, books, and papers covered the surfaces, and clothes were piled on a rickety Windsor chair. They talked all night in the cozy glow of two small incandescent lamps.

Toward morning, it started to rain and fog rolled in. At 6 A.M. Mark walked Chris out to her car. The ground was wet and hard and they heard little taps of water still dripping off the naked branches of the trees. Fog was everywhere; dense, mysterious, whitening with the morning. They held hands and walked around the house in silence looking up with awe at the towering pines disappearing into the fog.

Mark asked, "Will your mom be mad?"

"I don't know," she said. "When I called, I said I was at Claudia's." She smiled as Mark leaned over the windshield and wrote his name in the mist backwards so she could read it.

When she started the engine, he laughed and tried to hold back the windshield wipers. He watched and shivered as her car inched away, quickly swallowed in the fog.

She slept all day on Sunday and Mark didn't call. She went over the evening in her mind, and knew it was special. She thought about Phebe, feeling guilty. She wondered how Mark could be so cool and not call.

She was at school early Monday morning, and walked quickly to the Pinkham Building, pushing back a coughing spasm and trying to control the churning in her stomach. Would he be there yet? How would he act? Tenth-graders hurried past and two lower classmen came barreling up from the basement, laughing and careening around the landings. Chris made her way up slowly, stopping to rest. She leaned back against the door at the top. God—she could hardly breathe. So soon—this was happening to her again.

Phebe was taping a large picture of Mikhail Baryshnikov on her locker door.

"Hi Phebe."

She didn't answer and Chris went to her locker. God! she thought, Phebe's mad at me. She knows. Someone must have seen Mark and me leaving the square dance together . . . and of course they told Phebe. Everyone's going to hate me . . . I know it. The locker popped open and she stopped to pick up the empty pretzel bag that fell out. She smiled. So that's who unlocked her locker. Her friends had raided her pretzels. She didn't mind. She kept two bags stashed on the top shelf for everyone. Sometimes they surprised her and she'd find fresh bags replacing the ones they'd demolished. Everyone knew Christine's locker had emergency rations. They didn't know she was allowed to have food in her locker for medical reasons.

Mark's locker was deserted, and Claudia appeared. Chris was dying to talk to her.

"Hi Chris."

"Hi Claudia." Chris hesitated and said, "If my mom ever asks you, I spent Saturday night at your house."

Narrowing her eyes sagely, Claudia pulled Christine close to her, directing her lowered voice toward the lockers.

"Where *were* you?"

"At Mark's house." Chris kept her voice low. "I called my mother and said I was at your house."

"Chris, you should have called me. What if your mother had called back?"

"Oh, I didn't think of that." She shrugged. "Oh well, she didn't."

John came in and Chris went over to him. She never started the day without a hug from John. He'd gotten over his crush on her, and transferred his love to Olivia Newton-John.

"Hi Sweetums," she said, and John wrapped his arms around her, lifting her up off the ground.

"Hi Puffy." He looked down at her with a bright smile, "You didn't wear your pillows today." She laughed.

"No, it isn't cold enough." She'd started wearing my Perry Ellis ski jacket the week before. It was a gray paper-thin poplin with down quilting, so extreme and puffed out she looked like Mr. Marshmallow when she wore it.

John had said, "My God! She's worn her pillows to school," when he first saw the jacket and he'd started calling her "Puffy." Chris always wanted a nickname and hoped it would stick.

She heard someone say, "Hi Mark," and turned to see him twirling his lock. She held her breath as Mark looked for her and walked over to her locker.

"Hi," said Mark.

"Hi."

"Was your mom mad?"

"No . . . she doesn't know where I was."

He smiled, not taking his eyes off her. "Did you sleep all day?"

Chris felt a flush all over as she nodded and said, "Till three o'clock. Did you?"

He turned and rested against the locker next to hers. "No, I biked for thirty-five miles."

Chris blinked. "Really? For fun?" She loved the way he kept looking at her. "That's like biking to New York City."

"I think a lot when I bike." He studied her a minute. "When's your first free?" he asked.

"Third period."

"Wanna get an early sandwich at the Feed Store?" She nodded. "I'll meet you in the parking lot. The red pickup truck."

"Good," she said, "I'm hungry already." He laughed and left her as she dug her English notebooks out of the bottom of her locker. What a feeling, she thought happily—I may not make Cloud Nine, but this must be Cloud Eight.

11 · Cloud Eight

Christine didn't tell me about Mark right away and I saw a new cheerfulness at home that puzzled me. It was little things. She started staying up in the morning after her thumps instead of going back to bed for a few precious minutes. Her step was quicker and she dressed without complaining she never had anything to wear. She even laid out her clothes the night before. She began to arrange her physical therapy by herself, instead of relying on me. She asked me to go shopping with her at Macy's and Bloomingdale's and, more surprising, she liked the way clothes fit her now. Her shape hadn't changed, but she was wearing them with confidence. She began to use rose water and glycerine soaps and discovered the joy of soaking in a hot bath with scented oil.

But it wasn't just the way she was taking care of herself. She was more a part of the family instead of a grumpy recluse. She played Barbie dolls with Jenny. She didn't turn her stereo up as loud when Jim was home. Her room was just as big a mess, but since I'd learned from Claudia and Drea and John that their rooms were pigpens too, I stopped complaining.

All these little things added up to a big change but it never occurred to me that she was in love—and I didn't notice that our conversations about boyfriends had ceased.

Even more surprising, she wasn't depressed about her health, and there was plenty to depress her. She was losing weight again and was having trouble getting up the stairs. Her lungs were overgrown with a new organism. The congestion from this new disease made her so short of breath she stopped for air in the middle of her sentences, and her laugh was guarded—she didn't dare let go. When she came home from school, she fell into a heavy sleep for an hour yet she kept her spirits up and went to school cheerfully.

On Thanksgiving, she was soaking in a hot bubble bath and I asked her if she thought she should be in the hospital.

"No," she said, refusing to even consider it. Leaning back in the tub, and reaching up with her toes, she turned the faucet and let in a little more hot water. "I can't *live* in the hospital, Ma . . . I just got out."

"I know," I said, trying to open the door to the conversation we never had. But she closed it again.

"Well, I'm not going in—there's too much happening at school." She soaked and I sat. "I've added an extra set of thumps, though."

"Is it helping?"

"I don't think so. My cough is very dry and hard. I can't get anything up. But maybe I'm keeping the secretions moving around down there."

"Chris, you *should* see Dr. Ores before Christmas. You want to be well enough to visit your father in England."

"That's true." She thought for a minute. "I'll make an appointment, but next week."

Jenny came barging in the door, looking for me, and saw Christine's wonderful bubble bath. "Ooooooh, you lucky," she exclaimed in envy.

"Jenny"—Chris glared at Jenny in mock severity—"what are you forgetting?"

Jenny couldn't imagine.

"Close . . . the . . . door!" Jenny closed the door and knelt down on the carpet by the tub, patting the cloud of bubbles and scooping up little pieces. Chris looked at Jenny again—"Jenny, *now* what are you forgetting?" Jenny was baffled again. Chris explained. "I don't mind if you come in when I'm having a bubble bath"—she paused a moment, adding—*"sometimes,* but it's polite to ask first."

"Oh," said Jenny quickly, glancing up at me. "Well, can I sit and watch the bubbles? I could go and get my Barbie dolls." She sighed, her eyes hopeful. Christine gave her a patient look.

"Go get the dolls, but close the door after you." I left with Jenny, marveling at Christine's new forbearance.

Winter blasted its way into southern Connecticut in mid-December that year, not with snow, but with wind and frigid rain and ice storms. I lent my Saab to Chris. I pictured her getting stuck or skidding on the highway in her condition. Front-wheel drive in a heavy car like a Saab was much safer for winter driving than her tiny Datsun. She wore her puffy jacket everyday, carrying on and struggling with it, yelling at it, beating it into her locker, which was too narrow for the fat jacket. John told everyone the jacket was growing. One morning he said to Chris and Claudia, "Watch—I've got a new bit," and he borrowed Jamie's guitar and began imitating a punk-rock star named Sid Vicious. He was trying to make his voice snarl—six-foot-one, two-hundred-pound, redheaded and freckled John Egan, who didn't care if he looked ridiculous as long as everyone laughed. Christine mouthed the words along with him:

> and then I killed a cat
> and might I say,
> not in a shy way, oh no,
> oh no, not me—
> I did it—myyy waayyyy.

She'd taught him the song and she said, "No, John, that's not it at all—you look too wholesome," and John tried harder to look mean and rotten.

Christine laughed. She laughed too hard and started to cough. She knew instantly it was going to be a violent spasm. She waved "I'll be right back" to John and Claudia and as the cough went deeper into her lungs she hurried through the hall doors to the now deserted staircase where no one would see or hear her. She reached for the railing and held on with her left hand—her right one pressed flat against her chest. She coughed and coughed, struggling to breathe as her lungs expelled all her breath, not letting her take any air in. She felt that her lungs must be completely deflated, but the cough kept coming.

She gasped inward, got some air, and stepped down one step, clutching the wooden top rail with both hands. She saw John and Claudia watching her through the window of the door. Her back and shoulders curved inward and her lungs emptied again. She gulped a short breath, but the coughing started uncontrollably once more. She just wasn't getting enough air in—before coughing it out again. She saw John turn back to talk to Jamie, but Claudia didn't take her eyes off Chris. The hall started to spin slowly before her and she held tighter to the rail, as if to solder her hands to some support. Another wracking spasm came over her, and she saw black spots dancing in the air and knew she was about to faint. Her heart pounded and raced, pushing and banging against her breast. What was happening? Would her heart fail? Oh God, she thought, help me . . . She gulped again at the bottom of a cough, her lungs desperate to regain control. Suddenly, she felt a little easier, and coughed less violently. She knew she could stop now when she needed a breath. More coughing followed, but she took control, pushing down and squashing the cough impulse with her chest muscles.

Then her stomach started churning, and waves of nausea hit her. Her stomach heaved. She gulped hard and pushed the heave back down. The dizziness returned and she felt a cold mist crawl across her back.

"Oh no," she muttered, "I can't throw up here. I can't . . . not in front of my friends. I won't." Her heart raced and the queasy feeling rippled through her.

Her lungs still wanted to cough themselves clear but then she'd throw up for sure, so she blocked the cough with long slow breaths, expelling each breath through tightly pursed lips as Dr. Ores had taught her. And by doing it, she pushed down what she felt coming up from her stomach as well as the cough reflex. Trembling, she overrode her body's struggle to rid itself of the secretions.

"Thank you God, for not letting anyone be out here," she

prayed and her knees buckled and she slid her hands down the vertical iron bars of the railing, sitting on the cold cement step, resting her head on her wrists. Claudia opened the door at the top of the stairwell.

"Chris . . . are you all right?"

Chris nodded limply, and Claudia crouched down beside her, resting her hand on Christine's heaving shoulder. Claudia searched her face and saw that Christine's lips were blue, but she said nothing.

"Oh, Claudia, thanks for waiting. I couldn't breathe."

Claudia sighed. "Don't thank me. I didn't know what to do. I was so scared. I was afraid you'd bleed."

"I know . . . so was I." Her face was white and damp with perspiration. "Did John know what was happening?"

Claudia shook her head. "No. When you ran out, he was still doing his imitation."

Chris smiled. "Don't say anything."

"I won't," Claudia said. And Chris stood up carefully, still gripping the railing while Claudia held her elbow tightly. She blotted her forehead with a tissue.

"I almost fainted. I saw black spots."

Claudia didn't say anything, took a deep breath, and nodded.

They went back in and Chris walked slowly to her locker. Claudia said, "Will you be okay now?"

"Yes, I think so," Chris responded, and Claudia went to class, looking over her shoulder at Chris.

Chris sat down on the rug. It felt good to be able to get plenty of air into her lungs. John didn't have a class and was talking to Jamie. The hall was almost empty now and she lay back on the floor, resting her head on the books at John's feet. She decided not to go to class. She crossed her feet and looked at John upside down.

He crouched down next to her. "Are you all right, Puffy?"

She smiled, looking up at him. "Yes, would you get me my pillow?"

John looked at the books underneath her head, puzzled, then smiled and went to her locker and took out the Perry Ellis jacket.

He helped her wedge it under her head, saying, "Are you sure you're okay? Why don't you stay here with me and Jamie till next period?"

"Okay."

"Oh good," said John, "we can play."

We were at the hospital seeing Dr. Ores two days later. She stepped out of her office into the waiting room and beckoned to Chris warmly, as if she were her favorite puppy.

Chris walked down the narrow hall, the back vent of her gray velvet blazer flipping up and down over her faded jeans, keeping silent rhythm with her noisy stride . . . the undone metal clamps of her yellow fireman's boots clicked along. Three children in the office looked up from where they played on the floor and turned to watch Christine's galoshes jingling down the hall, the tops falling open like unruly wings on her feet.

Amused, Dr. Ores put her hand on Christine's shoulder as she guided her into the private office.

When Chris settled on the examining table, her feet dangled in the air and the boots slid off her feet with a final jingle. Dr. Ores came in the door and smiled at the sight of the boots sprawled like discarded banana peels.

"How do you walk in those?"

"It's not hard . . . as long as I don't run," adding, "but I don't run, do I."

Dr. Ores leaned over and examined a tiny replica of an electric guitar pinned to her blazer and replied, "Still, I would think shoes like that might create certain problems." Christine was silent, uninterested in pursuing the conversation. Dr. Ores inquired, "Is that a special guitar you're wearing? It's very well done."

"It's Sting's."

Dr. Ores stepped back and regarded Christine's expression of nonchalant innocence. Dr. Ores spoke six languages. The language of a teenager wasn't one of them, but she was a quiet listener and a sharp observer. And that was all she needed.

"Whose?"

"Sting's," Christine said more carefully.

"Sting's . . .," said Dr. Ores.

"Sting's," Christine answered, quietly.

"Is that a person or a thing . . . may I ask?" Dr. Ores knew to expect the unexpected.

Chris smiled, forgiving Dr. Ores for her ignorance.

"It's a person. He's the lead in a New Wave group, called The Police."

Dr. Ores studied Christine's color while she digested this information and she echoed slowly, "a New Wave group . . . you mean—are they artists, or surfers?"

Christine started to laugh. "I'm sorry. I should have said rock group. New Wave is a new kind of rock music that came from punk rock. Have you heard of punk rock?"

"Oh yes, I've heard of punk rock." She picked up Christine's hands and studied the color of the nail beds of each finger. Under the polish, they were blue from lack of oxygen.

Dr. Ores mused, "I should have known by the guitar that it wasn't surfers. The Police . . . do you think I'd like them or would the screeching guitars make me deaf?"

"New Wave doesn't use screeching guitars—that's heavy metal. You might like The Police."

"Christine, you always teach me something new." Chris looked down, embarrassed, not sure if this was Dr. Ores's dry humor that usually annoyed her, or if she meant it as a compliment.

"No, you just ask a lot of questions."

"So I do," agreed Dr. Ores, puzzled. Normally, the cheery small talk they engaged in gave Dr. Ores some clue to her state of mind, but not today. The white room with blond wood cupboards and new stainless steel was bright and silent. Chris liked the old offices better. Dr. Ores walked around her desk and sat down studying Chris.

"How are you doing?" Dr. Ores asked.

Chris didn't answer but gave a hint of a shrug.

Dr. Ores stood up. "Well, let's see . . . let me listen to your chest." Chris took off her blazer, her sweatshirt loose enough for the stethoscope to go under. Dr. Ores moved the stethoscope slowly over Christine's lungs. She listened a long time, expressionless, her head bent in concentration, sometimes saying "breathe—" "again—" "cough—" "again."

Finally, she straightened up. "Have you coughed up fresh blood during postural drainage?"

"Sometimes there's some old blood—dark," Chris said.

"You don't sound as bad as I thought you were going to." Dr. Ores sat back down, weighing the choices. "But you don't sound good."

Chris looked up, suddenly cheerful, and said, "I went to a square dance last month." She paused, thinking back, "But . . . I didn't love it."

Dr. Ores waited, sure this was going to lead somewhere, but nothing else was offered. She said, "It has its good points."

Chris was quiet again. Suddenly her back sagged into a deep curve and she slumped forward, resting one cheek in the palm of her hand. "Ohhh, what's the use—what's the use?"

Dr. Ores noticed the tremor in her hands. This was not the spunky girl she knew and she said, "You're feeling pretty sick, aren't you?" Chris nodded quickly, her lips tight. Dr. Ores proceeded slowly. "Is it on your mind a lot?"

"Are you kidding? It's all I ever think about! A hundred times a day—I'm sick, I'm sick, I'm sick and tired of being sick . . . and I'm never going to get well." Chris spat the words out like deadly poison. Dr. Ores was struck by her voice. It wasn't the voice of a young girl. Chris sighed, her face pale and drawn. "I just don't know what to do anymore. It's hopeless."

Dr. Ores matched her answer to Christine's mood and said, "I can see you're not having an easy time." It was too much. Christine's eyes started to fill with tears and her mouth tightened, turning downward. Dr. Ores spoke quietly and kindly, "Well, maybe there's something we can do about it," and she picked up the phone and asked for admitting.

Chris came to life. "I just got out of here two months ago. I'm not coming in!"

Celia put the phone down and said quietly, "Well, Chris, we

can talk about it . . . maybe we can wait till after Christmas." Chris didn't respond. "I'll send a sputum culture to the lab today and we'll see what grows out, and maybe we can make a dent in this infection with oral antibiotics, until you can come in for IVs."

Christine's face was bitten with anger, her eyes dry, her jaw tense and pugnacious, staring blindly at the boots on the floor. "Nooo—no—no—I can't wait. I know what'll happen. The same thing that always happens. I'll try to hold out and I won't make it, and I'll end up bleeding and I'll be in here at Christmas. No *way* I'm going to be in the hospital at Christmas—ever!" She stopped, out of breath, and then proceeded in a low voice, "It's got to be now. I can't go to school in this condition. Sometimes I cough so hard I turn blue and I start to shake and faint. It's terrible and it scares everyone half to death—myself included. Arrange a bed for Monday . . . I'll come in," and she muttered under her breath, "Shit . . . shit . . . shit."

"I agree," Dr. Ores said, and Chris wondered if she meant her decision or her language.

Dr. Ores could feel the burden of the illness settling heavier on Chris. She picked up the phone again and asked for admitting. While waiting, she said, "I think it's the right decision, Christine—"

And Chris explained, "I'm flying to England at Christmas to visit my dad. They'll be taping more Muppet shows and I just love it. You can't imagine how much fun it is. I just can't miss that." She was cheering up. It was only two weeks, after all, that she'd have to be in the hospital. It was a relief to know she'd be able to breathe again.

That weekend, before she went into Babies Hospital, I met Mark Read. A red Mazda pickup truck was parked in our turnaround as Jim and I drove up. Chris was standing next to a blond boy and they were peering under the hood as I walked over.

"Hi Mom, this is Mark Read. Mark, this is my mom." Mark straightened up, clanking a wrench down on the fender. He extended his hand.

"Hello, Mrs. Gordon, nice to meet you." His straight blond hair was sticking out every which way.

"How do you do. Problems with the truck?"

"No. I'm adjusting new parts. My brother's home for Thanksgiving and he put in a new transmission."

Jim heard Mark as he walked up and asked, "How long did that take? It's a big job."

"A couple of days. We did it together. It's not work for me. I like tinkering with cars."

Jim stayed and talked to Mark about the rotary engine, while I gathered up the packages and went in with Chris. As soon as we were inside, she asked, "Mom, can I invite Mark for dinner?"

"When?"

"Tonight."

I thought a minute. Jenny was at her father's for the weekend and we had no plans. "Yes. Tonight's okay, but it won't be fancy. I'm—"

Chris stopped me. "Oh God, I'd die of embarrassment if it was. I want to be very informal and eat in the kitchen."

I started putting away the cleaning supplies. "Isn't Mark Read the one who dropped you on your head a few weeks ago?"

"The same." She paused and walked over to the glass doors that opened onto the terrace. "I guess you could say he's my boyfriend." She turned to me, trying to be serious, but she couldn't hold back a big smile. Neither could I.

"Oh Christine, how wonderful," I said, letting the good news sink in. "He's very attractive—blond, blue eyes—"

She corrected me. "Green eyes."

"Didn't you say he was the president of the senior class?" She nodded, knowing it was impressive.

"Where has he applied to school?"

"He's applied for early decision at Amherst."

"I know Amherst. Your great-great . . . ummmm, I forget how many greats—your great-great-uncle Samuel Tuckerman was a professor of botany at Amherst. He spent years doing field work in New Hampshire. They named Tuckerman's Ravine after him."

"Really?"

"Mark sounds like he has a sense of direction."

"He wants to be a minister. He's Episcopalian." Now she had my full attention.

"A minister. That's interesting. Is his father a minister?"

"No, his father's a sailmaker . . . well, a rigger for a sailmaker."

"A rigger . . . for a sailmaker . . ." I was repeating everything she said. "Does Mark know you're Episcopalian?"

"Of course. He's asked me to go to church with him. He goes to Christ's Church in Rye."

"I hope you go. You haven't had the benefit of the religious background I grew up with. I failed you in that. I hope it won't embarrass you, not knowing the prayers."

"No, it won't, Mom. Besides I know some . . . well, one."

I put the last of the cleansers under the sink. In the year I'd heard about Andy Gibson, I never knew what his ambition was or what his father did for a living. When I finished arranging, I walked over to Chris and put my arms around her and hugged her.

"Oh Chris, I'm so happy for you."

She sighed. "I still can't believe it myself. I'm not used to having someone like me back."

"You waited so long, be careful, dear."

"Can I go ask him now . . . about dinner?"

"Yes."

She hurried back outside. I sat at the kitchen table, staring out the window. Cystic fibrosis wasn't going to keep her from being loved. I said a prayer and thanked God for letting her have this.

Our dinner went smoothly. We had a cheese fondue, which put everyone at ease. Mark was charming, polished, and polite, and so was Christine. It was a good beginning.

12 · Uneasy Cloud Nine

Monday morning we drove to Babies Hospital as planned. Chris was very upset but she made light of it to her friends and Mark. She couldn't let them see her coughing spasms. She was afraid they might start to feel sorry for her and that would destroy her friendships.

Journal Entry: Babies Hospital

Mark and I are getting closer and closer. We've been out together with the gang and the gang's seeing us as a couple.

I wrote him a letter Sunday, after Thanksgiving . . . Oh, guess where I am . . . BABIES HOSPITAL.

I lasted 2½ months.

Friday night after Thanksgiving, Phebe had a party. I went with Mark and I was such a tease. I wore my dusty rose silk and lace teddy (from Bendel's) under a smoky green chiffon shirt that Mom lent me. You couldn't really see anything, but . . . .

Mark went BANANAS. But I wouldn't go home with him. I just kissed him good-night.

I went over to Claudia's and straightened things out with Andy . . . I called him at Hobart. I'm sure our friendship won't end. I'm not the type of woman who can just not love someone because I have feelings for someone else. It's a strange feeling, because I've been in love with

135

Andy for so long. Now I can love him (which I do) and not be in love with him. Mom says that is not an easy transition to make.

Boy, I can't think of a worse time to be in the hospital. I hope Mark doesn't forget me.

But even so, there was a bright side. Babies Hospital had a life of its own and not all of it was bad. There were five staff nurses on the tenth floor and they ran things up there with understanding for and devotion to the youngsters. Some patients came once and returned to normal life, but many came back again and again.

The nurses liked Christine. They laughed at her jokes, listened to her music, and knew her pet peeves and eating habits. They'd met Jerry over the years and recognized him with or without his beard. They watched "The Muppet Show" on Monday nights and the next day always asked Chris what parts he played. Sometimes a nurse would come in the room as she was watching it. How Chris loved to say to them, "That's my dad."

When Jerry's recording of the little muppet Robin singing "Halfway Up the Stairs" went platinum she burst with pride. She told everyone, "My dad's record went platinum!"

And the nurses were experienced with the way cystic fibrosis destroyed children's lives and how the children sometimes took it out on those around them, and they made allowances. Because her attitude was so upbeat, they let her wander the floor freely. No matter whose room she was in, she was cheering them up. Dr. Ores called her the "social director." And when she returned and the nurses were glad to see her, she understood it didn't mean they were glad she was sick again. When she left, even she forgot sometimes and said, "Bye Ginny, see you soon." They knew she didn't want to come back, but she'd have to.

Journal Entry: Babies Hospital

Mark's coming to visit in a few days. I don't know if I love Mark, because I'm not used to being in a mutual situation . . . so I can't tell. Love is not a hopeless dream

this time, so there is no pain and it's hard to tell if what
I feel is love.

Maybe it's just too early to tell. One thing I know,
when he touches me . . . I shiver. (He does wonders to my
neck and ears.)

That may be the difference between love and hero
worship. Love is real. God, I hope I never have a bad
coughing spasm in front of him.

Christine was a master at controlling her cough, although it wasn't to her advantage. Her lungs needed to be coughed clear. She shared her room this time with a girl named Kendall, who also had cystic fibrosis. The girls were so different and it didn't escape Chris. When Kendall was out of the room, she asked, "Mom, do I look like Kendall?"

"No, you're pretty."

"So is she."

"But she doesn't act pretty. I mean . . . she looks so sick and depressed all the time," I explained.

"That's what I mean . . . do I look like that?"

"No . . . you look normal."

"Are you sure?"

"Yes, I'm sure." She always seemed to think I was flattering her, but I wasn't. "Sometimes when you're tired, your posture is all bent over, but so is Claudia's—mine too, for that matter. You don't sound like Kendall either, when you cough."

"You mean the way her cough is so violent and deep?" So Chris had noticed that, too.

"Yes, do you think she does that on purpose?" I asked.

Chris bit her lip in thought. "I don't know. I'm afraid to ask."

I said, "Her cough terrifies me and makes me feel nauseous." Chris looked at me in amazement.

"Me too . . . I thought it was just me. It sounds like . . ."

I knew exactly and finished her sentence. "like her stomach is turning inside out. It's so awful it makes me want to run from the room when I hear that ripping and tearing sound in her throat."

"That's what I'm talking about Mom. Do I sound like that?"

"No, you don't."

She shuddered. "I didn't think I did. You know, lots of times, in fact, at school, almost *all* the time, I stop my cough."

"I know, but maybe you shouldn't. Maybe your lungs would be clearer if you coughed hard like that." She looked annoyed.

"God, healthy people never understand. Not even you." She sat forward and said, "Mom, when normal people see a sick person they see . . . someone handicapped. They don't see that the person is normal like them, but stuck inside the handicapped body. They see a cripple. If I coughed like that, my friends would think I was different from them and I'm not. If they feel sorry for me, it's all over."

She was right. Even I made that mistake. I could look past cystic fibrosis, but other, more visual handicaps clouded my vision.

I tried to get to know Kendall, but she didn't say much. She acted different. She was blond and thin and hunched over with a haunted darkness around her eyes like the anorexic girls. And like them, she never smiled. I felt sorry for her the minute I met her and knew this was what Chris fought against. Pity. The sick look. But then, maybe some are more easily crushed.

The antibiotics Christine went to the hospital for have been called miracle drugs, and sometimes her improvement was miraculous. This was one of those times. By the fourth day, she felt her breath coming easily and her cough lessening. Even her sleep was undisturbed and her spirits soared as she told me with hope, "Mom, if this new Ticarcillin works so quickly, it'll probably work the next time and the time after that. Don't you think so?"

I agreed, though it was never certain. She was given as little as possible in the hope that the deadly organisms infecting her lungs wouldn't have time to build up immunity to the drug. Dr. Ores and Dr. Harold Neu, head of the Infectious Diseases Department, proceeded cautiously through this complex maze of protection, always trying to save something for the next time.

Twice Mark came in to visit, making the arduous trip on public transportation—the train from Rye to Grand Central, the shuttle subway from Grand Central to Times Square, the uptown subway to Columbus Circle, and then the uptown A train to 168th Street and Broadway. The trip took two and a half hours. She couldn't believe he'd do it. When I told her she was worth the effort, she remained incredulous. But Mark's love was giving her what neither my love nor her father's could give her now—belief in herself and in her worth.

Two weeks later, on December 11th, I brought Christine home on a bright cold Sunday afternoon and watched her climb steadily up the steep unbroken flight of stairs to her bedroom, carrying a pillowcase full of her stuffed animals. She didn't stop once and took a deep breath at the top, relishing the feeling of renewed strength. She didn't feel as well as she had this time last year, but the antibiotics had worked magic nevertheless. She looked down from the bannister and said, "Mom, I bet I'm the only person in my class who doesn't take this for granted."

I stopped on the bottom step and looked up at her in surprise. She'd complained very little before going into the hospital, but she knew that I knew what "this" was. She could breathe. She could go upstairs without "coughing her guts out." She laid her struggles at my feet—painlessly, weightlessly, choosing this happy moment instead of one of despair. My heart ached at her generosity of spirit.

I nodded simply. "It's a safe bet, Chris." And I followed her up the stairs.

Back at school, the senior Christmas tree in the Pinkham Building was decorated. Chris wanted to get there early. She knew her friends would ask her about the hospital and she was intent on deflecting their questions. She did it the way she knew best, with laughter.

Mark was the first to arrive and John was right behind him. Pushing open the hall door, the first thing they saw was Chris—sitting in her locker. Leaning forward, her rear on the raised locker bottom and her elbows resting carelessly on her knees, she was munching pretzels as if she'd been there since dawn. Mark strode over with a big smile.

John laughed at the sight of her and cried, "Puffy, you're back!

How'd you get in there?" He leaned over to look and she ducked as he stuck his head inside the locker. "Are you stuck?"

"Nope," she said, and got up and gave them both a hug—a huge affectionate hug for John and a little playful hug for Mark. Maybe because they were going together she was tentative, delicate, and restrained with him.

She sat back in her locker, her shaggy white fur boots like two big hairy paws on the carpet and John said, "I've been going to this school for six years and I've never seen *anyone* sit in their locker."

Chris looked at him innocently, popping another pretzel into her mouth as Claudia and Drea came hurrying over.

Claudia said, "Hi Chris, welcome back!" and Drea just stared with her mouth open.

"How'd you get in there?"

"Hi, Drea. I just fit. No meat on my bones."

Drea laughed and Claudia said, "That would have been a great picture for the yearbook . . . I wonder if I can do it."

"Me too," said Drea and they went to their lockers trying to squeeze their backsides into the bottoms of them, but no one else could do it and no one thought to ask her about the hospital.

Thursday, Chris asked me to go shopping with her at Bloomingdale's after supper. It was cold and she bundled up in her white quilted coat and white sheepskin boots.

Christmas shopping was under way and the parking lot at Bloomingdale's in White Plains was full. Walking up to the heavy glass doors, I realized I was alone. I turned around to look for Chris. She was standing a few feet back, near the closest row of parked cars, not moving, her hand over her chest.

"Chris?"

"Mom, I think my lungs are bleeding."

I caught my breath . . . it was impossible. I walked to her side and took her arm, tucking her forearm in over mine. She clutched the back of my hand, leaving little white patches on my skin where her fingers gripped. She wasn't coughing.

"Are you sure, Chris?"

"Yes, I can feel it. I'm going to need a paper cup." Then she started to cough—that low rhythmic bubbly cough that sounded like no other—and she dug into her pocket for a tissue. We walked in and stopped at the first counter, where a lone salesgirl was arranging glittering evening bags under a glass case. There were no customers here. Chris leaned both elbows on the countertop, her left hand still gripping my wrist.

I said to the salesgirl, "Miss, can you help us?" She came over, puzzled by my tone. She looked about seventeen. "My daughter is ill. I think her lungs are bleeding. Can you get her a paper cup as quickly as possible . . . in case she starts coughing up blood?"

The salesgirl looked at Chris uncertainly and then said, "Of course, I'll be right back."

Christine spit blood into her tissue while the salesgirl was gone. The girl was back in seconds with several cups. I handed one to Chris, who was trying to hold back the cough, breathing out slowly through tightly pursed lips.

"Do you have a nurse in the store?" I asked.

"Yes . . . on the second floor. Would you like me to bring you?"

"I'm sorry, but could you go and get her and bring her here? My daughter can't move when she's bleeding."

The girl looked at her again—in puzzled concern. "Would you like something to sit on? I have a stool behind the counter." Chris couldn't answer, but she nodded gratefully. The salesgirl brought out a tall stool for Chris to sit on and said, "I'll get the nurse . . . no wait. I can call. I'm sure she'll come right away."

So far, there were no customers near this counter and no one had noticed us. Christine was coughing quietly and spitting blood into the cup so expertly that no one would have known what she was doing.

The nurse arrived, only a white skirt under a Shetland sweater giving a clue to her status. I explained what was happening and asked her if she knew what hemoptysis was.

She nodded. "Can I help you to my office . . . or do you think you'll need an ambulance?"

"Thank you," I said, as Christine shook her head emphatically. "I don't think we need an ambulance, but she shouldn't move until the bleeding stops. Do you have any cough suppressant with codeine?"

She didn't, so the three of us waited there, talking little, and the nurse took down information for her report. It was only fifteen minutes, but it seemed like hours. Chris was finally able to talk.

"Mom, I think I can make it to the car now if we go slowly."

I thanked the nurse and the salesgirl, who came over and said in a discreet voice, "Are you feeling better?"

Chris nodded and said, "Yes, thank you."

We moved like somnambulant snails back to the car. All she cared about was that she hadn't made a scene and she said, "That salesgirl was so polite . . . she didn't even stare. She pretended not to notice."

Getting into the car was another story. Just open the door and scoot in, right? But Chris would have to bend and twist when the slightest wrong move might restart the bleeding. If she could keep her torso rigid, slide her left leg into the car, and drop herself slowly onto the seat, she should make it all right. Three times she stopped and put her hand over her chest, as if her hand could communicate with her lung. At last she was in the car. She seemed far away.

I started the car and let the motor run to get the heater working. Chris didn't move, her head back against the headrest and her eyes closed.

"How can you tell your lungs are bleeding?" I asked her.

"I can feel it."

"You can?"

She didn't open her eyes. "Sometimes it's a fluttery feeling—like a butterfly beating its wings, under my right shoulder." Her words came in soft whispers. "I can't talk, Mom."

"Don't talk—here comes the heat. We'll go." I should have remembered—she never talked when she was bleeding, and we drove home in silence. At home, I gave her codeine and vitamin K, when she was midway up the stairs to her room.

Dr. Ores was as surprised as we were, and said to wait, it might stop. Chris spent a quiet night and stayed home from school on

Friday. She stayed in bed and took cough suppressant. She canceled her physical therapy.

She spent Saturday in bed, too. With no more bleeding, she began to feel more confident. Her only complaint about the depressing turn of events was to deadpan, "I'm really glad I just spent two weeks in the hospital so nothing would ruin my Christmas."

She was worried about missing thumps and could feel the tightening in her chest as her lungs filled with secretions. It scared her. Congestion meant mucus—a fertile ground for a bacteria called pseudomonas. Pseudomonas meant illness and destruction of her lungs. She had to stop it. Talking with her therapist, Karen, they decided to resume therapy Sunday morning even though it might be too soon, because pounding her chest could start the bleeding.

Saturday she decided to go to the Red Barn. It had somehow become a special night. Everyone would be there. Except Mark, who was visiting a friend at Amherst.

She made her way down the stairs carefully, found me in the kitchen, and told me, "Mom, I'm going to the Red Barn tonight."

"Oh Chris, no . . ."

She interrupted me. "I'll be *careful.* I'll be very quiet. Believe me—I know what could happen."

I studied her while I thought it through. She was willing to take this chance, in front of all her friends.

"Chris, is it realistic to expect you to be anything other than your zany self under the circumstances, with Christmas and everyone back from college and drinking?"

"I'll just have to be careful. I have no choice."

"You *do* have a choice. You can stay home." But I said this in a small voice like I didn't mean it. I tried again, with more conviction. "I don't think you should do it."

There was a long silence. With every month that went by, I understood more that her friends were the key. It was all she had and I backed off when she said, "I probably shouldn't go, but I'm going to."

"Well, there's only one Christmas when you're a senior—just don't go alone."

"Claudia's going—I'm sure she'll pick me up. Mom . . . are you mad?"

There it was. That little voice pleading so sweetly. "Of course not—worried, not mad. How could I be mad? I love you."

"Oh, thank you." She crushed me with a hug. "Mom, you don't know what it means to me. You just don't."

I let her think I didn't and as she let go I said, "Chris, make yourself a little"—I stopped—"emergency kit. Use a cosmetic bag—you have plenty—and put in paper cups, Kleenex, your cough suppressant, some Valium, Dr. Ores's number, our number, and the address of Babies Hospital . . . And two sentences about what you need when you bleed, you know, because it's so hard for you to talk." I'd almost said "survival kit" but caught myself.

She nodded, full of new energy. "Good idea." She looked at me, smiling like Pilot Small. "Would you mind getting all the stuff together?"

My heart melted again. I could never spoil her. She just didn't spoil. "Okay. Leave a makeup bag on your vanity in the bathroom. I'll do it."

When Claudia came to pick her up at nine o'clock they went off so happily, talking a mile a minute, you'd never have known she was sick. I told Jim and he was shocked.

"You're letting her go out in her condition? That's crazy!" I was defensive.

"It's not crazy. I know what she needs to keep going, and it's not sitting home alone. It's her life. God, she knows what a risk she's taking better than I do, because she lives it. If it's more important for her to be with her friends, I'm not stopping her." Jim shook his head. He didn't agree. But I was very sure this time.

She was not to be spared. A little before midnight, Claudia called. Her voice was low and urgent. "Mrs. Gordon? Christine started to bleed a few minutes ago. We're coming home."

"Oh no, I was afraid of that. What was she doing?"

"Nothing," Claudia explained. "She was just sitting with me and Andy—she's been so quiet, a couple of people even asked if she was feeling okay."

"Is it bad?"

Claudia paused. "I . . . I don't know. Christine's waiting in the car . . . we'll be there soon."

Claudia's car came slowly into the driveway twenty minutes later and I ran downstairs, pushing the garage-door button. The door lumbered up slowly and noisily and Claudia pulled her car in right behind mine. She got out first and looked at me with silent terror.

I opened the car door for Chris. She was staring out the front window and didn't say anything. She seemed dazed—maybe in shock. Then I saw the reason. The eight-ounce paper cup in her hand was full of blood—not a few bloody secretions like at Bloomingdale's, but dark, red, liquid blood.

I felt my breath die in my throat and my heart began thumping against my chest. Reaching in, I took the cup from her hand, while Chris remained still and Claudia stared at the cup. Putting it on the cement floor, out of the way, I said, "Chris, can you move?"

She nodded slowly.

I knew she couldn't talk and I had to ask the right questions. "You're not coughing now. Do you think the bleeding's stopped?"

She nodded again, still not looking at me.

"Did you take the codeine?"

She held up two fingers. That explained her glazed look and her apparent calm. She wasn't in shock, she was sedated.

"Do you want me to help you get out of the car?"

She held up her hand and shook her head. She had more control and could hold her concentration better if she moved at her own pace. I stepped back and waited.

She moved very slowly, inching her knees around so that her feet almost touched the ground and then she slid a little forward, and touched the ground. She was moving like a statue, her upper body rigid as she took my hands, pulling herself very gently to a standing position. I wasn't sure what to do next.

"Chris, will it work if I put my arm around your waist—and you can lean on me and stop when you need to?"

She nodded, and I looked over at Claudia. "Thank you Claudia. Thank you for getting her home so quickly."

"Is there anything else I can do?"

I looked at Chris and she shook her head and whispered, "Thanks."

"Okay. Can I call in the morning?"

"Of course," I said.

"Thanks, Claudia," Christine said again, in a whisper. Claudia touched her arm, hugged her carefully, and left.

It took us a long time to go upstairs to the living room. We went two steps at a time and then waited. I suggested to Chris that she sleep downstairs, rather than go up another flight of stairs.

"No, it's too lonely."

Jenny and Jim were asleep, and when we finally got to the top of the second flight I helped her get into bed, and propped up her square french pillows so she could sleep sitting up. Lying down would cause more bleeding. We didn't know why—but it did.

Then I went to get my pillows, to sleep next to her on the canopy bed. I thought about calling Dr. Ores, but it was one o'clock, and I decided to wait. I didn't think about the emergency room at Babies Hospital. By the time we'd get there it would be two o'clock in the morning, and on a Saturday night it was unthinkable.

When I came back in the room, I turned out all the lights except the one by her bed. Her eyes were closed and her head was resting back on the pillow tops. She looked pale and exhausted and so thin. How did her frail frame withstand this violent disease? When I stepped to the side of the bed, to arrange her covers, I saw tears running down her cheeks. I was afraid to speak or touch her—afraid of releasing a torrent. Crying empties the lungs in such a stressful way, it would make the bleeding start. I stood there and closed my eyes and said a prayer to myself—Please God, help her.

And then I said simply, "Chris, I'm going to sleep here tonight—all right, dear?"

She said, "Thanks, Mom," knowing I could see her tears but not turning her face away.

I climbed to the far side of the bed and lay down, pulling the covers up to her waist, covering her hands, which lay at her sides.

I reached over and held her right hand. She squeezed my hand once and then it was limp again.

I kept hold of her hand and listened to the sound of her breathing—short and shallow. The house was quiet and I could feel fear, dark and tense, pressing against my rib cage and my throat as if it wanted to scream out. I looked up at Christine in the dim light, and said quietly, "Why do you have to suffer like this? It isn't fair."

"Sometimes, I think, God is punishing me." Her voice faltered.

I knew it. I felt like I was breaking inside. I couldn't let her believe that. "Oh no, Christine, he isn't punishing you, he isn't."

"I know," she whispered, "but, sometimes, I feel that way." She was taking gentle breaths, every two or three words.

"I know, so do I. But that isn't the answer. I don't think there is an answer. It's just bad luck."

"It's so hard to talk."

"I know dear, I'm sorry." I squeezed her hand again. My mind was full of questions that tried to push aside the fear. We waited to fall asleep. I thought of how many times I had been beside her like this, trying to comfort her, unable to help her or even share her burden—ever since she was a little girl, falling asleep in my arms in the batwing chair.

For so many years I'd asked God why, and the years of asking had revealed only that it was a stupid question. There was no answer. Neither of us slept for a long time, not even Chris with her double dose of codeine. I wondered what she was thinking. And I thought of her friends, back at the Red Barn, laughing, unaware, having fun together, while she lay beside me, fighting alone.

13 · Free Flight

We talked to Dr. Ores in the morning. She still didn't want Chris back in the hospital. The last two weeks with antibiotics in Babies had cleared her lungs and this was bad luck, but, unless it got worse, no hospital. I thought it was time Chris let Mark in on all this.

"Chris, since Mark knows you have cystic fibrosis, maybe you should explain to him what happens when you bleed." She started shaking her head. "Okay, it's up to you."

"I don't think he has to know everything, Mom. I want to give Mark my best, and never"—she stopped and said it again—"*never* be a burden to him. He can't love me if he pities me."

So I let her handle it, but I wondered how she could juggle the depressing turns of her illness with a growing romance. She never talked about it directly, but I found clues in her conversations about Mark. It seemed she was too busy and happy and in love to bother with anything so depressing as her illness. And as her illness kept pushing her down, love lifted her up, and love was winning. Could it be that simple? I began to think that love, and especially being "in love," might be a key to her survival. She'd said last time she was in the hospital, "You know, Mom, I feel like I get sicker in the hospital just from the loneliness." She was unwrapping a midnight roast-beef sandwich.

"What do you mean? You get better here."

"I know, but no, I mean, inside."

I'd sat in the wing chair thinking and said, "You're so different from me. I like being alone."

She considered. "I know, you're much stronger than I am."

She caught me by surprise and I watched her meticulously pulling the little fat edges off the roast beef in her sandwich and I said, "I don't think that's a strength . . . . . I think it's a weakness."

"No way," she'd said, and then the door had opened and a nurse came in to flick the IV lines. We never finished the conversation.

Entry:

> *My lungs started bleeding again. It happened in Bloomingdale's with Mom.*
>
> *Then later at the Red Barn—I was with Claudia—just a while ago. I had been feeling better and I guess I thought that if I was quiet and sat still I'd be alright but I wasn't.*
>
> *No big scene, but still it was hard. Mom was really upset when Claudia and I drove in—and she came out to the car and I was sitting there with a cup in my hand, full of blood.*
>
> *My friends at the Red Barn could tell something was wrong. Andy was there. What a dear. When Claudia told him what was wrong he just gave me a sweet look and held my hand while she got in the car.*
>
> *I'll always be sorry our paths didn't really cross. He just knows how to charm a girl and really make her feel special. I hope we see each other again.*

Then Dr. Ores told her that going to London to visit her dad for Christmas was out of the question and Chris was fit to be tied. Jerry sent her the British Airways refund from her canceled plane ticket with a note saying, "For a shopping spree." She went to Bloomingdale's and bought Christmas presents for all her friends and something special for Mark—a snowflake-pattern Scandinavian sweater.

To her surprise, though Mark loved the sweater, he was morose the night she gave it to him. He said he was feeling miserable and tired of his poor-as-a-churchmouse status and his own present to Chris couldn't compare. He gave her the new Pink Floyd album, *The Wall,* but he was embarrassed.

She didn't think of him as poor at all. It never occurred to her the sweater was too much and she told me she shouldn't have been so insensitive and egocentric, observing ruefully, "I never thought I'd see the day when being thoughtful would be thoughtless."

To Christine, Mark's living on a grand estate and repairing the old red pickup truck every few weeks not in his garage, but in the hangar where the family plane had been kept years ago, was romantic and mysterious. And she loved sitting next to him when he drove across the bumpy, overgrown landing strip to gas his truck at the old pump on the estate.

Mark found his predicament anything but romantic, but he wore his impoverished aristocrat role so gracefully Chris hadn't seen how self-conscious he was.

They wrote letters, handing them to each other in the halls, and Chris tried to cheer him up and put things back in perspective.

> *Dear Mark,*
>
> *I'm giving you this card because you're so down about Christmas and buying gifts for everyone. Don't be.* Please. *You don't have to get gifts for everyone—hardly anyone— no one in school if I recall. Only family. The only reason I'm giving presents to everyone this year is 'cause Dad gave me a lot of money and I have nothing better to do with it.*
>
> *Call me spoiled . . . I know it's terrible, but we were both so disappointed that I couldn't go to London, he said, "here—splurge."*
>
> *What do you think people are going to say?*
>
> *"Mark Read didn't buy me a Christmas present—I'll never speak to him again!"?*
>
> *Poppycock!! And the last person you need to buy something for is me.*
>
> *1) I have everything (Dad's fault)—except for a porsche and a white fox coat.*

2) You've already given me something—can you guess what it is?? No it doesn't begin with s and end with x (although that's part of it).

To give me a super Christmas present, you know what you can give me . . .

Well, anyway, again don't be down and stop feeling sorry for yourself . . . I don't! You're in for a great Christmas Buddy—you have ME! and I don't cost anything—except for:

$100,000 a year for medical expenses (actually could be more)
2,000 a year for clothing
2,600 a year—food
500 a year—for presents and needs
3,500 a year—for Rye Country Day School (Mom just told me that should be $4,000)
1,000 a year—for miscellaneous

$109,100 Total

and you don't have to worry about the miscellaneous.

love, chris

I saw less of Chris in the next two months. In fact, I hardly ever knew where she was except when she was taking care of Jenny or talking on the phone. She didn't need me now and I welcomed the time to spend with Jenny, who had still not adjusted to my divorce from her father. Jenny's beginning the first grade at Rye Country Day where her big sister was a senior was restoring a feeling of family closeness, so I tried to build on it by asking Chris to pick Jenny up from the Primary Building and drive her home a couple of days a week. More than that would have interfered with Christine's freedom. I hoped that Christine's upbeat feelings about our new life would have a positive effect on Jenny. And, while I tried to make Jenny's life better, I marveled at what a normal life Chris was achieving, more than I'd ever hoped for. Asking her to act as a mother's helper added to her confidence.

There was hockey practice every day from four to six and

Chris braved the icy dampness of the rink in the fieldhouse to watch Mark training with the team. Chris wanted Jenny to meet Mark, and she said to Jenny after school one day, "Jen, let's not go home yet, okay? I want to watch the hockey team practice in the fieldhouse for a while."

Jenny said, "Oh yuck," but took Christine's hand cheerfully and they walked through the school parking lot past Mark's red Mazda. Chris pointed.

"That's Mark's." Jenny looked up at Chris.

"How come he drives a junky truck?"

"He just does. I think it's cool." Jenny considered and agreed. "So do I."

They were almost out of the lot when Chris turned around suddenly. "Jenny, wait, follow me. I have an idea."

Chris went back to Mark's truck and plopped her bag on the hood and started fumbling through the contents. Jenny had left class minus her mittens and hat and with her coat undone, and now she shivered, digging mittens out of her bag and zipping up. Chris, still rummaging, pulled out some crumpled Kleenex and climbed up and wiped the front windshield clean with slow up-and-down strokes.

"Are you cleaning his *car* for him?"

"Nope, just wait." Then she took out her cosmetics bag and twisted a lipstick and, using the side mirror of the truck, applied it carefully. Looking around, she crawled back up on the hood and started kissing the windshield, leaving lipstick kisses all over it.

Jenny watched with a big smile and as Chris reapplied the lipstick and left more impressions, Jenny said, "Chris, is Mark your boyfriend?"

"Of course. I'm leaving him kisses." Jenny covered her face with her hand in embarrassment and then leaned up against the hood teasing Chris in a singsong voice.

"He's gonna be ma-a-d . . ."

Chris put the last few impressions on the window and said, "No he's not, he loves attention." She sat back and surveyed the lipstick kisses muttering, "Perfect," and then she jumped down and stepped back to look again. "It's pop-art, Jen—a pop-art love letter."

Jenny didn't know what she meant. She watched Chris gather up her things and said, "It looks neat—but you're weird."

"No, I'm not—I'm wonderful," chirped Chris, then quickly changed her mind and said, "Well, I shouldn't say that, I'm not wonderful, but I'm not weird either. C'mon, let's go." And they hurried to the fieldhouse as Chris thought out loud, "I wonder if he'll be able to see it. It's dark when practice is over."

Chris and Mark didn't have as much time alone as they wished, but Mark said not to worry, soon the hockey season would be over. They kept writing.

Dear Mark,

I'm sitting in the bathroom watching my sister Jenny take a bath. B-O-R-I-N-G!! Mom and Jim just left to play tennis for an hour and a half. Jenny asked who I was writing to and I told her "Mark." She just replied, "Oh, Lover boy?"

Thanks for hitting the puck over the side . . . Jenny wanted one so much. It's now sitting in the tub with her.

So far this letter is shit and I want it to be fiery and passionate. So let me now tell you that I found it very hard not to stay today. When you came out in your gear and your 'Star-Wars' shirt, I felt a twinge in my stomach. You always make a face when I compliment your body. I was thinking (while looking at you) how safe and warm I feel in your arms. Mmmmmmm, I wish I was there now.

I can't wait to watch you play tomorrow. I don't understand much about hockey and I don't care who wins, I just know that I love to watch guys play hockey (or football or LaCrosse)—and it's so sexy . . . you most of all.

I hope you're not too tired tomorrow after the game—'cause I'm gonna ravage you with kisses.

love, CEN

Almost eight weeks went by before I noticed a change in her health and then another sudden and rapid decline began, much like what had happened after the September admission. The shortness of breath was back, her cough was increasing, and she was bringing up fresh streaks of blood everytime she had thumps now—not enough to stop therapy, like at the Red Barn in December, but enough to keep us anxious and on edge. In our minds we saw the specter of a festering vein in her right lung that hadn't quite healed after the last hemorrhage and might start up at any moment. As her illness closed in again, she resented it more than ever. She felt like a bird with broken wings falling behind the flight. She refused to say a word to Mark.

She never told me in so many words they were having a love affair, and by the time I realized it in February she thought I'd known all along. As long as things were going well, I didn't hear a word. When their relationship slipped out of balance, we talked.

> *Dear Mark,*
>
> *I'm sorry I ruined your day. I hope it got better after we said—hell make that before we said—Good-bye. I ruined mine as well. I don't know why I'm like that. I told you I was insecure . . . maybe more than I thought. I told you of my inner nightmare, about life and college and my health . . . everything ties in to the last one. I don't know how to face it alone and sometimes, I need someone to tell me, "It's alright, Christine, you'll be fine, everything will be all right, I love you."*
>
> *Then I realized you can't tell me that—no one can and mean it . . . how do they know the future? I do this to myself most of the time.*
>
> *About us. I worry that you won't let anyone understand you . . . isn't that lonely? I'm just the opposite. I want everyone to know me because I'm so afraid of being lonely. It's terrible to be afraid of loneliness because it's an unavoidable state sometimes.*
>
> *You said I'd think you were a jerk if you reveal yourself? How can you say that? Self hate is the mind's (and soul's) most dangerous weapon. Please let me warm your heart. I'm like a fire—to live I need (thrive on) and crave love—just as a fire does oxygen. But unlike a fire, I can*

*control myself. Don't worry, you won't get burned. I'm
not going to try to change you . . . no Frankenstein syn-
drome.*

*Point! I love you, and I want to understand you better
if you'll let me. You're going to enjoy it, I won't hurt you
and I'll keep your heart and soul happy and warm, and I
won't try to take you away from your religion or God.
Love Him as much as you can and want for He is your
Savior . . . (or maybe Jesus Christ is—excuse my ignorance)
and that's the way things are in your heart. "Follow your
dream," remember? I can understand how you feel even
if things aren't the same for me. Who's my savior? I don't
know. Either I don't have one or I haven't found one.
Maybe it's love.*

*Does this clear any doubts . . . or does it raise them? I
hope I haven't said too much. Call me a gambler.*

*One thing—understand, and this is true. I have high
standards and good taste. I'm extremely picky and fell for
not a lot of people (crushes yes, but I'm talking heavy-
duty, real-stuff, I ain't just whistlin' Dixie—love) and when
I have, the person's been top quality . . . I mean crème de
la crème, thoroughbreds . . . ARRGGH!*

> *You know, da real BEEF . . . style, class,
>   looks, intelligence, passion, kindness,
>   everything!*
> > *ONLY THE BEST, READ—
> > THAT MEANS YOU!!*

> > > > *love, Christine Elizabeth*

Their relationship would right itself for a few days, and then
they'd lose their balance again.

Dear Chris,
    *I don't know what it is, but it's true, I was totally fucked
up all day. You saved it though. You cheer me up. I'm*

*prone to get into those moods every once in a while and
I thank you for not giving up on me. Some other people
I know would've said in a huff, "If you won't tell me then
I can't help" and left, which never helps. Thanks for stick-
ing around and working on me.*

*I was depressed because I was really wondering if you
liked me at all and sometimes it snowballs into my pulling
the "I'm poor" routine and everything else. I just seemed
to think that things weren't adding up right between us,
and then I just said, "Damn, here goes nothing." I was
bummed. ANYWAY . . .*

*I don't know what the hell to do after the game Friday
night, or for that matter, what we can do, seeing I'm broke
and will be tired from the game. Maybe we can just mellow out somewhere warm . . . with a fireplace.*

*We definitely don't have enough time or space for
each other. I wish we could Twilight Zone our way to
Tahiti. It would be nice, wild and crazy . . . Ricki, don't lose
that number.*

*Sometimes, I get mad at the fact you seem to think that
everything that comes out of me means SEX. In fact,
usually very little of anything that comes out of this brain
has to do with that three letter word. (And if you believe
that, you'll buy this watch . . .) No seriously, folks—*

*Basically, I want to let things flow, and not push a
thing! I'm going to let you do the pushing. No, I don't
mean that . . . I don't know what I mean.*

Okay Buzzy, this is it, this is the big one.

love
MER

Dear MER—
    *I'm listening to Tschaikovsky's Dornroschen Op. 66, a
very famous* peace. *Can you guess what it is in English?*
    *Your letter was nice and I'm glad you're not pushing.
Things never work out when they're pushed.*

John was soooooo *funny today, I couldn't stop laughing
. . . that Monty Python routine—"I wonder what's on the
telly"*
"Ooh, it looks like a penguin"
"No, no, what program!"

I hate school work—you know that???

DEEP HATRED

Well, this is a reel short note, sew, Good buy,

since Sara lee,

Chris . . . (HUH?)

14 · Gathering Clouds

Mark was very religious and it affected their relationship in odd ways. They talked about Christian ethics and morals and the lessons in the Bible. Mark gave her his copy of the Good News Bible and she started reading the New Testament, Matthew and John. Sitting on her bed with every light burning and her cat Ivy on her lap, she read till late at night. I heard the familiar sound of minimalist punk rock turned low on her radio as she read, and I was touched by her enthusiasm and the incongruity.

Mark assisted the curate in teaching the confirmation class at Christ's Church in Rye, and he taught Christine as well. In February, Mark and his friend Jamie went to Princeton for the weekend on a religious retreat, sponsored by FOCUS, a Christian Fellowship group. Mark asked Chris to come. She pondered the weekend for days and talked to me about it.

"Mom, I want to go, but how can I? I'm too sick. Who'll do my therapy?" She paced the kitchen—all the thoughts she'd gone over rushing out at once. "How could I just disappear three times a day? I wouldn't want them to see. God, it's so disgusting. Coughing up mucus and spitting into a cup. I'd be so ashamed. And if Mark ever saw it— God, he'd never want to kiss me again." She shuddered, recoiling from herself. She never talked this way, so full of self-hate.

"When someone loves you dear, it isn't so bad."

"Oh no, I can't take the chance. It's bad enough. Besides, what if I bled? My lungs are so terrible and I'm having so much trouble breathing." She stopped to wait for my answer but I was thinking and she sounded tired when she said, "I'll be in the hospital soon. I don't see how I can go, what do you think?"

She must be talking herself out of this for a reason. I followed her lead, saying quietly, "I think it would be difficult for you."

So she didn't go and Mark was disappointed. Trying to tell him the reasons, she felt like a hypocrite. She couldn't utter the words "I'm too sick." Not to Mark.

When he got back from Princeton on Sunday night, he called. He sounded odd and said they had to talk about what had happened.

Chris said, "Tell me now—what?"

She heard a long pause, then, "Uuhhh . . . hmmmm, well, let me see. Uh, well, how should I put it?"

Chris felt her heart tighten. Had Mark fallen in love with someone else? He found words. "Well, there was a discussion about premarital sex and the teachings of Christ, and, oh, I don't know—I can tell you when I see you."

"You mean tomorrow," she said, trying to pinpoint when.

"Uh, no, no, when we're alone, after the hockey game on Friday."

"That's a week. What's all the mystery about?"

"No mystery, no mystery. Just some heavy-duty things."

Chris was impatient. "What did they *say* about premarital sex?" As if she didn't know.

More silence, then he said, "They're against it."

She was ready and said softly, "What'd they say about making love?"

Mark made some sound she couldn't hear and said, "Same thing."

"Mark, it's a little late for us, wouldn't you say?"

He laughed. "Yeah, I think I'd say that. We'll talk Friday. I have more thinking to do." And they said good-night. Chris was uneasy.

The next day she went down to Jamie's locker in the basement. Jamie was a musician and spent more time playing his guitar on the third floor with her friends than he did by his own locker. Plus there was no rug on the floor down there. He was bending over as Chris approached and she bent over too, her eyes right next to his and said rapidly, "Zzz-boogada—boogada—boogada."

He popped up and smiled. "Hi Chris. What are you doing here—glee club?"

"No, I had to give that up. I wanted to ask about the Princeton conference. How was it?"

"Pretty good." He looked at her with interest. His friendship with her was growing but she rarely sought him out. "I had a good time. So did Mark—didn't he?"

She nodded. "I guess so. We haven't had time to talk about it." There was an awkward pause. "What went on anyway?"

Jamie wondered why she wasn't asking Mark. He leaned against the wall. "There were lectures and small study groups, walks around campus, talking, really good people, prayers, services, singing—you know, all geared to religion, faith, Christ."

"Were there many people?"

"About two hundred." She was surprised.

"That's a *lot*. Was it fun?"

"Fun? I wouldn't say it was a barrel of monkeys, but yes, it was fun. Maybe a little tedious at times."

"Was it ever really heavy?" He laughed, watching her pencil-trace the tiny graffiti on the cement seams between the cinder blocks.

"What do you mean heavy? It's supposed to be uplifting and enlightening."

"Yes, I'm sure." Chris tried to get back on her track. "I mean, did they have any serious talks about—sex or anything?"

"Sure. They do everything they can to keep us from having sex, but that's nothing new."

"Mark thought that part was pretty heavy."

Jamie stared up at the speckled ceiling tiles as the class bell rang. "I didn't think so." He was tempted to say, "but then, I'm not doing it," but he liked Chris too much and he knew Mark and she were serious. He envied them both. "Well, maybe it was for Mark," and he shrugged, embarrassed.

And Chris said, "Be sure to invite me to the next one."

"Will do," said Jamie, eyeing the clock. "I've got to go."

"So do I. See you later." She watched Jamie disappear up the stairs, gracefully taking them two at a time.

Left alone in the hall, she climbed the stairs slowly, knowing she'd be excused if she was late to class. She stopped on the first landing in a bright shaft of sunlight, turning her back to the window to let the sun warm her shoulders. She wished she wasn't so cold and tired. She thought no one was watching, and made no effort to hide her difficulty in climbing the stairs.

From an empty classroom the French teacher, Madame Amsellem, saw Chris standing in the sunlight. She watched Chris stop at every other step, hunching over like an old man and coughing repeatedly as she gripped the railing. She had never seen Chris like this. No one had. Chris hid these things—the wrenching episodes when she couldn't climb three steps and she listened fearfully to the scraping, rasping sounds in her lungs. After she was out of sight, her coughing still echoed down the stairwell. Madame Amsellem listened until she heard the door swing open at the top of the stairs; then she walked up herself, slowed only by her own thoughts.

After the hockey game on Friday, Mark and Chris were at our house, sitting opposite each other on her bed with the Harper's Study Bible between them. Mark finally explained the mystery. The conference leader had said that Christ's teaching forbade premarital sex and to engage in it was a sin against Christ.

"But that's nothing new, is it?"

"Well, he was so persuasive, it seemed new to me." He showed her some passages in the Bible, trying to make sense out of it. "How can I explain this? I just began to see it was . . . well, wrong to do. Try to understand."

"We don't live in 25 A.D., Mark."

"I know, but it's still wrong. We can't continue the physical side of our love affair."

Christine was shocked. It was ludicrous. She always thought cystic fibrosis would stop her from finding love. Now it was the Bible? He couldn't mean it.

Suddenly her cough spasmed and she flopped over sideways burying her face in the satin comforter. Mark knew she hated it when that happened. Sometimes when they were alone together he'd see her body tense and he asked her once what it was. She said, "Cough coming. I'm pushing it down." Apparently sometimes it came without warning. "Sorry," she said, and she pushed herself back up.

"Where were we?" he asked.

"No place good."

"Chris, I know it sounds weird. I mean maybe I'm weird. Let's face it I am. But I just knew when I heard it and thought it through . . . well, we should try . . ." He stopped. This was so hard, he was so unsure, he loved her so.

But Chris had a mind of her own and didn't believe she was a sinner. She tried to make him understand that what they were doing was natural and healthy for people in love and added grumpily, "And will you stop calling it premarital sex. It sounds like some kind of skin rash." Mark smiled.

"It doesn't matter what it's called. We're doing it."

"We certainly are," said Christine hotly, looking at Mark with conviction, "and I feel wonderful about it."

If he wasn't careful, Christine would humor him out of this. "Are you sure that's the real reason, Mark, and it's not something else?" He looked at her knowing she was about to wrap him around her little finger. She lowered her eyes. "Like maybe I have bad breath or something?"

"Will you stop it? Of course you don't have bad breath."

She was looking down twiddling her thumbs in her lap, and Mark said in a pseudo-suave voice, "Do I?"

She laughed. "I don't know. C'mere. Let's find out," and she reached to pull him over next to her. He laughed too and pulled away.

"C'mon, Chris. Will you be serious?"

"Okay, okay. You don't have bad breath," and she leaned forward looking into his eyes. Mark felt caught in her spell as she said slowly, daring to risk his anger, "Christ can't save you . . . if you don't sin first."

Mark dropped his head and covered his eyes. "This is no good. How am I going to resist?"

She looked through lowered lashes. "It's not going to be easy." But Mark wouldn't look, muttering something under his breath.

She stopped teasing and there was a long silence. Then she started to cry.

"Well, what are the ground rules going to be? How far is too far? And can we kiss, can we touch? And if we do, then what? It's crazy Mark, it's never going to work! We can't go back!"

Mark was confused. He didn't want to hurt her. They weren't breaking up. Nothing would change—he promised her—except one thing. In the end she said she'd abide by his wishes, but it wasn't what she wanted.

They cried, sitting on her plump satin comforter, beneath the eyelet canopy, like two children under a tree in a downpour, knowing it was going to hurt and test their love. Their feelings, which had been so clear, were plunged into confusion and torment, and problems began.

Their pledge of celibacy lasted for two weeks. Chris came home from school late one day, her eyes red and swollen. I was upstairs getting Jenny ready for a clay workshop at the YWCA when Chris brushed past me into her room. I said, "Wait here, Jenny, I'll be right back," and I followed Chris. She was standing at her window, staring at the leafless trees and slate sky.

"Chris, what is it?"

"Mark and I had a fight. I think we're going to break up," she said, not turning around.

"Do you want to talk?"

"Sure," she said, with no interest.

"I'll be back in twenty minutes. I have to take Jenny to art class."

"I'll come with you," she said.

"Okay." So we drove to the Y with Jenny, who was quiet in the back. We always had good talks in the car. I never knew why, except maybe it was easier for Christine to talk about hard things when she didn't look at me. On the way back home, she told me about the Princeton conference and their ensuing attempt at restraint. Then she paused for my reaction. I was momentarily speechless.

"What was the fight?"

"Our exercise-in-abstinence lasted two weeks. We don't have that much time alone," she glanced at me, her voice laced with sarcasm. I kept my eyes on the road. "But last week we broke it and today he blamed me. Damn him! It wasn't me. It was both of us. He said we failed and we sinned and I was a temptress." She turned to me as if I were accusing her. "I didn't do a thing!" She was about to cry. "One thing just led to another. We're human for God's sake." She stopped, afraid she'd gone too far, but she hadn't.

"He called you a temptress? A treasure, maybe—not a temptress. There must be more than meets the eye."

"You don't know the half of it. We share everything—our innermost thoughts. I know him, how passionate he is and how repressed, but even I don't understand this."

As I turned onto Cat Rock Road I thought back to my impressions of Mark when he came to dinner.

"Chris, when we met Mark, he was cool, charming, polished, *very* private, distant—you're telling me about his passion and religion. Which is the real Mark?"

"They're all the real Mark."

"Mmmmmm. If he's passionate *and* repressed, he must feel conflict over you." I pulled in the driveway and parked. "Chris are you, well, Mark's first?"

"No." I didn't have a next question, and she volunteered. "Last year he had an affair with an older woman."

I turned to Chris, studying her profile in the dark. "He had an affair with an older woman, when he was sixteen?" Chris nodded. I waited. She offered no more. "How do you know?"

"Everyone knows, and Mark told me." A long silence followed this interesting news. I didn't know what to say. Impatient, Chris said, "What?"

"How old was she?"

"In her mid-twenties."

"Was she . . . married?"

"Yes—but she was separated."

"Boy. How long did it go on?"

"Six months."

I thought she was going to say three weeks. Now I understood what was happening and it didn't bode well. This on top of Christine's illness was a lot for a teenage boy to handle. I asked, "How did it end?"

"I don't know." I had the feeling she did.

"Princeton must have blown his mind, Chris. There's the problem, guilt. It must seem like adultery to Mark even if she *was* separated. It's one of the ten commandments."

"But why is he taking it out on me? What we have is wonderful and honest."

"I'm sure it is. I believe he's sincere in his beliefs, but that kind of affair may be what made him seek out religion. Looking for answers and help."

She started to cry. "I can't stand this. I don't deserve it."

"No, you don't, but he may feel he doesn't deserve you." Her crying dissolved into hacking coughs. I waited. "Want to come with me to get Jenny?"

"Sure," she sniffed. "There's one thing this has taught me. Love does *not* conquer all." I started down the driveway and she said, "Wait, I'm going to stay here. He may call."

He called that night and apologized. But slowly, tension and uncertainty intruded and grew around their feelings like bindweed in a rose garden. Love still held them together but they couldn't recapture the joy they felt before the Princeton conference.

The month of February was bitterly cold and March brought no early signs of spring. I kept my attention on Jenny, who was having disturbing episodes of night fears. She'd seen *King Kong* several months before, and these fears had begun to take the shape of a giant gorilla monster she said she could see in the dark. I talked to a child psychiatrist on my own, trying to understand how to help her.

The fears were always worse the night after she came home from her father's, which puzzled me. Chris and I were both trying to help Jenny. Sometimes it took hours for her to get to sleep or she woke during the night and couldn't go back to sleep. She was exhausted, which made the fears worse. Then she began to hallucinate when she was awake and both Chris and I had the experience of Jenny staring out a window as it grew dark, letting out a scream and leaping into our arms, shaking and crying. The terror was too real and she couldn't be alone for a minute.

Chris was wonderful and never mocked her. Some nights when I was asleep she got up, brought Jenny back to bed, and sat with her, even let her sleep on the floor by her bed in a sleeping bag. Chris was usually up late, and Jenny was trying to control her fears and not come into my room all night, so she'd go into Chris's room first, where the light was on. Many a night, I thought things were getting better only to find that Chris had handled it. She showed such compassion and understanding, I told her she was going to be a wonderful mother.

Chris and Jenny drew closer that year. And they shared something else that I was the cause of and could be no part of. Chris knew what it was like to live with a stepfather she didn't love (Jenny's father), and now Jenny was living with a stepfather she didn't love (Jim). Jenny's relationship with her own father was so intense, and she saw him so much, that there was no chance for a relationship with Jim. When they talked about stepfathers, Chris chose her words carefully, since the stepfather she'd had to live with was the father Jenny loved, and Jenny had no idea of Christine's real feelings. But they shared a common experience and Jenny listened when Chris talked.

By March, Chris's pneumonia was gaining fast. The coughing and shortness of breath grew harder to control at school and violent and terrifying at home. Twice, she started to faint in the kitchen and her lips turned blue when her cough emptied her lungs of air, keeping her from catching her breath. We were terrified and I couldn't help her when it happened. There was nothing to do, except clutch her hand and wait.

I tried to get her to talk to Dr. Ores, but she was stubborn and defiant. School, her friends, and Mark were too important.

"Mom, if I go see the doctor, I know what I'll get—another

prison sentence." I wondered what she had now—a death sentence? "Next week the hockey season is over. Mark and I will have time for each other. I want that time—without pressure." So I let her make the choice, but I called Dr. Ores just the same and made an appointment for Chris to see her ten days later. Chris couldn't go on much longer, and by then she might be ready.

Rye Country Day's last hockey game was an away game against Brunswick, their archrivals in Greenwich. The skating rink in Greenwich had a roof but no sides and the frigid winds that blew up the hill and across the ice never let up. Chris dressed in layers for the game—to peel off later at Phebe's party. She coughed up fresh blood during her afternoon thumps, but she didn't tell me. She was fed up. She dosed herself with the codeine cough suppressant before the game, and put a small bottle in her purse with some wax paper cups.

During the game she could feel the bleeding in the upper right side of her chest. Hunched against the wind, she sat next to Claudia and John on the edge of the bleachers, in case she had to leave quickly. Amid the clatter of hockey sticks and the cheering and screaming, no one seemed to notice she wasn't joining in, and during the time-outs she came to life.

Between the second and third periods, while the Zamboni was cleaning the ice, Claudia looked at her oddly and said, "You okay?"

With her hand Chris indicated so-so and said, "My mouth is frozen." Then she leaned closer. "Claudia, if I feel sick during third period, could you bring me home?"

"I thought you were kind of quiet—what's up?"

"I feel nauseous," she fibbed. She'd put Claudia through one harrowing night; she wasn't going to scare her now. She felt more fluttering during the last period, but no coughing. If she was bleeding, it wasn't enough to spill into her bronchial tubes.

Waiting for Mark to change after the game, she bought a hot chocolate to warm her hands, but she was shaking so much she could hardly hold the cup. God, she thought, my nerves are shot, but I'm not going home. She took a Valium to stop the shaking and she and Mark went to the party. Half the senior class was there and it was one of Phebe's great parties. Mark drank Molson's Red Label and Chris started drinking Molson's, too. Dr. Ores had told her not to drink when her lungs were bleeding, but she thought, ale was mild, just this once. She forgot about the bleeding and the codeine and the Valium, having a good time clowning with her friends and dancing with Mark.

At 12:30, she started to feel light-headed and dizzy, as if she were floating. She remembered the Valium and said, "Mark, I think I made a mistake drinking on top of the Valium I took before we came." Mark stopped short.

"Whoops."

"I don't feel right."

"What do you mean?" He watched her closely.

"I think my heart's beating too fast. I feel like I'm tipping over and I'm shaking. But I *know* I'm not drunk." She leaned against him.

"How much Valium did you take?" he asked.

"Just one, a yellow one—five milligrams." She didn't look well. "I think we should go."

"Okay." He knew something was wrong and he hurried out in the rain to get her car, and then back in to collect the car keys for the three cars that were blocking hers, and then back out to move all the cars. She didn't talk on the way home. The rain was slowing down.

"Chris, you asleep?" Mark glanced over, as he pulled carefully into our rutted driveway.

"No, but I'm so tired—of everything, of everyone."

"Boy—I know what you mean," he said lightly. He shut off the motor and turned to her. She sounded strange, her voice faint, far away—from across a chasm.

"No, you don't know what I mean. I mean—" She stopped, opened her eyes without seeing, and closed them again. "I mean, I just hate my life and I hate this goddamn disease and I hate this stupid cough." There was anger in her voice, but no force behind the words. "I feel so weird. I'm not going to tell Mom I'm sick. Sometimes I hate so much, it scares me. Oh God, I hate my mother, she's always bugging me and hassling me. I go in the hospital and when she comes to see me, she just comes to make sure I'm doing my homework. And God, I'm so mad at my dad— he never bugs me but I might as well not have a father. I never see him. He writes, but I need him. I don't even know if he has his beard now or not."

She slumped over onto her knees. "I can't stand all this anger and hate. It's choking me."

Mark didn't say a word. She adored her father. He'd never heard her talk like this. Was it the mix of medicine and alcohol? They sat in silence and the rain stopped. The night was listening. Little rivulets ran down the black windshield. Chris rested her head in her arms and talked, her voice strange and singsong.

"Something's wrong with me. I can't stand anything any more, no pressure, nothing going wrong. I fly into rages over nothing and I get hysterical. What is it? And I'm so jealous of Jenny because she's healthy and she'll never have to have thumps. And I worry about her."

Mark put his hand on her back but said nothing. Maybe she'd needed to get this out. But there was more.

"And I can't stand Jimmy. He got all the best parts in the plays. And I can't even stand Jim. He's such a know-it-all and he hates my music and acts like I'm disgusting when he hears it. I'm jealous of Claudia because she has such a good figure and she complains she has to diet. God, she doesn't know how lucky she is. But most of all, I hate myself . . . I just hate myself."

She stopped crying and Mark sat speechless and silent. Then he said, "You hate yourself? Oh Chris . . ."

But she went on as if she hadn't heard. "You know, when I get out of the hospital I always tell my teachers I'll make up the work and when the day comes, I haven't done it. I'm such a fuck-up and Mom's right. If I don't study I won't get into Emerson, but sometimes I think I do it on purpose so I won't get in, because I'm so scared. I just hate the way I am and I hate everybody who isn't sick."

Now Mark didn't dare say anything. Maybe she hated him. Was all this coming from her unconscious? It was like a river rising and flooding its banks and he was overwhelmed. It started to rain again, a soft rain. Christine's eyes were closed and he thought she was asleep when she said, "Oh God. How can I plan for the future when I don't know if I even have one?"

She started to cry and Mark bent down and put his arm around her to hold her in and stop the flood. Her voice caught when she said, "Please God, why don't you help? No matter what, I can't escape. I can't get well. Not *ever.* I'm trapped in this body that's pulling me down, do you understand? I can't accept it and I won't accept it . . . but I have to accept it and I can't stand it. Why did it have to be me? Oh God, I hate you too, for letting this happen." She started to cry again, harder than before.

Mark sat in stunned silence. She seemed delirious and he hoped she was. Then she wouldn't remember this. She sobbed and sobbed, her head buried, her arms folded on her knees, her back shaking as she cried. Holding her as best he could, he said, "Chris, you have plenty of reason to feel the way you do. I wish I understood more. A little more at least, what it's like to be in your shoes. I've tried, but I can never know. My mind just can't understand. No one's can, Chris." His words sounded puny to him. She didn't answer. She breathed slowly, letting her sobs stop. He took her hand and her fingers were icy. "Chris?"

"What?"

"Are you okay?" What a dumb question he thought. She'd just finished telling him she wasn't okay.

"Yes, yes, I'm just so tired."

"Want a hug?" She sat up slowly and turned her head to him, relaxing her face, but unable to smile.

"That would be nice." Chris put her arms around his stomach and buried her face in his lumber jacket and Mark hugged her for a long time and thought. Here was this girl, *his* girl, who had everything. Brains, beauty, guts, determination. She was daring, nutty, and funny. She was sexy. He'd never known a girl like her, or at least he'd thought he knew her. How could God ignore her? She carried herself with such grace. She was so stalwart and un-complaining. He'd never dreamt she had all this anger. She usually laughed about everything.

"Chris, life doesn't make any sense. I only know I believe in you and I know you'll always win. You have too much going for you to lose because of one negative that's making things so hard. You'll never lose, I just know it."

He looked down. She was limp in his arms, asleep, or with the Valium and beer maybe passed out. He could have sat like that with his arms around her all night, but after a while the cold woke her and she said, "I'm going in. I'm sorry. I don't feel good."

He walked her up the steps and helped her to her room and into bed. She didn't say good-night when he hugged her once more. She was already asleep.

Mark never asked her about that night and she never said a word. We kept the appointment I'd made with Dr. Ores at Babies Hospital, and Chris was admitted immediately. Dr. Ores brought her up to the floor herself when she saw from the faint blue tinge on her lips how little oxygen she was getting. She told me before I left that Chris was in heart failure, the first time I'd heard the words. We didn't tell her.

It was a routine admission—if secretions in her lungs threatening to asphyxiate her could be called routine. We called it routine.

15 ★ Breaking Up

★
★ ★
Chris had an oral report due in Special Topics Biology
and she got permission from her teacher, Dick Brown, to do a
report on cystic fibrosis. She did her research in the hospital,
talking to the doctors like a colleague.

Dick Brown visited her in the hospital. He had special empa-
thy for Chris because he had diabetes and knew what it meant to
be ever vigilant of one's health in order to live. He wondered
about the report. She was usually laughing and clowning, charming him even when he didn't want to be charmed, but she
wouldn't be able to laugh about this. Maybe he'd see the other
side he liked so much, the girl who was so sincere and forthright
when her work was overdue, so determined to make good,
though she was late with every promise.

The report was due the day after she went back to school.
Drea and Phebe gave the first one that day. Their topic was drug
abuse and the class was in stitches the whole time. As part of the
report, they did a street scene between Phebe, a drug pusher, and
Drea, a square attempting to buy drugs. The report was deteriorating into a comedy routine, with nonstop ad-libs from the class
as everyone acted like they already knew all there was to know.
When Phebe pulled out cigarette paper and a packet of green tea
leaves and started picking seeds out of the tea with a tweezer, the
boys went wild. She laughed so hard, trying to roll a joint, that she
had to turn down raucous offers of assistance. Even Dick Brown
was laughing.

Chris was next and he called on her, not at all sure her report

would be serious. She'd walked into class with sticky spiked-up
hair and as she went to the head of the room, he mused at the
irony: What have I got now? A punk rocker going to joke her way
through a report on her own illness?

Chris began, "I did research at the Columbia Presbyterian
Medical Center on cystic fibrosis, where it was discovered in 1938.
The pathology of the illness was identified by Dr. Dorothy Ander-
son, who named it as well." Chris didn't use medical terminology
but didn't realize that even words like pathology and pulmonary
might be unfamiliar to the class.

"In Europe, there is another name for it, mucoviscodosis, first
used by a Swiss doctor named Franconi, at about the same time.
He didn't know he'd identified an actual disease. This name is
better because the main problem in the illness comes from the
thick mucus produced by the exocrine glands. But I've never
heard anyone use it. Cystic fibrosis is not a lung disease. It starts
as a malfunction of the exocrine glands. I'll explain how you get
it, how you treat it, the prognosis, and the complications."

She was feeling comfortable. Her clinical approach was working and the class quieted down. She had an odd sense of standing
outside of herself, watching with the rest. A window at the back
of the room was open and her eyes followed a trail of dust on the
floor stirred by the air and wafting back and forth across a square
of sunlight. It was better to avoid eye contact she thought. She
turned to use the blackboard, suddenly confident.

She drew a diagram to explain how the disease was inherited
from recessive genes which came from both parents.

Dick Brown leaned against the low bookcases at the side of the
room, listening to her voice, relieved she was serious. He watched
the class, pleased at how attentive they were after the craziness
before. Chris went more deeply into what happens when the
millions of tiny alveoli in the lungs get so clogged they can't
exchange carbon dioxide for oxygen, and he found himself drawn
in with the rest of the class, an odd role reversal taking place as
she became teacher and he student. This never happened in his
class.

She was saying, "Most patients get cyanosis. That's the clubbing of the fingertips. Though doctors know it comes from lack of oxygen, they don't know why the fingertips enlarge. It happens in emphysema, too."

Phebe and Claudia looked at each other and wondered why Chris hadn't left that part out. Wasn't she afraid everyone would notice her odd fingers? Phebe had never known it came from her illness.

But Chris was unflinching. She described the physical therapy she so despised as *the* most important part of treatment. It was hard not to color her remarks about the thumps, and she heard herself saying, "Children detest these thumps. The physical therapy is like a tyrant. The pounding seems like punishment, but, no matter what, the therapy can never be skipped."

Then she talked about mucus, and Dick Brown thought it was magical the way she handled the subject so delicately.

"Mucus isn't the gross, yucky thing we all think of. Mucus is a miraculous natural substance—thin, watery, slippery, odorless—that helps keep the body moist and germfree. It serves as a lubricant and cleaning agent, removing and flushing unwelcome and dangerous bacteria out of the system. Mucus is a friend to your body and your well-being. But for patients with cystic fibrosis, mucus is an enemy, because it's too thick.

"When the children are born, their lungs are normal. As I said, it's not a lung disease, but as the exocrine glands keep producing thick mucus, day in and day out, clogging up the lungs, it creates an ideal breeding ground for what doctors call 'opportunistic organisms,' that is, viral and bacterial pneumonias. And once these deadly organisms get a start under such fertile conditions they multiply and multiply. The patient's life is spent fighting them off, with antibiotics. That is the problem in a nutshell." She paused, pushing her hair back. "A small anomaly in the body upsets the balance of the entire system, and literally gums up the works. The most common cause of death is congestive heart failure.

"This term sounds like it means there's something wrong with the heart, but it isn't so. There's something wrong with the lungs.

They're so full of thick mucus—that's the congestion—and the heart can't push anything through anymore, anything being the blood that carries oxygen and carbon dioxide back and forth. Eventually, the heart fails.

"Hopefully the patient may lapse into a coma from carbon dioxide retention *before* it fails. Carbon dioxide is poison and as more is trapped the patient loses consciousness. This is probably for the best, since death is without struggle, like falling asleep."

If the class was quiet before, now it was hushed and motionless. Chris moved quickly into an explanation of the complications of cystic fibrosis—the digestive problems, the lung collapses, arthritis, diabetes, kidney failure, and dehydration. Touching on each one briefly, she left hemoptysis till last.

"Another possible emergency is hemoptysis. This is bleeding from the lungs, and it's the only time thumps are ever stopped. Sometimes the lung infections erode a major artery or vein. If that happens and the artery ruptures, the patient hemorrhages. There's not much you can do when it happens. Bed rest and tranquilizers are prescribed to halt the coughing, because coughing increases the bleeding. If the bleeding is severe enough, however, only coughing keeps the patient from drowning in his own blood in his bronchial tubes. It's touch and go."

Chris paused and stared at her notes, but the words were a blur. She didn't look up, waiting for the sound of someone stirring, but there was no sound. Did her friends know how often she bled? Claudia did. Had she ever told anyone else? She couldn't remember. She picked up the eraser and wiped the diagram off the blackboard. Then she turned—she had to finish—and said, "The reproductive cycle is not affected in female patients, but boys with cystic fibrosis are sterile."

Dick Brown looked around at his students listening to this pretty girl talk about what was killing her. He knew that was what they were all thinking. So was he. Even though her words held no emotion, and she referred to "the patient," not herself, the message was devastating. He never knew how deadly the lung infections were. She was saying, "For women, pregnancy is possible and women have borne normal children, but it's very difficult—and so far, infrequent. There's too much lung damage by the time the woman is at childbearing age." She stopped for a minute, and put her note cards in a neat pile on Mr. Brown's desk, behind her.

"There is no cure, and there are only partly effective controls to prolong life. A cure remains in the future." She asked if there were any questions.

After a minute of awkward silence, several kids raised their hands. Mr. Brown noted how superficial the questions were. Everyone was afraid to ask the question on their minds. Are you afraid to die? How can you go on knowing what's ahead? No one dared, but the question hung in the still air.

Then one of the girls asked, "How can a woman judge if she can have a child . . . and can she take antibiotics when she's pregnant?" The class bell rang, but nobody moved. Chris glanced at Mr. Brown. He nodded to go on. She was surprised and caught off guard. She thought a second.

"The answer to the second question is—no antibiotics. And as for the first—well, in my case, I'd want to talk it over with my doctor and then decide. It *is* my goal to have a child." She paused, not sure how to explain it. Claudia took a long slow breath and felt her throat catch, and Phebe closed her eyes, afraid to listen. Christine's heart started to gallop and she felt light-headed. Seconds passed and her friends watched. No words were coming. Why was she stopping, she thought. Then she began speaking again, her voice quiet and determined. "It will be up to me, to maintain my strength, to never miss physical therapy, to follow all the doctor's instructions."

She hardly recognized her voice as unwanted emotions stole through her. She was losing her detached feeling.

"The biggest danger will be the absence of antibiotics. Without them, the pneumonias will go out of control. Part of my lungs would be destroyed during the nine months. The question is, would I have enough healthy lung to last nine months. An X ray would help answer that question." Chris thought she heard her

voice wavering but she had to finish. She stopped saying "I." "It's
a critical decision that a woman would have to make with the
treating doctor. Because it's possible she'd be forced to decide
between her child's life and her own."

Chris knew the class was over but no one had gotten up and
bolted as they usually did. She was feeling overwhelmed. Dick
Brown moved to the front of the room.

"Thank you Christine. That was very well researched." He
dismissed the class. Chairs scraped and people moved to the door.
Chris gathered her things, trying to hold back her feelings. She
could hardly breathe. Out in the hall, Phebe rushed to her side,
her own tears spilling over. Phebe wanted lots of children and
when she'd heard Chris say she might have to choose, she'd been
horrified. She saw Christine's eyes flooded with tears and she put
her arms around her.

"Oh, Chris, are you all right?"

She nodded, keeping her head down. Several classmates
glanced in their direction. She swallowed hard. Seeing Phebe's
tears helped her stop her own. Funny how that happened.
Claudia hurried over as Chris was saying, "I had a hard time at
the end. I probably shouldn't have said what I did, but I was fine
up till then, so I thought I'd be okay. I hope I didn't embarrass
everyone."

Claudia said, "Are you kidding? I couldn't believe you had the
guts to do that. I never would have."

And Chris said, "I didn't have the guts, that was the problem."

"No one was embarrassed," said Phebe. "I don't think they
noticed. I'm just hypersensitive."

Claudia said, "It was a really good report, Chris."

Chris said, "Good, what a relief it's over," and slipped into a
Steve Martin imitation. She wanted to put it behind her, this
unwelcome dream unfolding, which wasn't a dream.

Mark's birthday was in April and for a week she carried on
about what she could give him that wouldn't make him feel
guilty.

On Sunday afternoon, I found her in the downstairs den, sitting on the sofa amidst scissors, string, Saran Wrap, and tissue. She was bent over, peering intently at a little bag of something as I walked over to take a closer look. I was always charmed when I came upon her doing something I knew nothing about— Christine living her own life. She was separating the ends of a jute cord tied around a little bag into a tassle.

"What's that?" I asked.

"Mark's birthday present." She held it up with pride, a little tan suede pouch, not much bigger than a plum. It looked like a pouch of spices a medieval prince might carry.

"It's cute. What is it?"

"Pot."

My mind went blank for a moment and my uncensored thought slipped out. "You're giving Mark *pot* for his birthday?" Now I *wasn't* charmed.

She smiled happily, "Yup," ignoring my expression of distaste and surprise.

"It's not even legal," I said, regretting the remark instantly.

Christine was glib and unperturbed. "What are you going to do, Mom, make a citizen's arrest?"

I laughed in spite of myself, then looked away in annoyance. I hated disapproving of Christine. I muttered feebly, "Oh, I don't know, Chris, it seems so—unsavory. He brings you the Bible, you bring him pot?"

"Oh Mom, Mark likes it—and everyone smokes it, even the square kids. Mark told me he's always embarrassed when everyone shares their pot with him, and he never has any of his own to pass around." She went back to fussing with the little pouch.

"I wonder what the Bible would have to say about Mark smoking pot," I observed ruefully.

Christine smiled and looked up. "Good question . . . we hadn't thought about it in those terms. I don't think I'll bring it up though."

"Interesting," I mused, "how we *select* the rules we choose to break . . ."

Christine was watching me, thinking it through with interest.

"And those we choose to *keep*," she added knowingly, and then she turned back to put the finishing touches on Mark's present.

I considered asking her where she got the pot, but didn't. "It doesn't seem like a very romantic present, Chris," I ventured cautiously.

"I know what you mean—but don't worry, I'm going to give him something else too—*very* romantic."

"Uhhhh, I don't think I'll pursue that," and I sat down, picking little scraps of jute off the upholstery.

Chris laughed. "Oh, Mom, c'mon. I don't mean"—she took a breath and said with great drama—"THAT!" pronouncing "that" like a two-syllable word.

I sat back and picked up the little bag. "Well, it's very appealing the way you've wrapped it. What's the Saran Wrap for?"

"So the pot won't stick to the suede."

I put it down and asked more seriously, "Can you smoke it?"

"No, but I don't care. When Mark smokes it, I'll get contact high."

I sat in silence wondering why I wasn't more concerned. Was she in with the wrong crowd? No, I knew her friends. Was this the beginning of her downfall? I didn't think so unless she and her friends were caught. Smoking pot had been a large part of the beat scene, when I was in college, a forgettable, nonaddicting, benign pastime for most of us. Now apparently teenagers smoked it. I didn't tell Jim. He knew Jimmy and his friends were smoking pot, and he disapproved but even he made no attempt to change things.

On April 16th, college acceptances came in the mail. Chris was shocked to find she'd been accepted at Emerson and Ithaca. She hugged me saying, "Mom, can you imagine, with *my* grades, I got in."

"I'm sure you were accepted on the strength of your interviews, just the way you were at Rye Country Day."

She listened and added, "Maybe they were impressed with my essay. I didn't mince words."

"You underestimate yourself, dear." I gave her a kiss and asked, "Is it going to be Emerson?"

She plopped herself lightly onto her bed and said, "Oh yes, I'll be near Mark, and John too."

Much later, when I read the recommendation Rye Country Day had written, added to her own essay, I thought she would have been accepted anywhere she applied.

SCHOOL RECOMMENDATION—CHRISTINE NELSON

There are few things in this world that would be nicer than for a college to have Chris Nelson. Chris is almost a saint. She is a wonderful girl with a great ability. In spite of the miserable deal fate has handed her, she looks at life positively and plans for the future. The reason for Chris's grades and low achievements compared to her SAT's is that Chris has spent many weeks at different periods of her life in the hospital.

Chris has Cystic Fibrosis. The type she has was supposed to take her away years ago. Chris is determined to live and be productive.

She does not complain. She lives more positively than most of us who think we are healthy. Her courage and her charm unmatched in any situation such as hers that I have seen. I love this kid, and you will, too.

Admitting her will be good for her and for you. She has already had a positive effect on kids here in school. She will do the same elsewhere.

This kid is so nice in spite of her situation that I would have to stop believing in people if I cannot get others to see the quality that we see in Chris.

I recommend her with all of the force that I can.

> *Herman W. Hall*
> *Director of College Placement*

HWH:r

Mark's birthday then came and went. I asked Chris the next day if he'd liked her present and she said yes, but didn't elaborate, which was odd.

Then Sunday night she came storming into my room in tears. "Mom, you're not going to believe this—you know the little bag of pot that I gave Mark for his birthday?"

"Yes . . ."

"Well, it's all gone, and guess who Mark smoked it with?"

"I don't know—who?"

"Jimmy!"

"You're kidding." Mark had no special relationship with Jim's son, and Christine had less of one. He'd been away at school all year and was home for spring vacation. Christine was seething.

"I just can't believe he's weaseled into my life again and smoking *my* pot—with *my* boyfriend."

"He probably didn't know you gave it to Mark."

"Oh yes he did. Mark told him. But that's not the point anyway." I knew it wasn't.

"What's the matter with Mark?" I asked. "How could he be so insensitive?"

"I don't know. Mark doesn't even think he did anything wrong."

"How do you know?"

"He told me. He apologized and said he didn't realize—I don't know." Chris started to cry sitting on my bed, putting her hand over her eyes, embarrassed.

I sat down next to her and put my arm around her—wishing she wasn't so thin-skinned, but then she'd probably lose the sweetness I cherished.

"What are you going to do?" I asked quietly.

She got up and walked around the room, going from window to window, staring out into the darkness and turning back to me and then staring out again.

"I think maybe we should stop seeing each other. I don't think he really loves me, even though he says he does. But he isn't showing it. First he said we could only go out once a week because of hockey practice, then after the hockey season was over, he said his parents were cracking down on him. There's always something—some reason why we can't spend more time together."

"Maybe he's just not ready, Chris. Eighteen is young for commitment."

"I guess so. I know there isn't anyone else. But I can't go on anymore. I'm starving."

"Then you're doing the right thing."

"But Mom," she cried in anguish, "it doesn't help if I'm doing the right thing. It's not what I want—I want *him.*"

"I know. It's no consolation when you lose what you want. But Mark is Mark. Sometimes you can't have what you want." I said it very carefully, so she'd know it wasn't a scolding.

She cried so hard she was unable to speak, mouthing the words, "I know, I know," and then she sobbed, "I never get what I want."

I sighed and agreed. "It certainly seems that way."

"Oh God," she cried. "I don't know anymore. Maybe there's something wrong with me, maybe I need too much—that must be it."

She sat up at the head of my bed and picked up one of the lace throw pillows, wrapping her arms around it, slumping over and burying her face. I sat thinking while she cried, waiting until she could listen again.

"Christine, even if that's it—there's nothing *wrong* with you. You have a great capacity for love, far greater than mine, or your father's. And maybe you need more love as well. I remember the way you loved your hamsters. To me, they were little smelly rodents—cute, but nothing worth loving too much. But you—you adored them, wrote stories about them, played with them. Most children tire of hamsters and don't take very good care of them, but not you. You loved those stupid hamsters like they were your own children."

Her head was still down as she studied the floor and sniffed, "They weren't stupid."

I laughed. "See, you still love them. And what about the little puppy, Nipper—you cried for three days when you left him that first summer on Fire Island." She was sitting very still, draped over the pillow, her face hidden, but I knew she was listening.

"You said you needed too much. It's not too much. What you need—you give just as much. But maybe it's too much for Mark."

She looked up for a minute, about to speak, and then slumped back down in a deeper curve.

"I love him more than I've ever loved anyone, and I think he's perfect for me—he's the one."

"Well, to me, he doesn't seem so perfect."

And the next day, Mark and Christine broke up.

School became an ordeal. Breaking up was so public. Mark was everywhere, but they didn't speak. The conversation we'd had the night before they broke up was the first of many. We analyzed every aspect of their relationship. Christine hadn't spent so much time with me in years. She needed constant interaction and reassurance and comforting. She was still totally involved with him.

I noticed something else, however, with alarm. Our conversations were getting harder and harder for her. Her sentences were quick and broken—breathy—and she interrupted herself to get air. Her lungs were filling up and each day her breathing was more labored. She didn't even seem to notice, but I did and I called Celia Ores.

"What do you think is happening to Christine, Celia? If she's admitted it will be the fourth time since September."

"There has been a marked deterioration in her lungs this year and there's nothing we can do at the moment to stop the infection. The last time the drugs had very little effect. She's done so well for such a long time."

"But how can she go to college if she's so sick? Are we being realistic?"

"I don't know. It's what she wants and I think she has to try, but I just don't know."

"Does she know how desperate it's getting?"

"Oh yes. She can feel it with every breath. She just refuses to give in. You know—her stubbornness and her impatience with confinement, her defiance of logical behavior, all work in her favor."

"I'm never sure."

"Lots of these young people don't do anything but mope. They're destructive. Families can be torn apart by this disease."

"Really? Then I'm not off-the-wall to let her do what she wants."

"No. Christine's spirit is as important as the antibiotics, sometimes more important, in keeping her out of the hospital. If she errs on the side of overdoing it, that's her way. She pays the price, no one else. She's a good judge of her limit, and she's not afraid to push beyond it."

"Celia, I'm sure we've talked about this before, but I feel like I'm hearing it for the first time."

"Well, you've experienced it now. I often have to explain the same things to parents over and over. And it isn't because they lack intelligence."

Later that night when Jim and I were going to bed, just before we turned out the lights, I said, "Christine's not doing well."

Jim looked up from his book and said, "She seems very frail and breathless again. I've noticed it. Sometimes her lips seem blue when she gets up."

I nodded. "I don't know how much longer she has. Dr. Ores told me there has been a marked deterioration in her lungs."

Christine knew, but denied it day after day. With six weeks of school left, she had no time for her illness.

16 · Tightrope

On May 4th, she was in her room working on an overdue English term paper when she felt a telltale flutter in her lungs. She waited till the coughing started and when she spit into the cup, there was blood. I was doing the dishes when she called and I went to the bottom of the stairs.

"Mom, I think I'm bleeding."

Not again. I hurried up to her room.

"I coughed up liquid blood, not just bloody plugs this time." But the fluttering sensation had stopped.

The senior prom was right around the corner. She didn't want to miss it—with or without Mark—and she cursed her fate, her voice low and tense.

"Why now God . . . give me a chance. Why now?" She sat on her bed. I sat on the arm of her deck chair and waited.

"Even if I bleed more tonight, do you think I could just rest in bed for a few days? That's all I do in the hospital . . . and maybe it'll heal over by itself. It's not *all* liquid blood . . . it's old blood too, and secretions." She paused. "Not as bad as at the Red Barn."

"That's good, but it's the antibiotics in the hospital, not the bed rest, that helps. But we can wait . . ." Bleeding came from lung disease, not exhaustion, and it was out of control again. She needed a new antibiotic.

In addition, there was a double bind. In order to stop bleeding, she had to stop thumps. But when she stopped thumps, it meant more congestion, which meant more lung disease, which eventually meant more bleeding. Chris called it her Catch 22. We both knew how quickly her lungs would fill with secretions . . . in a few short days, it would be life threatening.

I said, "Maybe after the prom would be a good time." The bottom was always dropping out of her life.

"As far as I'm concerned," she said, "there's never a good time to go into the hospital. If you knew how I hate it."

I started to say I knew how she felt but I cut myself short. I'd promised myself years ago never to utter those words. I didn't know how she felt and no matter how I tried I never would. I wasn't going to insult her now by saying that I did. She went on. "I'll go in tomorrow before I get worse. If I stay home, with my luck, I'll hemorrhage."

So I called Dr. Ores and asked if she could arrange a bed, and the night passed with no bleeding. That morning we were beginning to think she might not have to go into Babies after all. We debated whether or not I could leave to drive to school to get her books. There had only been that one flutter of fresh blood.

She had told me once that it was mind over matter. She'd taught herself to suppress the blood cough enough to let a clot heal over the site, though sometimes it took an hour or two to gain control.

Reaching to hold my hand tight and hard, she connected herself to life as if strength could really flow through my hand into hers. This, too, was a treacherous balancing act. When the blood came, her throat spasmed like she'd swallowed the wrong way. Violent coughing to clear the airway made the hemorrhage worse. But her will was stronger than her body's need to cough clear and all she allowed were little, bubbly, shallow coughs, enough to get a bit of air through. She walked her tightrope, nothing breaking her concentration, and her consciousness receded as she focused her mind inward, holding my hand.

But there was no denying the terror. It was her life flooding into her throat and we knew it. Blood came from her mouth as she choked and shivered, tried not to drown, tried to breathe. Helpless, I felt more than terror. Everytime, there was a sinister chill in the room, a third shadow, and if I reached out with my other hand, I could feel the sinewy figure of death, waiting, watching—as she fought for life.

There was no way I was going to leave now, I thought. Her schoolbooks could wait.

"Mom. I'm so far behind. I need the books or I'll never graduate. I'll be okay." Had we switched roles?

"No, I'll ask Claudia to bring them home for you."

"Mommm," she said, her voice dropping low, like a foghorn. "I'm okay."

So I went. She wouldn't let me go if she was worried. I put the phone on her bed, paper cups and Kleenex still there from last night, and I drove to school and back. I flew.

I was back in thirty minutes. When I came in the basement through the garage, I called upstairs.

"Chris, I'm back. Everything okay?"

No answer. My heart started to go faster. Hadn't she heard me? I ran up the two flights of stairs, stopped at her bedroom door, and stared—holding on to the door. She was leaning back as if asleep, a cup full of blood on the bedside table. My mouth opened, but no words came out. Oh God, what had I done? She hadn't heard me come up the stairs. Was she sleeping? I went over to the bed. She seemed unconscious—her face white, her head falling back on the pillows. Her hands were down at her sides with both palms turned upward. Her hands that way made her look as if she were pleading.

I found my voice and cried, "Oh Chris, I'm so sorry. I can't believe it. How did you manage? How did you stop it?" I sat down quickly and gently on the edge of the bed and took her limp hand.

She opened her eyes and said, "Oh Mom, I was so scared. There was so much blood."

There was another paper cup on the bed, with blood in the bottom. I'd made the wrong decision.

"Oh, Christine, please forgive me for leaving, for letting you go through this alone. It's my fault. Can you ever forgive me?"

She sighed and said slowly, "Oh, Ma—forgive you for what?" She took another short breath. "It was my idea."

But I was consumed with guilt. She'd been alone. She could have died . . . so much blood . . . a whole cup like the night at the Red Barn. There were tiny drops of blood on the sheet and her

GIVE ME ONE WISH

pale yellow sweatshirt. I sat next to her, holding her hand, still, shattered.

I picked up the phone, dialed admitting at Babies Hospital, told them Christine was on her way in, and asked them to try and have a wheelchair at the main door. The nurses on the tenth floor knew her so well, as did Rosa, who worked at the admitting desk, that with luck I could bypass the red tape that tangled up the admitting procedure when people who didn't know us were on duty.

Chris got dressed and I tied the laces on her bright yellow sneakers because she couldn't bend over. She seemed unafraid— but we moved in slow moton just the same. I helped her down the stairs and into the car, paper cups in one hand and a box of Kleenex in the other. Driving away from the house, I wasn't ready for what she said next.

"Mom, can we stop at school? I want to say good-bye to my friends."

I looked at her in surprise. "Darling, you just can't do that now."

She pleaded. "Mom, please, you know what it means to me. Suppose I miss graduation. Suppose . . ." She didn't continue. I knew what she was thinking. I stopped at the end of our driveway, looking at Chris, seeing more determination than worry in her face. How could I deny her this?

Finally I said, "Okay, we'll stop at school, but it's crazy." And so we drove to Rye Country Day.

When we got there, Chris asked me to wait in the car. "I'll take my time, Mom, I can do it."

I watched her go slowly up the walk on that cloudy spring day. It had rained during the night and there was still a damp gusty wind that blew her blond hair in swirling wisps. I was reminded of how many times over the years I'd watched her walk away from me. When she first entered kindergarten, I drove her to school and waited as she went in, cherishing the sight of her wispy little blond braids, her lunch box swinging in her hand, and her carefree footsteps, leading her away from me—on the way to her first classroom and the start of her independent life. Today, her steps were heavy and measured. She hunched over slightly as she walked.

Fifteen minutes passed. I hurried up the walk into school, and saw Chris coming shakily down the stairs, with Claudia. She had a cup in one hand, and the other hand gripped the railing. Her face was expressionless.

"Are you all right?" I asked.

Claudia answered, "She started to bleed when she was upstairs."

I looked at Chris. "What did you do, how did you manage?"

Claudia said, "There was a trash can in the hall. Nobody saw. Nobody knew what was happening. We went into the ladies room until the class bell rang."

I looked at Chris, but she wouldn't look at me. "It must have been terrible, Chris. I'm so glad Claudia was there." Was that enough to let her know I wasn't angry?

I asked Claudia if she could drive to the hospital with us to help Chris if she bled again. She said, "Of course, let me run in and ask the dean."

So the three of us drove to the hospital making small talk, pretending we weren't afraid. There was a wheelchair in the lobby as I'd hoped, and Claudia went up with Chris to the tenth floor while I went back out and parked the car.

Claudia and I spent the afternoon there and later, driving along the Hutchinson Parkway in silence, Claudia asked hesitantly, "Do you think maybe . . . it would be better to let her . . . go? To not keep holding on? I mean, her life is so difficult now?"

It had taken time for Claudia to find the courage to say this and she was afraid she'd made a faux pas.

I said, "It's crossed my mind, Claudia"—although it hadn't. "As long as Christine believes it's worth it to live—she will. She hasn't even begun to give up. And neither have I." It was odd to be talking like this with Claudia. I'd always wondered if one day I'd have such a conversation with Chris. "What Christine cares about now is getting out in time for the prom—and passing her exams—in that order." Claudia laughed and agreed. We drove the rest of the way in silence, each, I suppose, thinking about Christine's ordeal and the future. I noticed the first faint tinges of green on the still bare trees as we sped toward Rye.

After Jenny was in bed, I went back to the hospital and spent the night on the cot in her room and, at 4 A.M., she bled again. She woke me up, saying, "Mom, can I have the pan? I feel it," and I sprang up, put the pan in her lap, and gripped her left hand. She pushed the call bell and the nurse was there in a flash. She'd been expecting trouble too.

I sat on the bed in front of Chris, our fingers locked together, as she started to cough, trying to purse her lips and breathe slowly but not always able to—her back curving into the deepness of the cough, shaking and shivering. The stainless-steel pan caught most of the blood, except when she expelled it with a cough and tiny drops splattered around the bedclothes. The nurse remained at her side, handing her, as needed, a fresh Kleenex or a small glass of water. Christine's terror took her far away, even though she nodded in answer to the nurse's questions about what was happening. Alone inside herself somewhere, she kept her balance— fighting to breathe but not enough to aggravate the bleeding with her coughing, and it was over in twenty minutes. But twenty minutes can be very long. You can suffocate seven or eight times in twenty minutes.

It was a terrible admission for Christine. She'd never been so sick and her lungs bled for days. I spent many nights in the hospital, alternating with Jerry, who flew home from England. On the fourth day of bleeding, as I was getting off the elevator, I saw a medical chart sitting on the counter at the nurses station. It was Chris's. Always kept out of sight, it was thicker than the Manhattan telephone directory. I opened it and turned to the last page, skimming the newest entry. The handwriting was illegible at first glance, but I could read the last few words: "massive hemoptysis in the upper right lobe." I closed the chart and stared into space. "Massive" knifed through my mind. I turned like a zombie and walked slowly down to Christine's room. Death had left another calling card.

Christine was asleep, curled sideways over her pillows, the

bed raised as she slept sitting up. I sat next to the bed and watched the steady dripping of saline solution into the chamber that led to the IV tubing in her wrist. Her wrist was taped firmly to a narrow board. There must have been twenty pieces of puckered, beige-colored tape around the IV site extending to the board underneath and I knew she must be annoyed at the clumsy taping. Some nurses used too much tape. It hurt when they pulled it off and it was pulled off a lot when her IV was checked for infiltration of the fluids into the soft tissue around the vein. Chris used to make them wait while she pulled the tape off very slowly. And sometimes, with a new nurse, she'd direct the taping procedure, ignoring it when they bridled at being told what to do by a feisty teenager.

Something new had been added to her bedside, an IV pole with a bag of dark-red plasma, called a PRBC unit—packed red blood cells. Little drops of condensation on the clear plastic told me the bag had come out of the refrigerator. It wasn't hooked up to Christine. Dr. Ores had ordered a blood transfusion the day she came in and had told me on the phone she was ordering another. When she had the first one, there wasn't time to warm the blood to body temperature and the infusion of cold plasma was long and painful.

Chris slept for an hour, and when the nurse came in to start the transfusion, the blood was warm.

I spoke with Celia that afternoon and she told me a specialist was prepared to do an angiography, so they could see the hemorrhage. By injecting a radiopaque substance, they could check the condition of the blood vessels. A lung surgeon had been called in for a consultation. They were both standing by. We sat in the playroom alone, and she explained, "If the bleeding doesn't stop in the next few days, we may consider emergency measures. We have two options. The bleeding is coming from somewhere in the upper right lobe, which could be surgically removed. There is also a possibility that an embolization would be effective."

"Embolization? I thought an embolism was something that killed you—a clot."

"Yes, when it's in the heart—but the embolization will be an artificial clot made up of minute plastic beads that we'll inject into the area to seal off the bleeding permanently."

"Wouldn't that be preferable to a lung operation?"

"Yes it would, unless the bleeding comes from multiple sites. In either case, an angiography would have to be done first to help find the area to be treated."

When she described the procedure—the incision in the groin, the threading of a tube up through an artery and through the heart to the lungs, the injection of a dye, which could be seen on TV screens monitoring the procedure, to find the hemorrhage— she saw the horror on my face.

"The tube goes through her *heart?* And she would have to be still? Dr. Ores, she can't be still when she's coughing up blood— it's impossible."

Dr. Ores was silent a moment. "We're not at that point yet. She's having the second transfusion now and we'll wait and see. Her bleed last night was smaller than the night before."

"Does Chris know about the lung surgeon and everything?"

"Yes, he saw her yesterday and explained the procedure and so did I."

I was shocked. Chris hadn't said a word to me. I knew when Dr. Ores said "emergency measures" she meant last resort. I didn't ask her if she might die on the operating table, because I knew the answer was yes.

But after that night, the bleeding stopped. When we had waited seventy-two hours, without a recurrence, and we knew the crisis had passed, Chris told me about meeting with the lung surgeon.

"Weren't you frightened?" I asked.

"I sure was. But I didn't let myself think about it. No way I was going to let him cut my chest open, even though he did have an English accent."

"Who?"

"The lung surgeon, who else?" she said, and I had to laugh.

The network of people around her drew closer. Her father and my sisters Francie and Vanessa came. Cindy, Jim, Jenny, and her friends came to visit. Chris set the tone, joking with them on the phone—asking for beer, and food. She banished any maudlin overtones. They brought "CARE packages" of cards and tapes and posters and stuffed animals and snacks. They brought bags of jelly beans and hid them under the pillows of all the children and they smuggled beer into her room.

Chris told me there were eight kids visiting one day, sitting on all the extra chairs from other patients' rooms and on the bed and on the floor. At one point, Ginny, a nurse's aide, passed by, saw the crowd, and reached in, pulling the door to, but not shutting it. Everyone looked puzzled and when Chris said, "What's up?" Ginny said, "Administrator's coming up—could be a problem." Chris understood and her friends relaxed. She loved the way Ginny was always on her side. The rules said only two visitors— the heck with that.

John, Jamie, Phebe, Claudia, Drea, and Jill were coming the next afternoon and Chris sent me out to buy pretzels and Cokes before they got there. Her teachers came too. They knew it was more serious this time, but that was all. Chris told me ruefully, "I've never had so many friends come and visit, except that I *know* the one I want to see the most won't come."

But she was wrong. Mark *did* come.

As he was leaving French class, two days before, Mark was slow in gathering up his things and Madame Amsellem walked past the exiting students and asked him, "How's Christine?"

Mark shrugged. "How should I know?"

Madame Amsellem looked at Mark with displeasure. "How should you know? You've been going together all year, that's how you should know." She knew they'd broken up. Mark straightened up, instantly regretting his flippant remark.

"I'm sorry. I haven't talked to her in three weeks."

Madame Amsellem thought a minute. She kept her distance from her students' problems unless they were about French. Then she said, "You might want to give some thought to your feelings. Priscilla Funck told me Christine's lungs were still bleeding and she was given a second transfusion yesterday." She saw no sign of understanding, but she thought he understood. Mark was inscrutable and, just in case, she added, "A second transfusion

is not good news, Mark. I understand the situation is grave. I
doubt if Christine will be coming home again."

Mark suddenly spoke.

"Oh no, you're wrong. Not Chris. I know her. Nothing's going
to happen to Chris. She's too strong. She can beat it. She'll be
home in time for graduation. I know it." And Madame Amsellem
said no more.

But Mark was frightened and he went to the hospital with
Claudia and John and the group. When Chris told me about it the
next day, she was noncommittal, but I could tell she was pleased.

"Christine, it's not over. He still loves you." She started shaking her head with her eyes closed and I said softly, "I bet he's just
as hung up as you are."

She looked at me thoughtfully and said, "Mom, I'm just not
expecting anything. If I don't expect anything, I won't get hurt.
I always knew he was a decent person," and her voice drifted off.
Whatever she was going to say, she changed her mind, and I
didn't press her.

17 · The Prom

Chris wasn't well enough to come home for good the weekend of the prom, but Dr. Ores made arrangements for her to leave Babies for two days and return Sunday night. Excited but wistful, she wasn't angry. She was so glad to be alive. Everything was relative. She had big plans for the prom, and though she hadn't shared them with me, she'd written to Mark during her Christmas admission.

> *In here, I fantasize about you all the time. It's the best way to pass the time quickly. I keep on thinking about the prom—imagine you in your tux (go crazy—part your hair in the middle), me in white tails (jacket), silver joujous, and beaded hair and we discreetly drive up to the "before party" in a silver (or black) Porsche!!! We are the couple to share a table with. But we're not flashy (how gauche) (sp.?)—We've got more class than that. What d'ya think? Is it possible? Well enough dreaming for one letter. However we go, we'll be fine and we'll have a great time. Right sweetums????*
>
> *love,*
> *CEN*

But as the day approached, she avoided the subject of Mark, and made other plans. Her date was a sophisticated young man everyone called by his last name—Brummitt. His first name was Mark too, and he was good friends with Mark Read.

"Chris, how is it that Brummitt asked you so quickly and didn't have a date? I mean, after you and Mark broke up?"

"Oh, he didn't ask me, Mom, I asked him. I still can't decide what to wear."

I'd looked with dread on the prospect of finding a suitable dress. A prom dress had to be almost as perfect as a wedding dress. I was clipping dead flowers off a huge arrangement from the Muppets and she said, "The girls are wearing formals, but I'm too thin. I can't measure up to that kind of competition, and I can't wear a strapless no matter what, because I have nothing to hold it up." Discarding dead blossoms, I sat next to her on the bed. It was a real problem. Chris liked to dress in ways that attracted attention but didn't look weird—it had to be the right kind of attention.

"You can't get away with a décolleté either, I don't think," I said. We'd been all over this, but I didn't mind going over it again.

"No—I want something diaphanous, chiffon with drifting pale colors, unevenly hemmed and unevenly layered. Kind of like the White Rock Girl."

"Chris, the only problem is, I don't see how we can find your dream dress—not in one day. We won't have time." She wouldn't be strong enough to go tramping from store to store looking for it either.

"Mmmm," she said pensively, "I have another idea though."

"What?"

"Black tails. You know—what orchestra conductors wear—those cutaway tails. Marlene Dietrich did it—why not me?"

"Black tails," I mused. "With your Twiggy look, you'll be a knockout."

"You like it?"

"It's perfect. I never would have thought of it."

"I didn't think you'd like it. But Mom, my tails have to be real—not polyester. Real wool worsted. It can't be cheap."

"Don't worry, I know where to go."

I called A. T. Harris on Madison Avenue across from Grand Central where they sell and rent tuxedos and tails—no polyester. I said I needed black tails for a five-foot-four, ninety-pound young lady with a slim boyish figure but she couldn't come in for a fitting. No problem. Could they handle the final fitting on Saturday, while we waited? They said to come over and pick one out, bring her measurements, and they'd alter it to fit her—except for the trouser length.

I went the next day. The salesman seemed amused. This was a man's domain and I was fascinated by their clientele. Men of all ages and sizes were there, including college students. One young man in a navy blazer, fatigues, and dirty old Top Siders with no socks reminded me of Mark. Chris would have been in heaven.

She got out of the hospital with her weekend pass the morning of the prom. Dr. Ores came in before we left. She said quietly, "Don't drink—it may provoke bleeding."

"Can I dance?"

"Better not. That also could bring on a bleed. But have a good time." Chris looked skeptical; she couldn't have a good time standing still.

Our first stop was A. T. Harris. The salesmen were not as busy and they watched discreetly. Most of their clients had already picked up their rentals. The jacket with tails fit perfectly and a tailor hemmed the trousers in the back room while we waited. Chris wasn't cool or blasé, but her usual sweet self, asking her salesman about the different fabrics, should she wear a top hat (he looked at her blond hair and shook his head), and what about a belt. I watched her handle the whole thing and wondered to myself, How can Mark resist her? He must be crazy.

The tailor brought out the trousers and she tried everything on together, adding a black satin cummerbund. The salesman watched Christine studying her image in the three-way mirror and caught my eye with a look of approval.

She said happily, "I think it looks great, Mom, do you?"

"Yes—great."

We drove home in high spirits. What could have been a disastrous ending to her high school experience was turning into something wonderful. She was feeling lucky about herself and her life. Lucky that she had the date she wanted (sort of), lucky that she was pretty, lucky that the idea of the black tails was not a fantasy but coming true just as she'd imagined it, and lucky that she was out of the hospital.

At home, she curled up on her bed and talked to Jenny while she comforted Ivy. Jenny couldn't see how Chris could be so excited about wearing pants to the prom. After lunch, we drove down Greenwich Avenue to look for shoes. Chris wanted to look tall and I suggested black high-heeled sandals.

"Your slim foot in sexy strap sandals will be a good contrast to the tails."

We had no trouble finding them and while the salesman went in the back to get her size, Chris bent over impatiently to undo her sneakers. As I watched, she slowly raised herself back up to a sitting position. Looking straight ahead, she said quietly, "Mom, I think I'm bleeding." Our eyes met for a second.

"Oh Chris, we've been overdoing it. We shouldn't have rushed." I watched her. She wasn't coughing. Her hand was trembling as she put it over the spot where she'd felt the sinister flutter.

The salesman returned and fastened up the shoes. Chris sat still, saying they were perfect and she didn't need to walk around in them. He looked surprised and went to make out the sales check. We didn't move, and she said, "I don't feel it anymore. Let's just sit here until we leave."

I pretended to be looking at shoes until she was ready. Driving home, she didn't talk, her attention turned inward and, at one point, she said bitterly, "I knew everything was going too well."

"Maybe it's just a warning to be careful." I knew what her silence meant—how could she have a good time if she had to be careful. She was quiet the rest of the day and didn't feel the same joy and excitement. We were both afraid.

She called her friends, catching up on everything. When I went up to talk she was sitting on her bed, intent on polishing her nails.

"Is there a party after the prom?" She looked up from her concentration.

"Oh sure. It's called an after party. Then there's a breakfast party at Phebe's house and a beach party at Sherwood Island."

"What's the beach party for—lunch?" I joked.

"Yes, it's different. We're going home and change and pack picnic lunches." I studied Chris while she studied her nails.

"I guess I won't expect you till Sunday sometime then?"

"Well," she said, "I'm not sure I'll go to all the parties, but I think so."

I fiddled around her room picking up this, examining that, rearranging her stuffed animals. They overflowed the shelves. Her room was always full of small boxes and baskets and wonderful things—little mementos, bright lacquered boxes of earrings and delicate gold chains, makeup, tin buttons with impolite words and pictures of rock stars, funny toys for her cat, charms, special favorite issues of *Vogue* and *Bazaar,* rock magazines, rumpled lists of things to do, Muppets and puppets and pictures of her father with the various Muppet roles he did. She cherished everything anyone ever brought her. And she probably had more little things than most girls because so many people brought her presents in the hospital and her dad had one of every Muppet product sent to her—just for fun. To Jenny, Christine's room was heaven. She could spend an hour opening all the boxes, holding all the little things, asking Chris endlessly what they were and where they came from and if she still wanted them. When I emptied wastebaskets each day, hers were always empty.

I saw no sign of the fear she'd felt when she was trying on the shoes and when she'd inched her way up the stairs when we got home, and her excitement returned when she started getting dressed. She wore a white silk blouse under the jacket and her hair loose around her shoulders. She borrowed my antique war medals and pinned them on the lapel of the jacket. One was a World War I Red Cross Medal—her private joke. She put a piece of lace in the shallow breast pocket of the jacket and a white gardenia in her hair. Finally, since her blouse had no collar to hold a bow tie, she tied a narrow white velvet ribbon around her neck in a small bow. With the shoes and her narrow frame in black, she looked tall and patrician. I took some pictures with her camera, not knowing there was no film in it.

Brummitt picked her up at 6:30 in a gleaming white BMW

2002. He was an hour late but he came up the walk with an unhurried ease and I smiled at the sight of him, an impressive figure, six-foot-two, poised and handsome in his tuxedo, wearing black Ray-Ban sunglasses—definitely dangerous. Christine's young men looked like the heroes of her generation. Wedged on the back floor of the car were three quarts of screwdrivers Brummitt and Mark had mixed that afternoon—in Tropicana containers.

Chris appeared and I saw the flicker of a smile unbend his face when he saw what Chris was wearing. In the car, he said, "You look neat."

"Thanks, so do you." Trying to sound offhand, she said, "You're so late. We'll never make the before party."

"I know, Chris. I'm really sorry. I'm never late, it's not my style, but I couldn't help it." He didn't explain, though, and joked, "Let's skip it and have everyone wondering. We'll make a grand entrance in the ballroom."

The evening was balmy and clear, perfect for a prom, and the girls were wearing evening dresses with bare shoulders. Through the trees beyond the clubhouse, Chris could see the sun reflecting on the water. She'd planned her entrance for a long time, and her chin was high as she strode regally into the ballroom with Brummitt. She kept her eyes ahead, aware she was a standout and hoping her friends would like the black tails. They did.

The prom has since been referred to by the dean of girls as "the prom where Chris wore her tuxedo," even though it wasn't a tuxedo. Mark had worn tails too, with his scuffed and worn hiking boots. They greeted each other cordially at the table they shared, Mark and his date, Amy Segal, John and Claudia and their dates. Mark and Chris hardly spoke.

The faculty tables were set far back from the dance floor and the students flowed back and forth from the ballroom to the quiet darkness of the parking lot, wishing they could be in both places at the same time. The parking lot was seeing a different kind of action.

Chris and Brummitt and Mark and Amy and Claudia went out, and drained the first quart of screwdrivers. Chris ignored Dr.

Ores's warning, and told no one. Back in the ballroom, Mark boldly carried another quart in front of the faculty's suspicious glances.

Chris danced all night. Brummitt never danced, and he watched Chris, her feet leaping, shoulders dipping, and hair swinging in the wild aerobic dancing that was popular.

During the third set, she started to cough, and excused herself, leaving the dance floor, laughing and choking. She went to the clubhouse porch to cool off, standing in the dark. When her breathing was under control, she went back in, got a Coke, and saw Phebe sitting on one of the window seats overlooking the dark waters of Long Island Sound. Chris sat down next to Phebe and watched the shore and sea slide together in the night.

"The band's good," she said to Phebe. They were playing Pretenders songs.

"I know. I don't know where you get your energy, Chris."

"I don't either," she said, munching a handful of peanuts and looking out at the black water. They sat silently and Chris said, "Phebe, are you afraid of dying?" Phebe started to say "I haven't . . ." but changed midway, pausing carefully as her thoughts moved into deep and rarely navigated waters.

"I . . . I don't know if I'm afraid. I certainly don't want to."

"Mmmmmmm . . . I feel the same. I'm not exactly afraid, but it would be so terrible to miss everything. Reluctant, I guess—not fearful. Maybe we all feel that way."

Phebe nodded and Chris poured some of her Coke into Phebe's empty glass. Phebe turned toward the dark window again and said, "But I think some people are afraid to die."

Chris considered. "Maybe the same ones who're afraid to live. I don't understand people like that."

Phebe thought maybe Chris was talking about Mark and said, "Who do you mean?"

"Oh, no one, it's just a feeling I have." And Chris scrunched in, rested her chin on her knees, and wrapped her arms around her ankles.

"Chris, do you believe in life after death?"

She didn't answer right away, but looked at Phebe, thinking.

"I haven't decided that one yet. Wait—are you talking about immortality, or reincarnation?"

"Oh, not reincarnation. I just can't believe that."

And Chris said brightly, "Well, I'm coming back as a cat. No, seriously, I *do* think there's some kind of life after death. Maybe dying is another kind of birth."

Phebe leaned forward. "Chris, I think it's okay to be afraid of the unknown." She looked away and they both stared into the dark. Chris didn't answer and Phebe said, "Oh, I don't know. I don't know what's going to happen next week, but I'm not afraid of it."

Chris felt a rush of envy and her throat tightened unexpectedly. Making an effort to relax, she whispered, "Sometimes I get a little scared."

Phebe touched her arm gently and said, "When I'm depressed, my mom says, just take one day at a time."

Chris swallowed hard. "I know, I don't spend too much time thinking about it." But Phebe knew what was on her mind.

Chris got up and said, "I think I'll find Brummitt and try to get him onto the dance floor."

"Good luck," said Phebe. She was troubled by their talk. How many times had she heard Chris say she didn't like heavy conversations.

Back on the dance floor, Christine's enthusiasm took hold again, and for the rest of the evening she danced and joked with Brummitt and her friends, moving from table to table, her black tails flying behind her. Mark's eyes followed her, but she didn't see.

At one o'clock, they went to the after party at Donald Greis's house. There it was different. She spent most of the time crying. The evening was slowing down but intensifying, and so were her feelings. Mark and Brummitt were downstairs watching a pool game, and Chris sat on a sofa in the den, talking with John and Claudia and Jill and Drea, who tried to cheer her up.

Brummitt came upstairs, troubled to see Chris so upset. He thought Chris was the coolest girl in school and the only one who knew anything about people and life and the scene. He always thought she could handle anything. A keen observer and a gentleman, he said nothing. He was her escort, not her salvation.

After the pool game, Brummitt said to Mark, "Yo dude. We've got to talk." He led Mark up the stairs and into the foyer. Mark stared at the black-and-white tile floor.

"What's the scoop?"

"Chris is not in good shape. She's been crying. I don't know how you feel about her and I don't care, but you've got to talk to her." Mark started to say something but Brummitt wasn't finished. "I don't care who took who to this party. She loves you and she needs to talk to you."

Mark looked at his friend. Brummitt never offered advice and Mark knew he was right. He said, "Cool." And he went to find Chris. She was in the same spot, looking pretty and frail, clutching a white Kleenex smudged with black mascara. When she saw him, she knew he'd come to talk. He sat down next to her.

"Look, I know I've been an asshole . . ." If he thought he was going to find her weepy and contrite, he was wrong.

She interrupted in a low voice, "Don't give me any of your bullshit, Mark." He tried to ignore the others in the room.

"Chris, I thought we'd been all through this."

She softened a little. "You're avoiding the issue."

"I can't talk to you here." He got up and walked away.

She stood up, her hands trembling, and went into a bedroom to look at herself in the mirror. Her face was white and drawn, and her body felt shaky and panicky—odd. The night was dragging like a music box running down and her tails had lost their magic. She brushed on rouge and wiped the smudges from under her eyes, wondering why her hands were shaking. That was happening a lot lately. Maybe she hadn't eaten enough, but at least she hadn't bled. That was something.

She struck a pose, put her hands in her pockets to stop the shaking, and looked at herself, standing up as straight as she could. That was better. Sometimes she just had to fake it. She found Brummitt and they drove to the breakfast party at Phebe's.

The gracious white colonial house was set on the crest of a hill and the morning light had begun to touch the surrounding fields with thin blue color. There was a buffet breakfast and Chris had eggs, toast, and tea. Her hands were still shaking.

She talked to Claudia in the kitchen and decided to go for a walk. She opened the door and took a deep breath of the cool morning air, grateful for the warmth of her jacket.

"I'll be back," she said to Claudia.

"Do you want me to come?"

Chris shook her head and stepped out, heading into the field toward the lightening sky. She knew the wet grass would ruin her evening sandals, but she didn't care. It was comforting to be alone on the hill at sunrise. She imagined she was Juliet. She stopped frequently, feeling the first signs of tightening in her chest, uneasy about missing her morning thumps. Sometimes it seemed she was never going to have any rest from this illness, not even a day.

Mark came into the kitchen and said to Claudia, "Have you seen Chris? She's disappeared."

"She just left," said Claudia icily.

"What do you mean?"

"I mean she just walked out the back door." Mark opened the kitchen door and saw her standing by a split-rail fence. She was facing east and the sun had just cleared the horizon; misty cool rays of light touched her head and shoulders.

He called, "Chris—Chris!" and set out after her.

She turned and saw him hurrying along the bumpy ground. She started to shiver. When Mark reached her, he saw her soaking wet sandals in the grass. "Listen, put my boots on, okay?"

Chris started to resist but thought better of it. Her feet were like ice and she said, "Well, all right, but if I get smelly feet like yours, I'll kill you."

Mark laughed in spite of himself. This was hardly the response he'd expected, but when she bent down, he saw her smile. They walked out into the field, Chris tumbling along in Mark's hiking boots and Mark barefoot, gingerly trying to avoid the clumps of prickly thistles.

Chris blew on her hands. "My hands are like ice." Mark took one of her hands and squeezed it, warming her fingers. He reached for her other hand, unable to talk, wanting to hug her. Chris pulled back and looked up at him.

"I love you," she said. "I'm the best thing you've ever seen and I can't quit until you feel that." And she leaned up and kissed him.

He put his arms around her and said, "God knows . . . I'm trying."

They walked and talked as dawn turned into day. Mark told Chris the evening had been all wrong and they decided that breaking up had been a mistake. They loved each other too much.

Chris said, "We won't say anything yet."

But Mark said, "No, let's throw caution to the wind. Let's tell them now."

Chris turned away muttering to herself, "I threw caution to the wind weeks ago."

If Mark heard, he didn't respond, and Chris turned back to him and said, "We shouldn't—it's very bad form."

"C'mon . . ."

"Oh, all right." Mark went in and talked to Amy and Brummitt. Amy was mad and told Mark to stop using people, but Brummitt was relieved. Mark had found Chris irresistible.

They drove off in his red Mazda, to Crawford Park in Port Chester, and fell asleep in the truck. When they woke up an hour later, they drove to Mark's house, where he changed and they came to our house. It was 8 A.M. I was surprised and curious to see Mark Read instead of Mark Brummitt.

After Chris changed they went to Sherwood Island. They spent the day at the beach. Chris had forgotten her bathing suit on purpose. She didn't want anyone to see how thin she was. She wasn't strong enough to swim anyway, although she longed to join John and the others as they tried to brave the icy water—unsuccessfully. There was laughing, shrieking, and splashing, but no swimming. Chris watched on the shore and practiced skipping stones.

That morning was one of the few times ever that Christine skipped her early morning thumps. She'd been waking up to them for ten years, but not that morning.

18 · Headmaster's Award

But her reunion with Mark was short-lived and Chris never did understand what happened the following weekend or why.

They had a date to see the opening of *The Empire Strikes Back.* The plan was to sit in the third row center so they'd be enveloped in sound and immersed in spectacle.

There was a triple serpentine line when they got there but they spotted a girl Mark knew named Courtney at the head of the line, and when Mark and Chris went to say hello she let them squeeze in.

Christine knew Courtney liked Mark and didn't like her. They bought their tickets, hurried down to the third row, and Mark sat with Chris on his left and Courtney on his right. He turned to Chris and said, "Now, don't talk to me at all during the movie, okay? I want to be totally absorbed."

Chris looked over in agreement. "Right!"

But Mark was never absorbed and neither was Christine. Mark spent the two hours leaning over to Courtney, talking to her. He didn't say a word to Chris, or even turn in her direction. She might as well not have been there, and she endured the two hours in stunned silence.

Courtney left them when the film was over, and Chris and Mark walked out the back exit. Stepping into the clear light of early evening, Mark took Christine's arm and said, "WOW. *Great* movie. It blew me away."

Chris didn't say a word. Mark waited a minute and then joked, "Earth to Chris, earth to Chris, come in."

"Were you totally absorbed?" she asked slowly. Her voice was sharp with sarcasm as she pulled her arm away.

Mark looked at her quickly, "Yes, I was. Weren't you?"

Christine bristled, "With the movie—or Courtney?"

"Oh, come on, Chris," Mark protested, with an uneasy feeling. "She kept asking me questions."

Christine stepped in front of Mark, walking backwards and tossing her head back, mimicking his words exactly—as only she could. "She—kept—asking—me—questions." She stopped, her eyes icy black, her fury rising as she took a deep breath trying to control it. "You know, I can't *believe* the way you behaved during the movie! You told *me—me*—not to talk. But you spent the entire two hours talking to *her!*"

"No, I didn't," Mark said defensively, and rolled his eyes to heaven, adding, "What should I've done—ignored her? I was being friendly."

"Friendly—hah!" Christine spit the words like bitter cherry stones. "What do you take me for, your pet hosehead? I might as well not have been there. All I saw was the back of your head— selfish—insensitive—rude!" She underscored the last three words like chords at the end of a symphony.

Mark said nothing and kept walking, his head down in thought. Christine said scornfully, "I can't believe what I just heard you say—'trying to be friendly' C'mon Mark, get a *real* life-style." Mark stopped and turned to her.

"I think you're overreacting," he said evenly.

"Really?" she snapped. "Well, I think you're looking for trouble," and she strode away, heading in the opposite direction from where her car was parked.

Mark called after her, "The car's over here." He kept his voice light. He'd never seen Christine so angry. She wheeled around without missing a step, as if she'd known exactly where she was going, and they got into the car in chilly silence. Chris slammed the door so hard her window knob fell to the floor with a thud.

She left it there. She was dangerously out of breath and had to
fight hard to stop a violent coughing spasm. This was no time for
that and she squelched it, holding her breath and forcing it back.

On the drive home, she sat like a lemur, staring straight ahead,
her mouth set, grimly fighting back her tears as well as her cough.
Mark didn't apologize, and when he turned off the ignition she
reached over, took her keys, got out, and slammed the door again.
Mark got out too, but not quickly enough, and by the time he was
out she was halfway up the front steps.

He watched her go, thinking she might look back, but she
didn't. He put on the window knob that had popped off, and then
went to his truck, climbed in, and drove home.

It was over. Mark didn't call. Christine didn't call. An unhappy
ending to the year.

A few days later she announced without preamble, "Mark's
dating another girl." I was doing my monthly bank statement,
checks spread out on the kitchen table, and I looked up expecting
tears.

"You're kidding."

"Nope."

Christine sat down and doodled on my scratch pad, her blasé
facade crumbling.

"Who is she?" I ventured carefully.

"Courtney, what a stupid waspy name. She's pretty, but she's
one of those girls who's stuck up—stuck up about her body, stuck
up about her family, stuck up about her relationships, about
everything that's *hers*. She's an airhead."

"Sounds like the opposite of you. Mark's playing it safe." She
didn't respond for several minutes.

"I can't imagine what he *sees* in her. She's such a princess. Her
mouth is always open, because she starts every sentence with the
word 'I'."

I broke up. She could be scathing when she wanted. "Maybe
her mouth is always open because she can't breathe through her
nose."

Christine laughed for the first time in days. "No, he's fallen in
love with the perfect nose. What's he see in her?"

I tried again. "Nothing—that's the point."

"That doesn't make sense."

"Think about it."

Her foot started to jiggle and she made a face of dismissal and then said, "Okay, I'll think about it."

But she wasn't going to accept my suggestion for a while.

Two weeks before classes ended, Sylvia Hoag, the dean of girls, called me at home. She said, "Jacquie, at the Annual Awards Assembly on Friday, Christine will be receiving an award. I thought perhaps you might like to be there." She was mysterious and didn't say what the award would be. I assured her I'd come and she asked me not to tell Christine. She said warmly, "I think you're going to be very pleased."

I wasn't familiar with the awards Rye Country Day gave to the graduating seniors. It couldn't be a sports award if Christine was getting it. But I didn't think it could be citizenship or academics, either. We'd been arguing for two years over her study habits and I guess I still hadn't accepted the fact that she wasn't an A student applying to Radcliffe. She resisted and I insisted, reminding her till the work was done. More than just a conflict, it was a debilitating and destructive power struggle—she defiant and protesting that life was so unfair, and me agreeing with her, but telling her she had to do it anyway. I didn't yield and she didn't produce, and it was only in the last few weeks that I'd started to let up.

She'd read *Death Be not Proud,* in the eighth grade. She'd said, "Why can't I be like John Gunther's son? He was such a brain and he *liked* to study. I can't stand it, and I'm not a brain." By the time she reached her senior year, she was just going through the motions.

So I was mystified at Sylvia's revelation and I called Claudia and asked her if she knew anything about the award. She said she did but she wasn't supposed to say anything. I was surprised at her restraint.

I was in the auditorium that Friday morning, sitting quietly with a few other parents. The auditorium had been converted from the old gym with a stage at one end and a balcony with tiered seats at the other. The morning sunlight streamed in the windows on one side like nature's own spotlight on this festive occasion.

The upper-school students filed in, making the most amazing racket, and the seniors filled the balcony. I looked for Chris but couldn't find her. Dr. Pierson was in great form that morning. This was his first awards assembly at Rye Country Day, and this type of occasion was his métier. He enjoyed his role and set a tone of warmth and intimacy that made me feel like one of the family. He began with the American Field Service Award, which was won by Donald Kyle, who played drums with the band. He was a good friend of Christine's. I tried to guess as each award was described, if this could be the one, and I kept deciding no. There was a Math Award, a Science Award, prizes for Latin, French, Spanish, and English. All the extracurricular activities were recognized, too—Drama Award, Music Award, Photography Award, Art Award.

The endowed awards from foundations were all for recognition in science and math, none in the arts, except for the Harvard Book Prize.

And when Dr. Pierson spoke next, about the Headmaster's Award, it wasn't until he mentioned a "special person" that I realized this was what she had won . . . the Headmaster's Award. I'd never even heard of it. Dr. Pierson made the following remarks.

> *The Headmaster's Prize is the highest distinction conferred at today's award ceremony, and the most prestigious accolade given at Rye Country Day School, other than the Alumni Prize given at graduation.*
>
> *I have a special affection for this honor, for it's not decided by committee or by democratic vote, but rather by fiat. Yet I know this entire school community will have absolute consensus about the recipient.*
>
> *In past years this award has been presented for a variety of virtues—for academic excellence, or for outstanding leadership in campus extracurricular activities. This*

year, however, we are presenting this prize for even more
special qualities, to a very special person.

For 1980, the Headmaster's Award recognizes qualities
which should be more often lauded in any school, commu-
nity, or family. The prize will be given for spirit, spunk,
and a smile *to someone whose bearing has uplifted the*
faculty, classmates, the school. For spirit, spunk, and a
smile, to someone who has set an example for us to emu-
late and who has educated all of us in the most profound
sense—to Chris Nelson.

Chris made her way to Dr. Pierson's lectern from the balcony.
She was wearing white jeans and a white sweatshirt. Her classmates in the balcony stood up to applaud and by the time she got
to the podium and turned to smile at her friends, the whole
student body was on its feet, applauding as well.

She was radiant as Dr. Pierson hugged her with affection,
kissed her on the cheek, and shook her hand, and she walked
back to the applause of her peers, many of whom didn't know she
had cystic fibrosis. Rye Country Day, the school she knew and
loved and gave her whole self to, gave itself to her that day and
voiced its approval of the way she handled her life. All Christine
had done was to be herself.

I felt my throat start to close and I choked back the feelings.
But I couldn't hold back the thought. This day might be the high
point of her life. She wouldn't be able to turn adversity into
triumph forever. I tried to find her after the assembly but she'd
gone back to the Pinkham Building with her friends. She hadn't
known I was there.

Winning the Headmaster's Award didn't change Christine's
life but it did change mine, and the way I was with her. It took
this award, this recognition by her teachers, to teach me that
Christine's education was not the first priority. The way she survived and made her life meaningful was to give her best to her
friends, not her books. She invented the priorities that were right
for her. Rye Country Day understood and, at last, so did I.

The yearbook came out three days before classes ended. The

senior party was going to be at our house, and graduation was the following week. There were three hectic days of scribbling as everyone passed their yearbooks around. Mark walked up to Chris as she sat on the floor reading her yearbook, and lifted it from her hands before she could protest.

"May I autograph your yearbook?" She hesitated. "I'll give it back after next period," Mark said, and Christine nodded silently. Next to his picture he wrote:

> *Chris—You don't know me, at least that's the way I feel. But that doesn't matter. You see, Jamie and Claudia and John, they are all right. I'm not one to analyze myself or probe deeply into what I do. There is only one thing I know and that is—I love you. Probably more than anyone else I have ever loved. But even though we've shared everything and you have seen me at my best and my worst, I haven't been able to live up to the love you have given me. I feel, in a sense, that I have let you down more than anyone I have ever let down. I can't show you what you want to see. I can't give you what you truly need.*
>
> *You know this and so that is why we're the way we are . . . that is, hurting each other. I feel now unable to even talk to you.*
>
> *Brummitt and Courtney, they're not close friends, but they are the only ones I feel worthy to talk to.*
>
> *I can't talk to you. I fucked up and I can't ask for forgiveness. And so, even if I can't talk to you anymore, I hope you understand that it's over. That in the end, I'm sorry and that I'll miss you.*
> *Love, MER*
>
> *P.S. I hope things can be left at that—if not, well, I don't know anymore, it's not for me to say.*

Christine came home from school that day, and found me on the terrace planting portulacas in the cracks at the edges of the terrace steps. She sat on the steps and said, "Mom?"

"Hi Chris."

Christine, age 6, and Jacquie, Ithaca, New York

Buffy Sainte-Marie, Jerry, Christine, age 14, the Sesame Street set

Age 13, Martha's Vineyard

Cindy Beck

Age 17, Rye Country Day School

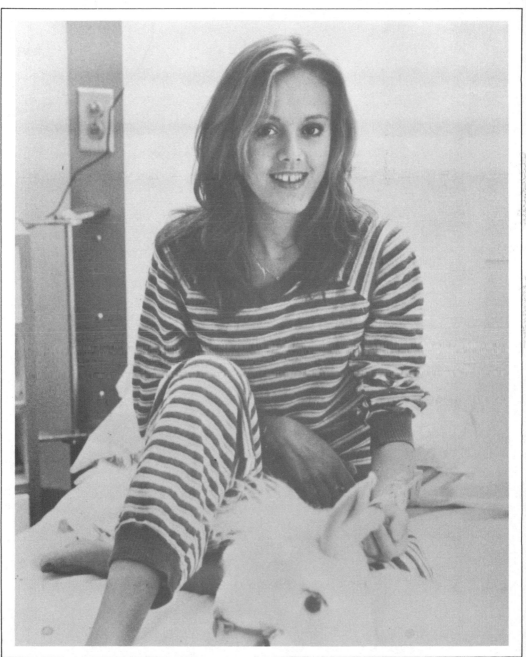

Age 18, Babies Hospital

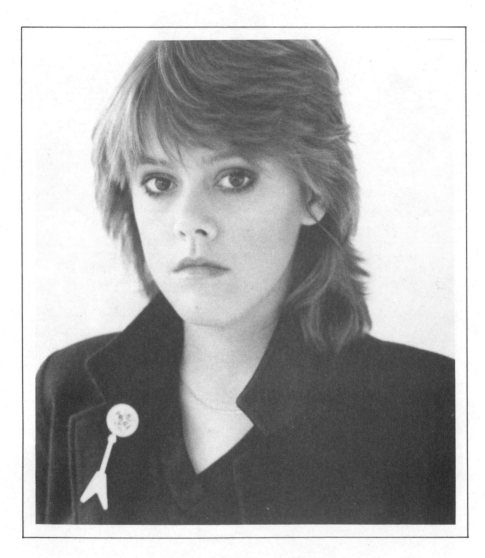

Age 19, Emerson College

Christine, age 20, and Jenny, age 8

Christine and Panic Scenery

Threepenny Opera

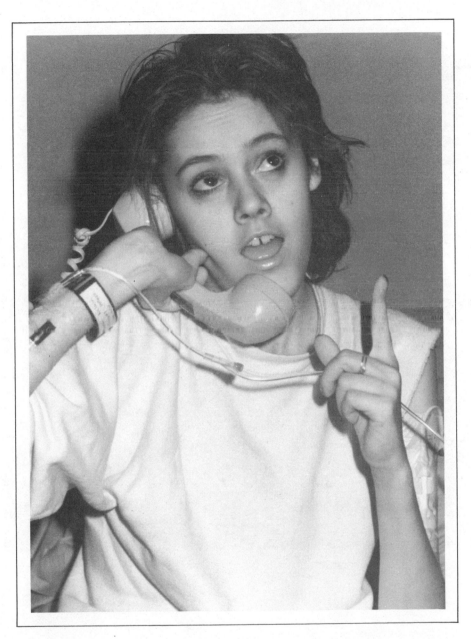

"E.T. phone home."

She handed me the yearbook, opened to a page with Mark's picture and a long inscription. She asked, "Would you read this?"

I took off my gardening gloves and sat down on the steps. I read it twice.

"I knew he loved you. I just knew it."

Chris looked sad and beaten. "What's the use, Mom, he's gone."

"He isn't ready, dear."

"I know. I thought he was. We talked about marriage."

I was surprised. She'd never told me this. "You did?" I wondered if this changed things. "Mmmm." She said no more. I went back to my planting and she watched me press the soil around the portulacas. When she saw spots I missed, she reached over, patting the loose dirt into place.

"Maybe it isn't over Chris. Maybe it's just the end of a chapter and he'll grow up." I didn't want to give her false hope, but it was possible.

"No, I think it's over. We can't go back. I don't know. Remember when we sat in my bedroom in the house in White Plains, and you first told me that you were going to divorce Jenny's dad, and you said you knew things were never going to get better, and leopards didn't change their spots?"

"Yes."

"Well, I don't think Mark's going to change either and that's what he's telling me. He even says it—what I need he doesn't have to give."

Christine wrote in Mark's yearbook the next day.

Dear Mark

I have a lot to say and I'm saying it here so it won't go where most of your important letters and papers go. I'm not sure where to begin except that words are pretty inadequate to describe my feelings over the past few days . . . anger, hate, remorse, love (believe it or not). I want you to know that I realize that a lot of things I've said about you these last couple of days, as nasty as they sound, they are said because I love you. If I didn't, I wouldn't care what you did or said.

Since that day in the leaf pile, I've really cared about you. I love you still—more than anyone else I've ever loved. We're just worlds apart in too many ways.

I've realized a lot about myself this year—one, that I'm too sensitive and do overreact. Going out with you has taught me much about you, myself, and people in general. I hope that we can be close again, but I know it will take awhile until our pain goes away. All I ask is that you don't give me the cold shoulder—just be natural. (You're a nature boy, it shouldn't be too hard.) About what you wrote me. Thank you for telling me how you feel. But you are wrong about only being "worthy" enough to talk to Courtney and Brummitt. Don't put the blame on yourself about us. What cannot be . . . cannot be . . . I think I'm just starting to realize that.

You see, because of the way I feel about life, I feel the same way about relationships—never give up. But it's different with relationships.

I'll never forget you because you were my first in many ways. Don't block me out of your mind forever. Be happy. Look for good things and good worthy people. Wish me happiness and remember how much fun we did have! Sometimes I thought we'd never stop laughing. Remember these things with a smile (not remorse . . . we're mature people, remember?)

. . . December 17th, the leaf pile, our brook, my stitches, my Valentine cards, our walk in the woods and my poor white pants, the evening we had success (do you understand what I mean?), my poor abused satin comforter, Beaujolais with my family—the next morning . . . our snow fort that never got built! These and all the other happy times are what we should think of, not the hurtful ones.

p.s. the day I surprised you in church.

mellow, mellow
oo-xx love Chris

If I thought the Headmaster's Award was the high point in Christine's year, she'd pick her senior party.

The school band was playing at the party. They weren't really the school band, but two boys from Rye Country Day and one from Rye High, who had a rock group. Stu and the Pids was their name that year. There was Stu-pid, Cu-pid, and Arm-pid.

They brought their equipment over—speakers, amplifiers, mikes, and drums—two days before the party, set it up downstairs in the den, and rehearsed. It was quite a scene. I met the leader of the group, Bruce McDaniel, a winsome young man with a broken tooth and a rubber duck in his hand. When Chris introduced him, he waved the duck with a cheery "Hi, Mrs. Gordon."

I met Donald Kyle, who won the AFS award and played the drums, and Jeff Davis, who played bass guitar. Bruce sang, wrote, and played lead guitar. They started testing and tuning and Jenny appeared with a mayonnaise-jar terrarium in her hand. Chris rolled her eyes and said, "This is Jenny, everyone. She likes toads, snails, and puppy dogs' tails."

I glanced at Chris and Jenny wailed, "I do not!" But she did like to make little homes for grasshoppers, crickets, and peepers.

Bruce looked in the jar. "What's in there?" he asked.

"Green grasshopper," Jenny said, then clammed up.

Bruce looked closer, "Oh—looks like a puppy dog's tail."

Jenny laughed. Chris gave me a look to remove Jenny and I gave her a look that Jenny could stay—for a little while—and I stood and watched for a few minutes. Donald plopped a red plastic fire hat on Jenny's head and they went around saying "aargy bargy" to each other in a voice like Mr. Magoo. Everyone was laughing but me. I didn't get the joke.

The music was deafening. I'd been hearing Christine's New Wave all year and recognized some of the songs but I felt like an old stick-in-the-mud. Every sentence out of their mouths was a joke, or an imitation with a funny voice, or a double entendre or a reference to something I didn't know about. I couldn't keep up with them. Had my life been that much fun when I was seventeen? I didn't think so.

To my surprise, Chris was singing with them, and they were

rehearsing songs for her, calling her Peach-pid. No wonder she was excited.

The day before the party, I left notes in the neighbors' mailboxes, telling them we were having a live band, and inviting them to come over. No one came, but no one called and complained either. The party was a success and Chris was the star. I wondered how her friends felt about her starring at her own party, but they seemed to like it.

Down in the den before the first set, she said, "Mom, I'm so nervous. I'm shaking inside and my mouth is all dry. Could you go up and get me a Coke?"

She didn't look nervous and I teased, "Chris, am I your maid?"

"Oh please Mom, I don't want to go up the stairs. I've been coughing up fresh blood all day."

"Oh no," I said and went to get her a Coke. Now I was nervous.

She sang songs by the Pretenders, "Mystery Achievement" and "Brass in Pocket," and she sounded like Chrissie Hynde. Deborah Harry had a group called Blondie and Chris had met them in London on the Muppet set. She sang "Call Me," "Hanging on the Telephone," and "One Way or Another." She sang Pat Benatar's "Heartbreaker." Once when I went down, they were all singing a song Bruce and Jeff had written called, "My Duck Is Under the Firehat."

Their version of "Mystery Achievement," a Pretenders song, was the best. I'd never heard Chris sing like this, all out, sexy, sure of herself. Her voice sounded like Pat Benatar and Chrissie Hynde and I could see why she picked the songs she did. Jim watched for a while, standing at the bottom of the stairs focusing on Chris. I was surprised. He couldn't stand rock 'n' roll. We both watched when she sang "Brass in Pocket." It seemed to have been written for her. Claudia was nudging Mark and saying, "Listen to the *words*, Mark."

> I'm gonna make you see
> nobody else here
> no one like me
> I'm special
> so special
> gotta *have* some of your

at-ten-tion
give it to me.

Mark whistled when it was over and her friends clapped and screamed their approval.

Jenny was sitting on the floor rapt, and Jim said, "Boy she's good. Where'd she get that voice?" We went back upstairs.

That was the only time I saw her sing with the band. I felt none of the pain I'd felt when she won the Headmaster's Award and there were no tears at this party. Mark wrote her a poem and left it on her bed upstairs, telling her again how much he loved her but how he loved God more. What an odd ending to the best two years of her life.

At least I thought they were the best two years. I was in her room a week later, helping her sort through her books. She wasn't saying much.

"It was such a good year for you, Chris—the prom, the award, and Mark, and getting into college."

She didn't answer. I put the textbooks on the bottom shelf of her bookcase, remembering how she used to giggle and chortle on the phone with Claudia or John. I always wondered what was so funny.

Suddenly she said, "Oh Mom. It was the worst year of my life. I wouldn't wish it on anyone," and she crumbled into the deck chair and started to cry.

I stared. I felt like I'd been hit in the chest with a bag of sand.

"Chris, how can I be so far off—when I'm with you everyday? I guess I just don't understand anything."

She shook her head and her hair hid her face. But she was having so much fun I thought. I crouched down and leaned on her knees. The gulf between us was not of our own making, but it seemed uncrossable.

"I'm sorry, dear . . ." My voice started to trail off helplessly and I pulled it back. Don't give up—stay with her. "I'd thought it was so good. I'm sorry. Sometimes I don't think . . ."

It *was* good. But I underestimated the power of her illness and the long downhill slide. I didn't know yet how much she was tangled in the same inner monologue I was about her health. Only it was ten times worse for her.

BOOK III

THE
ROAD
HOME

LODGED

The rain to the wind said,
"You push and I'll pelt."
They so smote the garden bed
That the flowers actually knelt,
And lay lodged   though not dead.
I know how the flowers felt.

—Robert Frost

19 ⋆ Wasted Summer, Wasted Fall

When she found herself on the tenth floor of Babies Hospital again three weeks after graduation, she couldn't believe it.

"What kind of life is this? How can I go to Emerson?"

"Chris, you got over the worst bleed you ever had five days before the prom. It takes time."

"I know, I know, but I can't take much more. On top of everything, I've been in this dump for three days and they still haven't hooked up my phone."

How could she change direction so quickly? She never let her defenses crack for more than an instant. She had fewer visitors this time. Her friends were either working or traveling in Europe. She said wistfully, "Those are the lucky ones."

"I don't know if they're so lucky."

"What do you mean? They have it easy."

"It's been my experience that having an easy life isn't very lucky at all."

"Oh *God* . . . ," she said, exasperated.

"Young people who have it too easy never develop any strength. They're soft . . . spoiled. They hate themselves. If nothing is hard, they don't know what it means to want, to overcome, to work for something, and they feel worthless because they're deprived of success."

"Bull," she said. A moment later she asked, "Is that why there's so many rich alcoholics?"

I laughed, and she said, "Look at *me*, Mom, I have everything.

It's embarrassing we have so much." I waited for her to wake up. She stared back at me. "Okay, okay, I see what you mean. I already have a struggle, right?"

"Yes. and it certainly hasn't made you a rich alcoholic."

Mark and Brummitt were both working, but they came to visit. They threw the leftover butter pats from her dinner tray onto the ceiling and Chris taught them to ride the IV poles like skate boards and somehow avoiding the nurses, they zoomed back and forth down the halls.

The summer was slipping by and she wasn't gaining weight. She drank Vivonex, a chemical food supplement that was absorbed directly into her bloodstream like medicine. It killed her appetite for solid food.

Soon her mind was elsewhere. Her roommate was a handsome eighteen-year-old boy named Rolf Schrama. He was a patient of Dr. Ores and she had arranged for them to room together. Chris couldn't get over it.

"Mom, I can't believe they're letting us share a room. He has c/f too. He's so nice. I think he's a real brain."

Chris and Rolf shared the same room for one happy week and then the administration moved him to a room across the hall. She was furious but Dr. Ores was resigned, and even Rolf hadn't improved her appetite.

Dr. Ores knew of another way for her to gain weight. She could be fed through a central venous line with a broviac catheter.

The other bed was still vacant when Dr. Ores went to discuss it with Chris, and every surface in the room was covered with papers and laundry, magazines and tapes, stuffed animals, opened medical supplies, and wilted flowers. There were glasses of unfinished Vivonex everywhere, the straws still in the glasses.

"What happened to this room?" asked Dr. Ores, amused.

"I haven't let the maids in for two days," Chris said happily. "I thought I should have the right to run amuck after they moved Rolf out."

"How did you get them to stay out?"

"I just asked them to come back later and they never came

back." Chris was rummaging through the traincase next to her.
Dr. Ores looked into the case and thought to herself, There must
be enough makeup in there for all of Hollywood. Chris knew what
she was thinking and said, "I just play with it. These are my toys."
She was opening little quilted bags, pulling out eye liners impatiently.

"What are you looking for?" asked Dr. Ores.

"Ash rose, an eye color. I had it yesterday," she said angrily
and began throwing things all over the bed; lipsticks, brushes, and
little containers flew around the covers. Dr. Ores didn't say anything. Chris looked up, expecting disapproval, but seeing none,
said, "Oh, I know you think I'm stupid, but I can't bear it. Nothing
is going my way today, and I have to deal with all this." She
gestured at the IV poles, the Vivonex, the lunch tray. "Nothing
ever goes my way."

Dr. Ores said, "Let's look for it together. What does it look
like?" She saw Christine's shoulders relax.

"It's a pencil with a pink stripe." Dr. Ores sat on the bed and
they scrounged around together in the train case searching for
the bizarre exact color Chris had to have.

"Here it is," Dr. Ores said, at last pulling it out of a side pocket.

"Oh God, I put it there last night. I must be getting senile."

"Senility is not one of your symptoms. But I want to talk to
you."

"Uh huh," said Chris, bending close to the mirror.

"I'm not happy that you've gained no weight."

"That makes two of us."

"I'd like to put a broviac catheter in your arm to feed you a
nutrition concentrate for a month." She saw Chris mouth the
words "a month" in horror. "I want you to put on eight or nine
pounds. Then you'll have some reserve when you go to college."

"Is this catheter different from an IV?"

"Yes, it's a surgical procedure with some risk because you'll
have to go under general anesthesia. You'll also have to move to
the eleventh floor for the month."

"Anything else?" Chris had learned to keep questioning.

"Just the tedium and the time upstairs."

"This floor is where the boys are."

"We can't do the procedure down here, Christine."

"What's my mother think?"

"She said it was up to you."

"What do you think?"

"I wouldn't ask you to do it, if I didn't think it would be a good idea." Dr. Ores spoke slowly to give Chris plenty of room. She'd do better if she was for it from the start. The procedure was called hyperalimentation. (*Hyper* = super; *alimentation* = nutrition.)

"Have any of the other kids had it?"

"Yes."

"Does it hurt?"

"No, not at all. Once the catheter is in place, you don't feel it."

"I'll think about it."

Dr. Ores listened to Christine's chest with her stethoscope, and left.

It was easy to see why bizarre colors were important to Chris when I found her eye-makeup formulas.

EYES Wild Blue (dark)
1. Gold Verde (under eye)—Borghese
2. Midnight Blue pencil (line top lid)—Arden
3. Light Bagdad Blue (almost into corner)—Mono
4. Blend with Blue Violetteo—Borghese
5. Orange (inner lid)—Dior
6. Pink (brow)—Barone
7. Gold dust on eyelashes (or turquoise)—Stagelight
8. Bedouin Bronze (inner lower corner)

She kept them on pink 3 × 5 cards in her vanity. She used to call them recipes. That was how she spent her time in the hospital—small investment, big return.

Chris got the broviac catheter and went to the eleventh floor. Dr. Ores went on vacation. Unfortunately the eleventh-floor staff did not understand cystic fibrosis. The hyperalimentation fluids caused edema; her bronchial tubes swelled so much she had trouble breathing.

Then Chris caught the flu. She felt like she was suffocating.

The skin between her collarbones caved in with every strangled breath. Oxygen was prescribed, to be used as Chris desired. But an arrogant young resident decided that Chris did not really need oxygen. When she asked for it in the middle of the night, he refused her. Chris called me at home, and there were frantic phone calls at two and three in the morning for several days until the situation was put right.

What a disaster. When Dr. Ores returned, she prescribed diuretics for the edema and, for the bronchial blockage, a broncoscopy and an endoscopic lavage.

Broncoscopy is a simple process that lets doctors look into the lungs through a tube with a light and a mirror, inserted down the throat. The endoscopic lavage is done under anesthesia. First secretions are suctioned out of the bronchial tubes to let the patient breathe and, second, an antibiotic wash is flushed in. Dr. Ores said it usually helped.

But it didn't work, and worse, it wasn't painless. Christine's throat and bronchial tube were so irritated from the broncoscope going down her throat they were swollen and raw for days. She couldn't swallow, she couldn't talk, she still couldn't breathe, and now she had pain to deal with. She was so exhausted she lay on the bed like a lump, staring at nothing, immobilized and beaten. I stayed with her, but I felt helpless, like I was bound and handcuffed. Sometimes words helped—but not at times like this.

20 · Emerson

Christine finally left the hospital on August 15th, the day after her nineteenth birthday. She would have two happy weeks with Jerry—and with Vivonex, thumps, and antibiotics. On September 5th, we'd pack Jim's station wagon with her suitcases, trunks, her stereo and records, load the roof rack with small furniture, and drive to Emerson College in Boston. Jenny was coming too. I wanted her to know where Chris was.

We'd done all we could to ease the transition for Chris. Dr. Ores had persuaded Dr. Harold Shwachman, a semi-retired pediatrician known for his work on cystic fibrosis at Boston Children's Hospital, to care for Chris while she was at college. I'd already interviewed and hired physical therapists over the phone and opened a charge at the nearest pharmacy. Dr. Ores said Chris should not be without a phone, so while other freshman waited their turn, hers was installed before she arrived. Food was not usually allowed in dorm rooms, but Chris was going to be permitted a small refrigerator for food and antibiotics. She was also the only freshman with a single room, which she considered a penalty. She wanted roommates.

Chris would barely settle in at Emerson before she left. The first weekend she skipped a freshman mixer and flew to London to be in the new Muppet movie, *The Great Muppet Caper*. She was going to be busy.

Journal Entry—August 1980

I just found a piece of beach glass for Jenny. I'm on Fire Island for a week with my Dad. I saw Matt Murphy at the Casino last night. Matt is (needless to say) as gorgeous as ever. What a gorgeous hunk of spunk. I'm in a party mood tonight. Even though I'm tired. "Get yer yaya's out!"

I miss Mark. This place would be so perfect if he was here.

Oh well, Emerson must have someone waiting for me. Let's see, handsome, funny, tender but powerful.

Monday 11:45 p.m.

I wish Mark were here. It would give the island so much more meaning. But at this point we're too distant to get back together—even after the evening of Phebe's party. When I left his house, I knew I would never hold him or touch him that way again. I wanted to turn back and kiss him good-bye. Just once. Very intensely, with a holding back passion. A good-bye kiss. Something to re-member me by. I wish I had left something personal of mine in his room, better yet his bed. I'm so romantic.

Not only am I romantic, but I want to be. I try as hard as I can to be the type of woman that men think of as a true woman . . . delicate, sensitive, loving, devoted, ap-pealingly independent, sexy but innocent, changeable but always feminine. I'm bound to be disappointed because I'm always searching for fairy tale love, undying, passion-ate, needing, forever. I feel it often but I won't receive it often (I don't really want it often, just once—) but it must be forever. Ah well, maybe I'll come close.

Wednesday.

Matt's eyes are blue, not that washed out, pale dry color, but deep, a rich periwinkle. They can pierce into someone's deepest thoughts. They are the type of eyes one likes to have eye contact with, it's almost impossible not to. Brummitt was like that. I could say so much to him with my eyes. Some people's eyes are available, not hidden. I'll always, always be sorry that things didn't work out with him. Too many obstacles in the way, plus bad timing.

    I finished my hot fairy tale . . . the Princess Bride. It was great—extremely funny. (hee hee)
Good-night.

Journal Entry—leaving the Island

    Matt took us for a farewell dinner at the Casino last night. My Dad left early to pack but I stayed. After a while it was just Matt and I and some other women. Anyway, Matt was a bit drunk so we started dancing and having fun. Matt's a very physical person, I never really realized that, but the whole time (once we started dancing) he had his arm around me. And when we said good-bye, he wouldn't stop kissing me (not that I minded—at all!). This was interwoven with a few hugs, and during one he kissed me again and again. Strange the whole thing. (I'm not gonna make it into anything, he was drunk.) However, I've been around him many times when he'd drunk too much beer, and never this.

    Basically, what it is, is people are always more affectionate towards friends then, which is why. Plus I'm going off to college so I won't see him for a while. However, if I had been a little more daring, and let my lips, oh say, linger, I don't doubt he would have been more daring. (kissing wise)

    Now, the reason for this change in him (it's never happened before when we said good-bye) is because of my change. I've grown up tremendously since last year. Last year I was becoming a woman. But because I'm facing college, my health struggles this year, and because of Mark, mostly Mark, I am a woman. (I think I can safely say *that.) So Matt must have seen that and maybe in that sense he's attracted to me, but of course he's watched me grow up and I'm his friend's daughter, so it would go nowhere. Also he's 13 years older than me, I'm only 19. If I were 20, it wouldn't be as bad. Maybe it shocked him a little bit that I'm a woman. I mean he really cares about me. He told me he loved me (first time he's <u>ever</u> told me that).*

I guess I'll always wonder what would've happened. Still, it's neat. Night.

Journal Entry: EMERSON COLLEGE!!
My new address is
132 Beacon Street
Boston, Mass. 02116

Well I got through the first day. I'm very homesick and I guess a little unsure of myself. I know I'll make friends, it's just going to take a week or two to feel comfortable.

After the freshmen meeting this evening, I didn't feel like going to the dance so I came back here. I was so depressed. I cried and said I wanted to go home. I was thinking of staying where Mom's staying, but I realized I couldn't.

I miss Claudia, I miss Mark, I miss John, I miss Matt. I miss anyone and anything familiar. What a wonderful feeling to have friends and a place where you belong.

Mark is so mature about so many things. I feel so much older than so many of these people and also so much younger.

Well, I'm all unpacked.

Entry:

It's been a good day so far—met five really nice guys (very funny) (all seniors). Also said good-bye to Mom and Jen. (sniff) Tonight a bunch of us are partying in Michelle's room. I met a guy tonight (Chris) who reminds me of Andy. We're going to dinner at 6:00 tomorrow.

Entry:

Dinner was fun. He's a really nice guy. I'm now on the Concorde. What a trip! I took a shuttle from Boston to New York. This jet is awesome. We're now going at Mach 2 (1,345 mph!) And the feeling of the take off was incredible. "inconceivable."

I'm writing letters with the pen they gave me. I just wrote Mark a real hot-shot "love ya" type postcard. He should get a kick out of it.

My scene is going to be shot on location in Hyde Park. (Hyde's my Mom's middle name.) My head is spinning . . . ach! This is the most amazing experience I've ever had. I'm so lucky to be me—Thanks God!

Jim Henson had written a small part in the movie for Chris. She called it a walk-on, but she had a line and that meant she'd get her union card for the Screen Actors Guild. She'd be a professional.

Jerry and I thought it was too dangerous for her to go alone so he flew from London, she flew down from Boston on the shuttle, they met at JFK Airport, and flew back to London together on the Concorde. A car was waiting at Heathrow Airport and they drove to Jerry's cottage in a tiny village called Letchmore Heath. The romantic stucco and wood house was shrouded in a drifting English fog as the car pulled in and Chris said, "How beautiful. Just like in the movies."

"Except for one thing," Jerry said, as the limousine drove away.

"What?"

"There's supposed to be a car here." He sighed. "What the hell's happened this time." He stormed in, picked up the phone and tried to rent one, but nothing was open on Friday night.

Chris went to the refrigerator and her heart sank. Empty except for beer. She hated to ask her father for anything when he was angry, but she didn't dare miss a meal.

"Dad, I think I should eat," she said tentatively. Her father stroked his short beard and studied Chris. Damn, he'd forgotten about dinner. Well, nothing was going to ruin this weekend.

"We can walk into town to the pub. It's not far."

"Okay."

"We'll go slowly. If you get tired, I'll carry you."

The pub was a rustic place called the Battle Axe and they sat at a table near an empty fireplace and ordered beer and steak-and-kidney pie. At last, they both relaxed.

"Nothing like warm beer and burned kidneys to warm you on a damp foggy night," said Jerry. Chris always thought she'd love steak-and-kidney pie, but after taking one bite of the kidneys she ate around them. She talked happily about school and her plans and Jerry noticed she hadn't coughed at all.

She said, "I auditioned for the glee club last week. My voice is a little stronger."

Spending the summer in the hospital was paying off he thought. They missed the evening thumps but did them in the morning. The Muppets sent another car for them. Chris loved being on the set again and this time she really felt like one of the group. Everyone was glad to see her. Richard Hunt lifted her up in a bear hug. Then he stepped back and said, "Hi, Gumbelina. You've gotten so beautiful," and she blushed happily. Richard had given her the nickname on "Sesame Street."

The company was on location in Hyde Park. Rows of giant spotlights burned like platinum, brighter than the sun. Technicians stood around talking, and Chris smiled to herself. It was always like this—everybody busy but nothing happening. Setting up shots took forever.

They were ready to film the scene with her one precious line. She had to walk on screen with her dad, look over at Kermit the Frog sitting on a park bench, and say, "Oh look, Dad, there's a bear."

And her dad would say, "No, Christine, that's a frog. Bears wear hats." It was a running joke through the movie that the way to tell a bear from a frog was, "Bears wear hats."

The wardrobe lady gave her some slacks, a blazer, and a blouse to wear, saying, "Here, put these on in the trailer." Chris took a deep breath. The clothes were terrible—shapeless. Did she dare? Yes, she did.

"Oh, I'm sorry," she said sweetly, "these aren't right for me. I can't wear them." The lady looked at her in surprise.

"Well, go ask Mr. Henson what he wants then." Chris went to her father instead.

"Dad, you should see the stuff they got for me to wear. What'll I do? Can't I wear what I have on?" Chris was wearing her white jeans and a yellow sweatshirt with yo-yos on it.

"C'mon," he said, smiling, and he walked over to Jim Hensen and said, "Jim, the clothes wardrobe gave Chris to wear aren't right. She can't wear that stuff. I think she looks fine the way she is."

Jim looked Chris over and nodded. "I agree. Tell Rose it's okay."

Jerry nodded and Chris heard her dad say, "Oh, and the clothes they have for me are all wrong too. So I'm going to wear what I have on."

She wondered innocently how he got the nerve.

They went to get a mike taped to the small of her back. They rehearsed and the afternoon was spent shooting the scene. After they finished Jerry said, "Chris, we have time to shop. Do you want to go to Harrod's or the Hyper Market?"

"No. I'd rather stay and watch." The sun felt wonderful on her back and she curled up like a warm kitten on the back of a sound truck.

The next day, Jerry flew back to Boston with her. He hugged her for a long time and his eyes were moist when he let her go. He wished she could have stayed in England. Everything was so much fun when she was with him.

Journal Entry—

I spoke to Mark this evening. I might go to Amherst for a weekend. He'd have to do my therapy of course. That would be very difficult for me to endure. But I could do most of the positions and then have him help me with the ones I can't reach. I'm on my own now. I have to learn to

ask people I love for help. I read some of the New Testa-
ment. I'm so confused. Sometimes I see nothing but what
will happen to me if I don't do certain things, but then
again he came so our sins could be forgiven. But, it doesn't
always sound that way.

(Mark said, "I wish I could carry your smile in my
heart.")

I'll have to ask Mark. If he doesn't know, I'll ask his
roommate and if he doesn't know I'll ask my minister at
home. I wish I could find a fellowship here. Seek and I
shall find, I guess.

Guess what. I was asked out—my first college date. I
really hope I can handle what's cut out for me here; mus-
ter up the discipline demanded from my courses. It's late.
I need sleep. I love Mark! There's still some hope, I think.

The second weekend, she was off campus again—this time
with Mark at Amherst. Wearing her new green satin *Muppet
Movie* jacket, she took the Trailways bus and Mark met her at the
station. He wore the Muppet jacket and Chris wore his old cordu-
roy blazer. They felt like the coolest couple on campus. They
stayed up late, went to fraternity parties, watched soccer practice, did everything. Mark was so proud of her. People stared at
them in the cafeteria but Mark knew it was the good kind of
staring and Chris leaned over and said, half joking, "Mark, what's
everybody looking at? We must look like movie stars."

Mark gave her a droll look, "Some of us *are* movie stars."

Mark slept on the floor in his room so Chris could have the bed.
He was touched when she asked for his help doing thumps and
he felt very close to her. After all they'd been through, she'd
never shared this with him. Chris had never felt so free.

When she got back to Emerson late Sunday night, she had a
cold. She called me.

"Mom, Mark and I are best friends now. It's *so* great."

"How do you do it, Chris? This is the second time you've
stayed good friends with a boy after you've broken up. People
always say they're going to, but no one but you does."

"I can't stand the thought of losing someone I love, I guess."

I asked, "How'd you get to Amherst?"

"I took a Trailways bus." There was a long silence on my end.

"You took a Trailways? By yourself? You got the ticket and found out the times and all that?" I was floored. She always acted so helpless at home.

"Of course. Why are you so surprised?"

"You never did things like that at home."

She laughed. "I didn't have to, Mom, you always did them for me."

"Hmmmm. So I did."

On Monday night she called again and I knew something was wrong. Her voice was a forced whisper.

"Mom, I'm sick." I sat up in bed.

"Chris, you sound terrible. I can hardly hear you. Do you have laryngitis?"

"No, but I can't breathe—enough to talk." I could hear her struggling, saying, "It started last night, and it's gotten real bad."

I spoke slowly, trying not to sound frightened. "Chris, when I talked to you yesterday, you were fine. How could—"

"It happened fast," she rasped.

I paused a minute, keeping my voice level. "Chris, go to the hospital. Can someone get you a cab?"

"I'm going tomorrow to see Dr. Shwachman. It's probably just the flu." There was a crackling sound in her throat.

"Dear, do you think you should wait?" Just the flu; people died of the flu.

There was silence, then, "I'm scared too, but the last few hours—there's been no change. I think I can wait." I prayed she was right.

"Okay, but don't be a hero. If you start to feel worse, get help. Tell the girls across the hall what's happening."

We stayed on the phone a little longer, then hung up. I lay awake nervous and wondering, praying useless prayers.

The next morning she was admitted to Boston Children's Hospital. The door that had opened and seemed to beckon her to a new life closed and locked.

She spent the next two months in the hospital. And as the days turned into weeks, symptom after symptom appeared. New viruses grew in her lungs. She fought viral pneumonias and bacterial pneumonias and fevers, searing pain from raw chest linings inflamed by the violent coughing and thumps, a fungus in her lungs, bronchitis, and strep throat. Worst of all, even worse than the pain in her chest, was the feeling of breathing through a pinhole, of suffocating.

Journal Entry: Boston Children's [1980]

> *9/29 I haven't gotten any sleep for a couple of days. I just cough and cough like crazy. It makes me hot and feverish. The doctors think I have a virus. Damn. Antibiotics won't help. I can hardly breathe. They're giving me Demerol.*
>
> *Last night I slept . . . a drugged codeine sleep. Terrible headache. Drugged sleep isn't restful. I woke up disoriented and in pain. Coughing never stops. I can feel the wheeze in my lungs.*
>
> *I can't get enough air. It's frightening. They moved my bed over to the open window. A wind comes in off the river I think. It does make me feel better, even if it doesn't help me breathe.*
>
> *Mom's coming tomorrow. I'm glad. I'm so tired and frightened. Desperately uncomfortable, hot, dizzy, congested. I can't wait till Mom gets here.*

She withdrew from Emerson. I went to Boston on Amtrak every three days, stayed for two, came home, and then went back up a few days later. I called Jerry in England and he flew to Boston. He found her despondent. They held each other and cried. They talked, and she made an effort to hide how bad it was.

When Jerry left, he was uneasy. She appeared heartened by his visit but when he talked to her on the phone a few days later she was worse, and he realized what an actress she already was. She was protecting him.

Journal Entry: Boston Children's Hospital

> *When I get out, I'm going home. I think I'll apply to Barnard. I don't feel so great today. I had a fever this*

morning and I can't breathe. The nurse's note said "respiratory distress." I'll say.

It's Friday. What a day. Woke up without a headache, but felt nauseous all day. They drew blood gases. You should see that needle—huge! Sooo painful to have. Got novocaine twice, but it still killed.

Became nauseous from bleeding and coughing till I threw up. TERRIBLE pains in my chest. What's that from? New symptom. I feel so ill. I tremble sometimes.

After four weeks, Dr. Shwachman said she could be transferred to Babies Hospital. When we left, she couldn't walk and an orderly brought a wheelchair. I helped her into the car. We sat in silence while I studied my map, and as we passed Emerson she said, "Good bye, Boston." On the way home, she told me, "I'm not going back to Babies Hospital, Mom. Never. I can't face them. Dr. Ores is going to have to get me into the Harkness Pavilion." I didn't know what to say.

"Do you think she will?" she asked.

"Of course."

"Will she still be my doctor?"

"Yes."

"And I want a private room." This was new.

"Won't you be too lonely?" I asked.

"Maybe, but I'm too tired to deal with roommates now. My days as social director are over."

She didn't say much more and there was more than tiredness in her silence. There was something dark and bleak.

Her decision to go into Harkness turned out to be wise for the worst reason. Two days after she was settled in the private room, I learned that all three of the girls with cystic fibrosis that we'd known, Kendall, Sarah, and Cory, had died. They were her age. When the nurses came over from Babies to do her thumps I asked them to say nothing to Chris, even if she asked how they were. I was afraid if she knew she might give up and die too.

21 · Bumps, Fits, and Starts

I brought her home just before Thanksgiving on a wet, gray, blustery day. A hard rain had beaten the last of the leaves off the trees and they lay flat and slippery, a mottled carpet on the back roads. Jim was home when we arrived and he picked Chris up in his arms and carried her up to her room. Jenny was at her father's.

Everything from Emerson was still in boxes when I went up to help her start to unpack. Chris was lying on her stomach, her head buried in her arms. Ivy was curled up on her feet and a wet branch tapped on her window. It was cozy.

"When's Jenny coming home?" she asked, not looking up.

"Tonight."

"Good. When's Thanksgiving?"

"Four days. How do you feel?"

"Not as good as when I got out before Emerson."

"I was afraid of that."

"Each time I slip a little. I remember how I was in eighth and ninth grade, and I guess it was normal. I was tired all the time then, had those colds and fevers and aches and stuff, but I didn't have this congested feeling all the time."

I took a long breath. "I asked Dr. Ores once how you could have so much lung infection and still be well, relatively well, I mean."

She looked over at me. "What did she say?"

"She said we don't need two lungs. We can get along with one."

She stared at the floor while I cut open the cartons. "Oh, Mom," she sighed.

"What, dear?"

She was slow to answer. "After this summer, I thought I was going to make it. I'm such a failure."

I knew it. I sat down next to her. "You know, I don't see it that way at all."

"How do you see it?" She sounded beaten, like she didn't want to hear. She buried her face in her arms again.

"If you're defeated, there's a lot of victory in your defeat."

"Oh sure," she scoffed.

"Chris, you *did* it. All by yourself. Not for long, but long enough to see that you could. Don't forget, you had the courage to face what no one else did."

"But I didn't make it."

"Your health failed, *you* didn't." She got up off the bed, slowly nudging the rubble at her feet. I said, "You're confusing failure with disappointment, Chris. You were cheated and it's not your fault."

"I know it's not my fault, but it doesn't change anything," she argued.

"Yes, it does. It changes what you know about yourself." I saw her mind whizzing through a mental list—what new things did she know about herself?

She said softly, "You mean how sick I am—sicker than I thought?" I winced inside.

"No dear, how strong you are, in spite of how sick you are." We were both right. She shrugged to herself and I bit my lip and got busy with the boxes. "Dear, you made all the right decisions. It was a glorious flight of freedom."

"Till I was shot down," she said bitterly.

"Yes, but you didn't fall down, and don't forget it."

She sat on a cardboard carton. "Aren't you just saying this to try and cheer me up?"

"Chris, you're nineteen, not six. I'd love to cheer you up, but I wouldn't try to fool you with lies. I believe it. I'm proud of you." Don't overdo it, I thought. She got up, stepped over boxes. She pulled up the flaps, looked in one box, then another, putting nothing away, making no decisions, like an archaeologist picking through a ruin.

"Chris, you know what I'm afraid of?"

"What?"

"Well, I know you don't want to be here, home with your *mother*. I'm afraid you'll get to hate us, and hate home and hate me. People hate their traps and home may seem like a trap now."

"I'm glad to be home, Mom. Well, sort of—"

"A refuge now, a trap later. But you know, there's a lot of ways you can have the freedom you had at college."

"Like how?" She sounded interested.

"Let me organize my thoughts tonight, and we'll talk tomorrow." I wanted to give her time to think about something positive.

Journal Entry November 23, 1980

It's my third day home from the Harkness Pavilion. Altogether, that must have been four weeks here and three in Boston Children's—a long haul.

And it's not over yet. I'm 88 pounds. Sooo very thin, and so embarrassed by it too. I just have no appetite. It's hopeless I think. But I hope not. I haven't called Mark in a while. I hope he's terribly worried about me. He sure hasn't bothered to find out—bloody two-faced bastard, little shit.

John's been a real friend. I saw the Rocky Horror Picture Show last night. I'm in love with Tim Curry! He's so incredibly handsome.

I want and need someone to help me be happy again. I've had such a grueling, miserable rotten six months. I never stop worrying about my terrible health. I'm so afraid, alone and scared and lost. I feel so little in an

endless angry ocean. Donald, John, Mark, and Andy,
someone help. I'm very frail and what I really need is a
long relaxing (but regulated) vacation.
I'm having a very hard time.

She did have an inner voice. Why didn't I try harder to find
it? We always talked about life and love. We were so good at that,
but we skirted around the dark edges—afraid to talk about death.
Maybe it wasn't me she had to share it with. Maybe, too, she was
protecting me.

That night I lay awake, wondering if she could rebuild with
her stage at school gone, her friends away, and no place to meet
people. Her life had been so full of love and energy before—it
kept her well. She'd have to start all over.

After I drove Jenny to school the next morning, Chris
wrapped herself in her comforter and I fixed her tea.

"Chris, it isn't going to be the way it was before. The main
thing is, *you* can run your life—as if you were away at college. You
don't have to ask my permission to do things. And you'll have
financial freedom. I have duplicate charge plates for you, for
Bloomingdale's and Macy's, and I got you signing privileges on
my Visa card. I have a Citibank card for the cash machine in Rye
where I keep your account. There's no reason you should feel
poor, you're not."

She raised her eyebrows. Good, I thought, I want her to be
pleasantly surprised. "Do you want to hear more?" She nodded
like a little girl waiting for me to put more honey in her tea.

"The bank account in Rye is in both our names, but it's your
account. When you're twenty-one, it will be *all* yours."

She was listening carefully, waiting for something. I had a
feeling what it was. "If you have friends over, and they stay late,
use the utmost discretion. Remember Jenny looks up to you and
you set an example."

"Don't worry."

"I don't. You've never been a user or a taker."

"Thanks, Mom." She sipped her tea. "It'll be nice not to have
to worry about money. It wasn't always that way."

"No it wasn't, we're very lucky."

It was also luck that I took up photography that fall. When she was in Boston Children's Celia Ores had had the courage to say, "Christine needs you. Would it be too much of a hardship if you were to stop working?"

In order to spend more time with Jenny, I'd left my position as fashion director of the Allied Stores the year before and was working part time for a fashion service. But even that was taking me to Europe twice a year to cover the ready-to-wear collections. When I asked Jim how we'd manage if I stopped working he said, "We'll manage just fine." Jim never put pressure on me to provide extra income and I was grateful.

Knowing I'd need some creative outlet, I took class once a week at the Y in darkroom techniques.

The third week of class, the teacher said, "Jacquie, I want some new negatives, something recent."

"Oh, I'm not a photographer. I just want to learn to print old negatives and make blowups. I don't even own a camera."

"Doesn't your husband have one?"

"Yes."

"Well, say no more and bring me some new negatives." So I was stuck. I asked Christine to be my model.

"Oh boy," she said, "We can take some great pictures and I'll send one to Mark and he can eat his heart out when he sees what he's missing. I can't believe he hasn't called to see how I am, that bastard."

He knew she'd been in the hospital a long time. She didn't know that Mark was consumed with guilt, sure that she'd gotten the flu at Amherst and he was the cause of her illness. He thought if she'd waited to visit she would have made the close friendships at Emerson that would have helped her stay well.

She wanted to start right away. "I'll go upstairs and fix my hair," she said.

"Okay." I hadn't seen this much spunk since she'd been home. I called after her, "It has to be a portrait, Chris, not a snapshot. We'll be working for a while." If I was going to do this, I might as well do it right. She was upstairs for an hour deciding what to wear, and we had a wonderful time shooting two rolls of black-and-white film.

"Let's go outside," I suggested. "We could take some Bonnie-and-Clyde pictures with the shotgun."

"Oh, cool."

Jim was a gamebird hunter and had given me a light 20-gauge shotgun. I was learning to shoot skeet, so I could go hunting with him.

"This is getting interesting," she muttered when I handed her the open shotgun.

The next day I got the contact sheets and looked at the little prints with a magnifying glass. They were wonderful. I raced home to show her.

"They're so small," she said.

"They're the size of the negative, see?"

"Oh, that's what you mean by a contact sheet."

"Right, I just enlarge the good ones."

So we started. And posing in front of my camera cured her ennui on many a lonely day that winter. The pictures were telling her about herself, giving her back the confidence she'd had at school. She tried on different moods and looks, and liked what she saw. And there was something else. The lens saw her beauty, not her sickness. That didn't even exist in the pictures, as if some miracle had cured her. She needed to know that she could still look normal.

When I brought the contact sheets home, we'd have scream sessions. We liked the pictures so much, we'd scream back and forth to each other, bending over, peering at the tiny pictures through a jeweler's glass like a couple of hunchbacks, and then bolting upright to point to a good one, shrieking, "Wait till you see this one, it's so great!" and we'd quickly trade sheets. The excitement wouldn't last, and she'd slip back into her depression, but it was helping.

Christmas was precarious that year. She went back to Rye Country Day with her friends, carrying on the tradition of seniors before her—strutting around their old turf, proud and grown up. Chris was relieved to be able to tell her friends she was transferring, not dropping out. She'd applied for admission to the spring semester at Manhattanville and had been accepted. The campus was ten miles from our house.

Mark wasn't back yet, but Claudia, John, Brummitt, Drea, Phebe, Jamie, and Amy were, and they went to the Red Barn afterward. Andy Gibson was there, too, and for a few days it was like old times.

Then the bleeding started again, an ominous setback. We were on the phone with Dr. Ores, ready to go into Harkness.

Journal Entry: Monday night

On my way to John's, going out the door, I felt it. Not much—a small bleed, but still I couldn't go out. So John and everyone came here. What dears.

Mark called today and wanted to see me before I leave for Virgin Gorda with my Dad. We were going to go to a movie (Flash Gordon), but I thought it might be foolish, so I'm going to ask him to come over and keep me company. I hope no bleeding.

I don't see how this can stop on its own though. Whenever I've had recurring bleeding (not streaking, real bleeding) in the past, I've had to go to the hospital.

Oh dear Lord, please not this time. I'm so very tired of living like an invalid. I want to enjoy life. I want to do something and be something. sigh. . . .

Well, tomorrow's Christmas Eve Day. Today I felt horrible all day, but I washed my hair and took a whole bunch of pills and started to feel better. It was nice having Mark over, but it was a little strange not being able to hug him or curl up in his arms. That's one of the things I miss most . . . not being held and touched by a man who really loves me.

So far tonight (11:13) no bleeding and I'm amazed. (knock on wood) I've been laughing and coughing all night long and my cold's much worse. Hope my luck keeps up.

Two things saved her. When her friends came to spend the evening at our house, because she couldn't go out, they had a slumber party in sleeping bags on our living room floor. Second, the bleed stopped and she joyfully canceled the admission. And the day after Christmas she was well enough to go to Virgin Gorda.

Journal Entry:

Dr. Ores says I can go. I have to have a wheelchair and no carrying any bags and Dad will have to leave Virgin Gorda and meet me in Puerto Rico for the hard part of the trip. But at least, I'm going. I can't wait.

Virgin Gorda (Biras Creek actually on the island . . . down a ways from Little Dicks Bay) was wonderful as usual. One problem. I can't lie in the sun anymore. Would you believe! Because I now take such huge doses of antibiotics, continually, it induces a reaction in the sun . . . a ghastly case of huge red welts . . . that itch. Like hives. Damn, I get cheated out of everything because of this stupid disease.

22 · *Purple Hair at Last*

Then came more good luck. Because of the photography, she reconnected with Bruce McDaniel's band from school, Stu and the Pids, only now their name was Panic Scenery. They were seniors, playing at school dances and local clubs, and they needed publicity pictures. They couldn't afford a professional photographer.

Chris asked me if I'd consider taking pictures of the band. The experience would be good for me, and I was glad to do it. Chris wanted to know how much it would cost. This was really for Chris and I didn't want the band's money. But I'd get better pictures if they didn't feel like a charity case.

"Tell them I have an assignment, they'll be a big help to me."

"Oh, Mom, that's great. Thank you."

I noticed Chris's hair was getting blonder.

"What are you doing to your hair Christine? I love it."

"Lightening it so I can dye it purple."

"You're kidding. Purple?"

"I'm not kidding."

"What if you ruin your hair? What if you don't like it?"

"It's only a vegetable dye, it'll wash out."

"Oh." I thought, Only a vegetable dye—like a henna rinse, nothing major. I forgot about it.

Bruce McDaniel came over that weekend to hang out with Chris and listen to records in the den. Bruce had a copy of *Rolling Stone* with a picture of Sting on the cover.

"Chris, what's he doing with his hair?" He held up the cover. "It was never that white before."

"I know," she said, "he bleached it."

"Not bad." Bruce studied Sting's hair. "If he can do it, so can I." Chris was all for anyone looking more like Sting.

"I've got the stuff. I could do it for you."

Bruce didn't take this seriously, but Christine had done a good job on her own hair. He said, "Mmmmm, I suppose you know what you're doing."

"How 'bout tomorrow?"

It was like a dare. "Yeah, okay." Bruce said. "How mad can my parents get? Hey, I've already got an earring. They almost threw me out of the house when they saw that."

"Nooooo, it'll look great." She got up and looked closely at a strand of Bruce's hair. "It's like black thatch. Do you have Japanese blood? I'll have to strip it first. Bleaching won't do it."

"*Strip* it? How do you do that?"

"With Clorox." Bruce opened his mouth but Chris said, "I'm kidding, I'm kidding. Don't worry, I know what to do. We just have to be careful you aren't blinded," she deadpanned.

"Blinded?"

"He's okay. You're in good hands," she said. They did it the next afternoon. Chris prepared me. "Mom, Bruce is coming over and we're going to spend the afternoon in the bathroom." She paused, relishing my look. I knew she was teasing for once.

"I'm bleaching his hair white blond, like Sting. He's shy and he'll be embarrassed so try to be—not around too much."

"Bruce shy? What are you talking about? He's a consummate performer and very friendly." Bruce was anything but shy.

"You don't know him, Mom. That's an act. He's really very shy."

I laughed and didn't pursue it. Chris and her friends described as shy anyone who was not obnoxiously brash. The important thing was that, involved and happy in the photography and the hair, she had not coughed at all in the last few days.

How much Bruce liked the bleaching I don't know. When he left the house, he looked radically different, with platinum blond hair and black eyebrows.

The next weekend Chris walked into Jenny's room and said, "Jen, could I have one of your blond Barbie dolls?"

Jenny looked at Chris in surprise. She handed one to Chris. "Is this okay?" "Yes." "Do you want one so you can play with me?"

Chris paused, thinking what a sweet question it was. "Partly, and I want to dye the hair purple?"

"Oh, wow. Can I watch?"

"Sure. Come on. I'm doing it now." Jenny scrambled up. In the bathroom Chris opened a small blue plastic bottle labeled "Crazy Color" and squeezed it carefully. "Look." Brilliant fuschia dye bubbled up like a pink lavadome and Jenny gasped, "OOOooooo, it's beautiful."

"After I do the Barbie, I'm going to do mine." Jenny stared at her sister, speechless. Chris applied the dye and while they waited, she invented a Miss America game with the other dolls, playing on the edge of the bathtub with Jenny. But when she rinsed off the dye, it all disappeared.

"It didn't work," said Jenny, disappointed.

Chris shrugged. "That's all right, it'll work on *my* hair."

The next day, she disappeared into the bathroom and came out two hours later with every strand of her hair colored a brilliant fuschia. She was ecstatic, and walked into the living room where Jenny was watching figure skating on "Wide World of Sports."

"Oh Chris. It's great! Can I touch it?" Chris bent over to let Jenny pat her purple hair. Then she looked at herself in the mirror, jumping up and down singing to herself.

"It's so great, it's so great."

"Let's go show Mommy," said Jenny.

I was in the kitchen and heard Chris say quietly, "Mom?" I turned around and smiled slowly. It looked wonderful, and I said so.

"You *like* it?" said Chris.

"I love it. That's a vegetable dye? I never saw a vegetable that color."

She smiled happily, "No, I meant they dye the vegetable this color."

I laughed. She always had a comeback. "It's a knockout."

"I know. It's perfect." She looked at us both a minute and said, "Do I look cheap?"

"Cheap? You could wear spandex pants and polyester leopard prints, and you couldn't look cheap. You have too much class."

"Oh good." She chirped and danced back to the mirror to look some more. She was going to get a lot of attention with that hair.

In January she started classes at Manhattanville part time, still living at home. Her hopes were high and so were mine. But I noticed from the start she didn't talk about it the way she had about Rye Country Day.

A frigid Canadian air mass pushed through New England in February and temperatures dropped below zero at night. Chris was afraid to go out because the bitter cold made her lungs spasm. But on one of those crystal cold Saturday nights, she talked me into going with her to see *The Rocky Horror Picture Show*. The 1976 movie was a cult film shown at midnight on Saturdays. She'd seen it three times with John. Jim tried to talk us out of going, but we didn't listen.

She wrapped a thick wool scarf around her neck, pulled it up over her mouth, and we drove to a decrepit movie house in New Rochelle. I put my arm around her firmly so she wouldn't fall as we picked our way through patches of ice in the parking lot. If she fell, she might rupture part of a lung and hemorrhage. We were taking a big chance.

The audience was full of raucous young people—a few girls, mostly boys, some dressed bizarrely with makeup and crazy hair and many in drag. It was like a private party. I turned to Chris in surprise as she said, "It's a musical about a transvestite, Mom. You'll see." She reached in her coat pocket and handed me a fistful of rice.

"What's this for?" I asked.

"You'll find out in a minute." Such mystery.

This was no normal movie experience. Four boys jumped up on the proscenium in front of the screen and started to lip synch and mime the action as the film began. Some lines were called out in unison by everyone. In a wedding scene, everyone started throwing rice. Chris laughed and yelled over the din, "Close your eyes!"

In a scene with pouring rain, people put newspapers over their heads and then lit matches in the dark as the actors did on the screen. I noted with horror that there was only one emergency exit down front. Chris had no newspaper, but she had matches in her pocket. Kids were prancing in the aisles to the music, but when Tim Curry, the star, sang his first outrageous song, the theater fell silent. He stepped out of an elevator on the huge screen—larger than life—wearing a black corset, black net stockings, a garter belt, stacked red high heels, and heavy makeup. I was fascinated too. He was gorgeous and it was fun and I felt lucky to be included.

Months later, we coaxed Jim to come to a midnight show in Greenwich. From the wild but more clean-cut audience, someone yelled, "Anyone here seeing the movie for the tenth time?" Several kids raised their hands.

"Anyone here seeing it for the eighth time?" More raised their hands.

"Anyone seeing it for the fifth time?" Chris raised her hand and started giggling, knowing what was coming.

"Anyone here seeing it for the third time?"

"For the second time?"

"For the first time?" And Chris stood up and pointed down at Jim. We didn't know what was going on till kids came prancing around Jim, pointing and chanting, "A virgin! A virgin! A virgin!" I laughed and Jim stood up and bowed from the waist, smiling broadly. He was a good sport, though he didn't love the movie as much as we did. But then Jim was grown up and Chris and I weren't.

A few days after that cold night in New Rochelle, I bought her tickets to see *Amadeus* on Broadway. Tim Curry, the *Rocky Horror* star, was playing the role of Mozart. She went with John Egan and, during the first-act break, she said, "Let's go backstage afterward and say hello to Tim Curry."

John looked at her. "How do you do that?"

"Just go through that door over there on the right, I guess."

"No, I'm chicken. I'll get the car. You do it."

"Oh, c'mon." Chris was surprised. John never said no. She'd

met so many famous people with her dad on the "Muppet Show," she thought nothing of it. "C'mon," she urged John again.

"No. I'm too embarrassed," he said.

"John, people go into show business because they *want* your approval. Celebrities are just people like us, you of *all* people should know." But John wouldn't go and he filed out afterward to get the car, thinking it would never work. Tim Curry wouldn't see her. When he pulled the car up to the stage door, where a few people were waiting, the door opened and out came Chris with Tim Curry. John watched in awe as they spoke to each other and shook hands good-bye.

John said, "How did you *do* that?" But Chris just smiled and didn't answer.

The vast rolling landscape of the campus at Manhattanville brought Christine her first experience of being officially handicapped. The long hill from the student parking lot to class was a killer; she could never make it without a terrible coughing attack. The college gave her an H sticker for the handicapped spaces up top. She hadn't told me about it but it must have set her thinking. She asked me one afternoon when I came into her room with a pile of clean laundry.

"Mom, who pays my medical bills?"

"Your father's major-medical policy at the Muppets."

"Does it have a limit?"

"No. The Muppets' policy had a $300,000 ceiling two years ago and we were afraid we might reach it, so Jerry talked to Jim Henson and they improved their coverage, and now there is no ceiling."

Her eyes opened wide. "They did that for me?"

"Well, I think it was you that triggered it. I'm not sure, but it benefits all their employees."

There was something else. When she was a senior at Rye Country Day, Jerry and I and his business manager, Arnold Sundel, realized that when she was twenty-one Jerry's major-medical insurance would no longer cover her.

I'd said, "But she's practically an invalid. She'll never be able to hold a normal job and get her own coverage."

Arnold Sundel had said, "There is one case under which she'll always be covered—if she's handicapped. Dr. Ores would have to write the company."

"I'll talk to her," I said. "I'm sure she'll agree with us." And she had but I didn't think Chris needed to know about that now.

I set down the laundry in different piles and Jenny came bombing into the room, climbed onto the bed, and kicked off her sneakers.

There was a beige sticker curling like a potato chip on top of Christine's schoolbooks. I picked it up and saw the bright green H on it. "What's this?" I asked.

She gave me a quick look and glanced over at Jenny. I nodded and kept still. Of course, it was a handicap sticker. No reason Jenny should know.

Chris sniffed the air. "What's that smell?" Jenny looked at her, sniffing too. Chris sniffed again, made a face, and turned to Jenny, narrowing her eyes, "Jennyyyy, it's your *feet.* God!"

Jenny protested. "It is not!"

"It is so. Would you please leave? Go wash your feet in the tub and get your sneakers out of here."

Jenny's eyes got that hurt look, knowing she'd made a mistake. She said, "My feet don't smell," and reached down to put her sneakers behind her back. She wasn't wearing socks and lifted a bare foot high in the air under Christine's nose, hoping to make her laugh. "See?"

Chris grimaced in horror and keeled over sideways onto the bed with a long "OOhhhhhhhhhh!" She held her nose. "My God, it *is* them. GET—out—of—here—now—Jennifer Saltonstall."

Jenny fled to the bathroom. I knew what she'd be thinking in there. How was she supposed to wash her feet? Chris and I waited until Jenny reappeared in the doorway.

"How do I wash my feet?" I tried not to laugh.

Chris looked shocked. "With soap and water, silly. Hot water."

"But where?"

"In the tub, I *told* you."

"Will you help me?"

"No."

"C'mon," Jenny pleaded, twisting in the doorway, trying to be cute. "I'm a helpless pipsqueak."

Chris and I burst out laughing. "Like *hell* you are," she said. "You're a hopeless case," and she went into a laughing/coughing spasm. Jenny was used to Chris coughing and didn't notice.

"Puh-leese, Chris."

She got the cough under control, breathing with quick catches to hold it back, and said, "You know, Jenny, you're supposed to wear *socks* with sneakers. Everybody's feet smell if they don't."

"I know, Mommy told me, but I *hate* socks. I can't stand the seams on my toes."

I turned away and put my hand over my mouth to stifle another laugh. In the morning, she put her shoes on again and again, trying to get the seams on her socks right.

Chris said in disbelief, "You can't stand the *seams on your toes?*" Jenny nodded. "Turn your socks inside out."

"I can still feel them."

Chris shook her head slowly. "God, are you a princess. Look, I like it when you sit in my room, Jen, but *never* with smelly feet. I'll run the hot water in the tub, but you have to wash your own feet. Understand?"

They trooped out and I looked at the sticker. It was for her car—a good idea. But Chris faced a new humiliation from that damn H sticker. Because she was pretty, she attracted attention. She didn't look handicapped. Most of the time she didn't even look sick and students glared at her and made snotty remarks when she parked in the handicapped spaces on the way to class. Disgusted, she said, "I feel like jamming the handicap sticker in their stupid faces and saying, 'What do *you* know?' "

We tried to laugh it off, but it was a no-win situation and she was deeply hurt.

"It's so unfair," she said, "I'm being punished because I don't look sick. I think I should get a medal, not a handicap sticker."

But living off campus and taking only two courses, she never connected at Manhattanville. She was despondent.

"Oh Mom, it isn't working out. I haven't made friends and I miss Claudia and I don't have a boyfriend. I'm alone again. It must be me. There must be something wrong with me."

"Chris, stop that. There's nothing wrong with you and it's not your fault. You're loving and funny and open, you're the best. But you're not a pushy show-off and you're not on campus enough. I'm so sorry it's not working."

Letter to Mark,

It's a good thing I'm too smart to use drugs, otherwise I would—a hell of a lot. I'm beginning to feel that pent-up-pissed-off-no-release-I'm-gonna-explode-soon-in-a-very-nasty-way feeling. Too many things have happened and I haven't been able to get rid of the hate and anger that's been building up. I really feel like a time bomb. Do you ever get that way? I mean last night I was so frustrated I kicked a brick wall over and over in rapid succession (I think I almost broke my toe). Very strange, I'm such a hot head. Me mum yells at me about it often. I think what I'd like to do is somehow find a job—(not just a part-time behind-the-counter job. A real one doing something that has to do with media, acting, music or performing of some kind. I'd still go to school but I think only part time. I'm not enjoying it at all cause I'm not meeting any people. Of course I don't really have any idea about how to go about getting a job, especially when I haven't finished college.)

I feel very disillusioned about everything. When I was at Rye, I never thought my life was going to lose it's direction so totally. I just don't know what to do. I wish I could go back and start over and change it, but that's just stupid thinking. I'm really at a loss and nothing seems to interest me.

If you have any advice let me know. And don't say pray about it cause that doesn't help me. All that goes wrong

in my life is chance or my own fault. So is everything that
goes right with it.

love Christine

She was also soon back in the hospital for three weeks and we
began to wonder if it was going to be possible to find a niche on
this sprawling country campus. Emerson had been so perfect.

That same spring of 1981, the house we rented on Cat Rock
Road was put on the market. We didn't want to buy it and looked
for another rental. The National Conference Center of the Epis-
copal Church spread over sixty-four acres in back-country Greenwich. Dover House, the country residence of the Episcopalian
bishop, was on the same property. He'd moved to the city. This
is what we rented. We moved in May while Chris was in the
hospital. Beautiful meadows and gentle hills surrounded us. The
gnarled and twisted remains of an old apple orchard still bore
fruit and behind a stand of pine trees were broad lawns, a tennis
court, and a playground.

To the south were a grove of lilac trees and a grape arbor
leading to more fields, and a strange spill of boulders that led to
a lake. Wildlife was everywhere, living undisturbed, and our nature walks became an everyday occurrence. The house boasted
front and back stairs, three floors, and three fireplaces. Chris and
Jenny's bedrooms were next to each other and Christine had a
sunroom all her own. Three walls of french louvered windows
with 164 panes of glass let the sun in all day long and all year long.
Our housekeeper quit.

Best of all, the walls were thick plaster and absorbed every
sound. Chris could play music at any hour of the night and no one
could hear. What a welcome release. We'd forgotten the peace
and privacy that plaster walls provide. Sheetrock just doesn't do
it. Chris told me, "Mom, Jenny was so cute last night. I was playing
a Stranglers album kind of loud and Jenny came in, dragging her

pillow, rubbing her eyes. I said, 'Oh sorry, Jen, want me to turn it down?' and that little squirt said, 'No, I want you to turn it up.' "

We all loved living there and explored every acre. I learned that land gives you a sense of permanence and substance. Always silent but always there and always changing, it fills some of the empty places in your soul.

23 · Summer for Gumbelina

There was something glorious about that summer of 1981. It was the fun Christine had. She was almost twenty and, though her health was running her life, we didn't see her slip closer to danger. She imposed her will and stayed out of the hospital all summer.

She was easily exhausted and reeled with sudden dizzy spells. She was breathless and cyanotic—her lips bluish from lack of oxygen. Small bleeds kept her anxious about physical exertion and there were odd fevers for no reason. But she focused on her friends and, except for an occasional mumbled barrage of four-letter epithets about how nothing ever went her way, she didn't complain.

On the contrary, she was always laughing, always changing and growing—full of surprises, throwing caution aside and dancing in her room. We moved her furniture around looking for a new arrangment. She needed room to dance wildly up and down—"pogoing," she called it. She changed her hair from fuschia to lavender and back to light blond, the color she'd been born with. Her moods changed too: one day buoyant, another day fatalistic and defiant, the next day buoyant again. What a comedienne. She made us laugh. Oh, how she tried, and those little victories she didn't believe in were everywhere.

She struggled to gain the weight she needed. One morning she said, "Mom, I really want to get to a hundred pounds this summer. I'll make a deal with you. I promise I won't be abusive when you come with Vivonex if you'll bring me a glass of it every hour, as cold as you can make it." She looked at me sweetly. "Would you do it?"

"Okay." But she still had to eat. "I have steaks defrosted in the icebox if you get hungry." It was often after midnight when her appetite suddenly appeared, and I threw a lot of steaks away, but I cooked a lot too, whatever the hour.

She was out every night, it seemed, at movies and parties. She made guest appearances with Bruce's band and went to rock concerts and clubs with Bruce and John or her stepsister, Lysa. The Ritz, CBGB, and Studio 54 in Manhattan and the Left Bank in Mount Vernon were her favorites. We took pictures, too, all over our beloved sixty-four acres. She enrolled at the Westchester Conservatory of Music to study voice in the fall.

And when she wasn't out with her friends, she was home taking care of her health. She slept till noon, did extra thumps, took antibiotics, and did her aerosol masks. In the early evening, she took short walks with me in the south meadow watching the rabbits poke their noses out of the woods. She told me pogoing on the dance floor was good for her lungs, that it made her cough more productive. Yet she couldn't walk to the lake anymore, it was too far. Instead she sat on a grassy knoll under the old maple in the meadow while Jenny chased butterflies with a net, her little legs going as fast as a roadrunner. Chris even developed a relationship with Jimmy. She'd never given up on him and, now that he was at college, he relaxed about her and even liked her. She brought out the best in him, as she seemed to do with everyone.

One night in August, Lysa picked her up on the way to the Left Bank to see a hot new band from Georgia called Pylon. Chris came down the stairs in a Betsey Johnson black jersey dress with long sleeves and a flounce skirt. She had black tights and pink ankle socks over the tights. Anyone else would have been hot— not Chris. She was always cold. Her blond hair was back-combed into peaks and the last of the purple Crazy Color that remained on the tips looked like a pink halo. I knew she was no angel. Her small gold dagger earrings were flashing in the light.

Lysa could hardly keep up with her that night. Chris danced and jumped with the band and the lead singer, a girl, pogoed in unison with her. When Chris noticed the singer following her, they both broke off and smiled at each other.

After that Chris and Lysa danced every dance and Lysa kept forgetting there was anything different about Chris until the music stopped and she fled to the dark corners of the room coughing and gasping.

After one number, Chris couldn't leave the dance floor. She collapsed over the speaker, coughing to Lysa, "Could you get me a Coke?"

"Sure." Lysa ran and got a Coke and Chris downed it in ten seconds. She stood, drawing in rapid, even breaths, and Lisa heard the ice rattling in the glass. She looked. Christine's hands were trembling.

"Oh please, don't look at my *hands.*"

Lysa blinked and hugged her lightly. "Don't be silly, everyone shakes after pogoing. God, it's heart-attack time."

But Chris hadn't cared about that, not then. She meant her funny fingers. She hated the yucky clubbing at the ends.

At Phebe's party before school began, Chris sang with the band. Bruce said, "Hey guys, Chris is singing. Let's pretend she's a rock star and you're the roadies. We'll surround her and muscle everyone out of the way when she comes in."

John said, "What do you mean pretend? She is a star." And that night she made a grand entrance to the cheers and whistles of her friends.

And then there was her Adam Ant caper. She and Bruce had tickets to the Adam Ant concert at Pier 47 on the Hudson River. She wore Adam Ant clothes and so did Bruce. She had an antique soldier's uniform from a thrift shop, a brown velvet jacket with tails and gold epaulets, and pirate boots. Her hair was very purple again and she had tiny braids along her forehead. When I expressed amusement, she said, "Dressing like the star is a way of saying you're a fan, Mom. Bruce is doing it too. I have a letter I'm going to try to get to Adam Ant."

At the pier, they waited in line all day, ate hotdogs, drank beer, and sat in the sun. A couple of guys behind the fence looked like crew members and she took her letter out to give to one of them. But it wasn't a crew member, it was Merrick—one of the band. What good luck. As he took the letter through the fence, a couple of girls watched and one asked, "Do you *know* him?" Chris said, "Nope."

When dark clouds rolled in, vendors appeared like magic selling plastic ponchos. Bruce bought one, but Chris had faith in the day. When the gates opened, they crashed down to the front together. The opening act was an all-girl do-wop group called Schoolgirl and the fans kept yelling, "Get off!" and "Nexxxtt!"

Chris and Bruce looked at each other and she said, "Suppose that was us up there." Bruce shrugged.

"Hey, no one said it was easy. You just keep playing."

And then as an incredible pirate ship sailed into view, with Adam Ant standing on the bow, lightning flashed and the skies opened up. The fans screamed their approval and love as Adam Ant played, sang, and pogoed in the rain, his rings flashing. The rain lightened to a drizzle, but too late—the purple in Christine's hair ran and pink rivulets streamed down her face and throat onto her white blouse. Bruce's poncho ripped, so he was as wet as she was, but they stayed till the end.

The next night, she went back alone for the second concert. People in the audience were friendly so she didn't feel too lonely. Afterward, she went to Studio 54 by herself and at the door saw one of Adam Ant's band. He struck up a conversation with her and she pretended she didn't know who he was and got in with him. They talked a little and then she sat down at a table next to a young man with bleached white hair. She recognized Billy Idol. His famous song "White Wedding" was being played on New Wave stations, but most people didn't know him yet. They watched the scene, commenting to each other. She had a good time that night, but when she told me about it the next day, I heard a wistfulness in her voice. She wanted so much to be part of the music world and that night she touched the edge of her dream. Bruce was envious when he heard what she'd done.

Ten days later, she got a thank-you postcard from Adam Ant, on tour in Hawaii.

With the deepening of summer, her friends talked about going back to school and she comforted herself with her new weight and new hope. Maybe she could make it after all. We drove into Greenwich Village and walked around the campus of N.Y.U., such as it was. She wanted to study drama, but when we applied, we learned it was only for graduate students. She was disappointed. She'd been fantasizing about an apartment in New York. She would have loved N.Y.U.

But she bounced back. After all, she hadn't been in the hospital since May. She was a hundred pounds. All she needed now was someone to love.

Someone appeared, but not the right one. We had a dinner party for her twentieth birthday, and among the guests was my youngest sister, Francie, and her "engaged to be engaged" fiancé, Steven. During the party I noticed that wherever Chris was, Steven was, and Francie and he were the last to leave. The next week, he called her and wanted to come over and show Chris some new lyrics to a song he was writing. She discouraged him. Then he started writing and sending his work. Song after song arrived. She didn't respond but then he began to arrive unannounced. Chris was mortified and realized that Steven had fallen in love with her. She finally discouraged him and discussed the problem with Francie, who understood Chris hadn't done anything but was hurt just the same. Chris said over and over, "I love Francie, why did it have to be her boyfriend?"

On a hot Saturday night before Labor Day, I sat on her bed watching her finish her makeup. She opened a little vial of tiny silver stars and tossed them in her hair.

"Ooooo, those are neat." I went for a closer look. "Don't they fall out though?"

"When I dance, they tend to fly off, but a few stay in." She and Bruce were going to see *The Empire Strikes Back* for the fourth time and then to the Left Bank to see a group called the Rockats. They stopped at a cluster of convenience stores Chris used to call "robot vomit," saying a giant steam shovel had a bad day and threw up a pile of junk. There was a discount beer distributor, a Carvel, a gas station, and a Cumberland Farms grocery store.

They went in together, wandering the aisles looking for inspir-

ing things to eat, and were about to leave when Bruce spotted a
copy of *Swank* magazine on the display rack behind the cash
register, where he couldn't thumb through it. Written across the
cover in yellow was "EXCLUSIVE! Tatum O'Neal—Nude—12
years old."

Bruce was shocked. He grabbed Christine's sleeve and pulled
her away from the checkout counter back behind the pretzel and
Fritos rack. "Chris, I've just got to have that copy of *Swank*! Did
you see it?"

"No, what?"

"*Swank* magazine has nude pictures of Tatum O'Neal at age
twelve. We've just got to see that."

"What do you mean *we*? You mean *you* do. I don't." Then she
laughed and said, "There's nothing to see at age twelve anyway.
Why don't you just get it?"

"Who me? Chris, you know me. C'mon, I can't. I'm a wimp
and it's too embarrassing. Would you?"

She looked him up and down, amazed and amused.
"Cheeky—it's too embarrassing for you, but it's okay for me."

He implored, "C'mon, do it for me. Next week's my birthday."
Christine shifted her weight to one hip, putting her hands in her
pockets and tilting her head back. She studied him.

"You are *not* a wimp. But you *are* chicken." Bruce looked at
her, all wide-eyed innocence. How could she refuse a friend on
his birthday? "OOhhhh, all right," she said, "I'll do it, but I'm
going to have to be someone else."

"What do you mean?" Bruce asked, but she was already walking back to the cash register.

She waited until the customer who was paying had left the
store, then she walked casually to the register, adopted a cheery
English accent, and said to the man slouching behind the counter,
"Could I have a pack of Kents please?" Bruce hung back. The
man looked up at Chris, noticing her for the first time. She went
on, getting up her courage, making her hesitations sound natural.

"Uhhhh, I'd also like a *TV Guide*. Thank you, one of those
packs of hairpins—yes, those, mmmm, oh, some matches of
course, and a copy of *Swank* please."

The man took the items from the display behind him and rang them up. Chris stood looking absently around the store, casting her eyes in Bruce's direction with a "How'm-I-doing" look. The man put everything in a thin brown bag.

Bruce headed for the door, still acting as if he didn't know her. But Chris didn't move. She picked up the bag and faced him, pulled out the copy of *Swank* with a flourish, handed it to him, and said, still using her accent, "There you are, luv', is that what you wanted? Happy Birthday."

Bruce felt the man's eyes on him. Wishing the floor would swallow him up he said quickly, "Oh, you shouldn't have," and rushed out of the store.

Chris followed at a leisurely pace, turning around at the door to say "Cheerio" to the man.

After the movie, they ambled into the Left Bank at the end of the Rockats' first set. At one o'clock the band played again. The Left Bank is a small club with a three-foot stage and the bands are accessible. In the middle of dancing with Bruce, Chris catapulted herself onto the stage and kissed Smutty, the bass player. Cheers erupted as she danced breathlessly back off the stage to Bruce, who took it in stride. He leaned into Chris and said, "Cheeky move . . ."

"Mmmmmmm, market research . . ." She laughed and kissed him too.

That night they were quiet when they drove home. Chris sensed something and wondered if Bruce wanted to be more than friends, after all this time. And Bruce wondered if Chris knew how he felt. He wished he had the courage to tell her then, but he didn't, and Chris knew he was dating another girl, so she said nothing.

But with all her merriment, bravely going out to rock clubs, overcoming the awkward moments, her happiness was fragile. One day of missing contact with her friends and she seemed to lose her footing and fall into depression and silence. She wasn't as self-reliant. I thought it was because she was confused about what to do in the fall. And then I made a mistake.

I'd met a woman psychologist in town. I suggested to Chris

that perhaps counseling would help her find the way. We made some appointments. After the first one, Chris was depressed, but didn't comment as to why. She went out with John and Drea instead.

The afternoon of her second session, I found her crying in her room afterward. When I asked what was the matter, she was tight-lipped and mumbled, "Nothing I can't handle."

The third appointment produced the same result but the tears and solitude lasted longer. I pressed her this time. Something was wrong and I finally came right out and asked her, "What's going on in your sessions?"

"Oh, she's trying to get me to face reality."

"But you *do* face reality. What does she mean?"

"I don't know."

Chris had her own reality. Surely the psychologist understood this. I asked, "Do you mind if I go and talk to her?"

"Okay." So I did. The psychologist seemed to make sense, but I wasn't the patient fighting for my life. She must not have made sense to Christine.

The next time, Chris came home black and hopeless again and said, "I'm not going back to see her again."

"I think you're right. I was hoping she'd be helpful." Chris didn't answer and I felt uneasy. What had gone wrong?

Labor Day Weekend she went to the Cape to visit her dad for two weeks. She was proud to be driving up all by herself and happy about her hundred pounds of weight and I helped her pack her car with Vivonex, Cotazyme, antibiotics, and the machines for her aerosol masks.

Four days later she called to say she was coming home. She and her dad weren't getting along and she'd forgotten her blender to make the Vivonex.

I said, "Your father will get you another blender, dear. Don't waste a day."

"He won't. He's mixing it up by shaking. He's mad at me and says I'm old enough to remember these things."

I didn't know what to say. Maybe their relationship was different now that she was a woman. Parents don't always have logical

reactions to cystic fibrosis, and he was right. She was old enough
to take care of herself.

"You'll have to work this out, dear. I don't think leaving is the
answer."

"I know. If I lose the weight I gained, I don't know what I'll
do." She stayed and lost the weight. She scrawled across a page
in her journal:

> *the walls are closing in*
> *just, just, I just really do*
> *loss*
> *all you ever think about*
> *weight loss—fudge*
>
> *fits of depression*
> *pits of despair*
>
> *just took me so long to get there.*
>
> *and now, it's wasting away*
> *92 pounds down.*

But Jerry had observed a change. She wasn't taking her pills
or doing her aerosol masks. What troubled him more was that
when he asked her, "Chris, did you do your mask?" she'd say yes.
Then he'd find it on the sink by the pump, still full of the antibiotics. She'd never done that before. But he didn't confront her, so
he didn't know why. Nor did he discuss any of this with me. It
wasn't his way.

24 · *Shadows on the Screen*

There was no glory in the fall. Doors were closing every-where. No sooner had she started her voice and piano lessons at the Conservatory than she was back in the hospital on September 15th. Only for two weeks she hoped, but she was there a month. She asked for oxygen and used it every day. I noticed how she always checked to see where the oxygen mask was, making sure she could reach it.

Then she lost her voice and she just fell apart. The nurses had no idea what singing meant to her and why she took it so hard. They were annoyed with her sudden bursts of temper, her long silences, and her infuriating eating habits. She'd order large meals and then eat nothing on the tray. She wasn't perverse. But she was trying so hard that when she filled out the next day's menus, she circled everything, vowing to eat. Then she couldn't.

But Dr. Ores understood. She met the residents and nurses at Harkness to explain the disease.

"Look, this young lady knows that nothing is going to save her. And she doesn't know how to deal with it, so she deals with the little things that she *can* control; like how many ice cubes are in her Vivonex, the kind of bread on her sandwich, how her pillows are arranged, when she wants her thumps, what time you wake her up, how much tape you put on her IV. She needs *something* to go her way. She needs your attention and patience. I assure you she won't abuse it."

And her talks with the nurses made all the difference. They were kinder, more attentive, not peevish with Chris even if *she* was with them. Soon she relaxed and stopped fighting them. She won their hearts.

It was a gentle Christine who came home in mid-October. Not beaten, but less feisty. She left her anger on the doorstep and went back to her voice teacher. She seemed to be absorbing life, music, books, television, films, everything the media could bring her at a faster rate. She read *Dune*. She bought a used electric guitar and took lessons. And when she wasn't practicing or writing songs she followed me around the house like a wound-up chatterbox. When her singing voice returned, she was hoping to sing with Bruce and his new band, The Life of Riley. It was becoming more and more important to her.

She said to me one day when we were driving to pick Jenny up from school, "Mom, what'll I do if my voice doesn't come back?"

"I'm sure it will dear. Dr. Ores said be patient."

"How can I be patient? You know, even though it seems like I'm busy, it isn't enough. Listening to music, reading, watching movies. I'm just a spectator. I'm not living. I'm watching other people live. I don't want to watch. I want to *do*. I have something to say."

I bit my lip. Those were the options that were disappearing. The doing things. She sighed and Jenny came running out the school door.

On my birthday she gave me a plain white sweatshirt and said, "I was going to have a message printed on this at one of those shops on Broadway, but you know, the stupid hospital."

"Oh, what message?" She knew I'd ask and she gave me a droll look and pulled a folded, dog-earred paper out of her blazer pocket. I opened it and read, I'M NOT ALWAYS WONDERFUL. I laughed and hugged her.

She taught me about rock 'n' roll or New Wave, as she called it, in all its forms: reggae, ska, punk, and others. She played records from groups in New Zealand, Australia, Jamaica, Los Angeles, England, and Scotland. There was a whole world I knew nothing about. In the beginning I had to make an effort, but it was worth it. These were things she'd be sharing with her friends, not her mother. Her illness was stealing from her life and giving to mine. But guilt was foolish now. She needed to give to someone. I was the lucky one.

When she walked the floor of her sunroom at night, brushing her hair back, gesturing and bobbing up and down in little bursts of energy, I couldn't take my eyes off her. Sometimes she moved cautiously, as if she were measuring the amount of energy she could use, and she was always a little breathless, like air was escaping somewhere, but night was her good time.

"New Wave isn't pretty, Mom, but new classical music isn't either." She twisted a paper clip out of shape pensively. "You know that minimalist composer, Phillip Glass, the one Jimmy liked who wrote 'Einstein on the Beach,' well, New Wave is minimal too—and dissonant."

She got up and picked out a record album. "Like the Stranglers. It's bare bones rock. Here, I'll play you the second cut, 'Threatened.' It's a good example. There's always a wrong note sounding but it's on purpose . . . like a bug in your ear." I listened and liked it.

"Go on," I said.

"Well, like the B-52s and the Sex Pistols. They don't want to sound nice. They want to sound terrible like a bunch of garbage-mouth boys playing their guitars too loud. They'd lose their reason for being if they got good." I smiled and shook my head.

"I should have known."

"The point is to get people riled up. They aren't commercial. They hate the Top 40. That would be selling out."

"You don't think they just say that because they aren't there yet?" I loved it when she started pacing.

She said, "Maybe some, but not most. The assumption is they won't be successful so to get success would be offensive."

"I wonder if some of the groups have talent." She was taken aback.

"Talent. Of course! I admit it's easy to pass lack of talent off as intentional. You have to know the difference. But it can be charming too. Part of the fun of the B-52s is how inept they sound musically, but you have to be very good to sound so inept. When they're bad, they're better. Do you get it?"

"Yes."

"Here, listen to this Adam Ant."

I listened to Adam Ant shrieking, "Qua, qua, qua diddly qua qua."

"I like the Stranglers and the B-52s better. Why is he screaming at the top of his lungs?" I asked.

"It's energy. He doesn't want to sound boring."

I laughed. "Well, I can't get used to it. I think I like this music because I like you."

"Nah, you're just learning. You known how grown-ups are. They don't give it a chance. They never like what they don't know about."

"I wouldn't say never."

She gave me three tapes to listen to in the car, Devo, Siouxsie and the Banshees, and U2. I still thought it was her I loved more than the music and I told her. But she said I concentrated more when I was listening with her. I handed the tapes back the next day. She was listening to a raucous song called "Bad Boys Get Spanked" by Chrissie Hynde and she sat me down to listen.

"Look, anything that's good isn't easy. Like James Joyce. He isn't easy but what a great writer. Jackson Pollock's dribble painting isn't easy either. God, it looks like a joke, but he was a serious artist." She paused again, gathering her thoughts like a young professor. "I think man is at his best when he's making music, even if it sounds like an awful racket, as Jim calls it. It's a new sound, and some of them are serious artists. You should listen to Peter Gabriel." And she gave me a tape that said Genesis.

Bruce, whose whole life was music, said Chris knew more about what was going on, the new groups, the new sounds, than anyone he knew. She pushed on, ahead of the rest, riding the wave, with nothing to distract her, and I've never stopped listening to her music. To this day. I must be the only middle-aged mother in Greenwich who calls WLIR Radio on Thursdays to vote for "screamer of the week."

When Cindy and Ted and Lysa came for Thanksgiving that year, we laughed through our turkey dinner. Chris knew how to get us all going, turning ideas upside down and inside out, engaging in naughty repartee with Jim but never giving up her innocence. We all went up to my studio and took pictures, filling six contact sheets. We were very silly and Chris was never more beautiful. How she loved being the center of attention.

That night, I lay awake long after the house was quiet praying this would last. Our roles had changed during the summer, but Chris never saw it. When she was little, I taught her to be strong and now I was learning from her. I had everything yet I couldn't give life the love she did. As her illness dragged her down, she taught me and I rose to meet her.

Christine said once she'd never spend Christmas in the hospital, but another viral pneumonia put her there on December 9th. IVs were started, not to treat the viral pneumonia, but to hold back the bacterial pneumonias while the other one ran its course. She couldn't breathe. Terrible fevers came, sapping her strength, leaving her limp and delirious. Ten days passed with no improvement and Celia was alarmed. Chris was on a fever seesaw, her body out of control, her system fighting the infection with fever.

When they took new X rays, I asked to see them, but they were mysterious. Gray blotches speckled the negative image of her lungs like craters on the surface of the moon. Dr. Ores called them cavities. They didn't look like much, just shadows. But at last I understood. There was a war going on and the fighting was getting desperate. Her lungs were the arena, abnormal secretions were the weakness, bacterial infections were the enemy, and antibiotics were the weapons. But the bacteria were cunning, mutating to become stronger versions to resist the antibiotics. We'd treat one infection and this would leave the field open to three more that were waiting to begin a new campaign of destruction—carving those awful cavities out of her lungs. They were big trouble. The bacteria could kill her as the infections tunneled through her lungs, until the lungs collapsed or until the spreading infections ruptured a blood vessel. They couldn't find antibiotics fast enough to destroy all the bacteria competing for healthy lung tissue and feeding on it. I'd explained it many times to people who'd never heard of cystic fibrosis, but, seeing the shadows on the screen, I understood as I never had before.

Dr. Ores was grim and there were tears in her eyes when she said, "I think Christine should be home for Christmas, but you'll have to have oxygen upstairs and down. It may be difficult for the family."

I was leaden inside. "Difficult? For us? It'll be worse for Christine." Celia agreed.

The next day I went to Harkness and brought a live Christmas tree I'd found in a pot at a nursery. While we decorated, I noticed she wasn't struggling to breathe.

"You don't have a fever today?"

"It broke last night. I woke up wet and shivering and it hasn't come back. It will, though."

She climbed back onto the bed slowly and put the light-blue oxygen tubing around her head, delicate nose prongs directing oxygen into each nostril. Moving someone's stethoscope off the end of the bed I sat down. "Whose is this?"

"A resident left it so I could listen to my lungs."

"What do you hear?"

"Noise—like radio static." She clicked through the TV channels before switching it off. She dropped her head forward and covered her eyes with her free hand. "Oh Mom, it's Christmas and here I am." I wondered if I should have brought the tree, and she dropped her hand, staring at the wall.

"I know," I said, "we never wanted this to happen." I picked up her hand gingerly. It was still puffy and swollen from yesterday's IV. The back was purple and black and yellow. I could see the needle puncture mark and when I touched the purple edema gently, my finger left a dent in her skin.

"It isn't fair," I said finally.

"That, and *why*, why me? That's all I think about," she said.

I nodded. "So do I and there's never any answer, is there?"

We were quiet again. The oxygen unit bubbled over the hiss of the humidifier. The dripping IV chamber made no sound at all. Chris shifted her position and the rustling sheets sounded like sails luffing in light air. I heard the steady footsteps of a nurse go down the carpeted hall.

"You know what Andy said once?" she asked.

"What?"

"It was the night we said good-bye at the Red Barn before he went to Hobart. We were talking and I asked him the same thing. 'Why me?' I wasn't complaining, it was just a rhetorical question." She wasn't talking in quick little spurts, but easily and quietly with no struggle. The oxygen helped. She went on.

"He said, 'I think God chose you, Christine, because you're strong. I think he knew you'd pass the test.' And I asked him what test, and he said, 'He knew you'd still know how to live and how to laugh, in spite of everything. Sometimes I feel sorry for myself over nothing. My folks don't understand me, or my girl gets mad or I blow it at the hockey game—you know, small stuff that gets me down. But you, you've really got a reason and you don't let it get you.' I'll never forget him telling me that. Sometimes I believe it."

She fiddled with the sheet, smoothing the creases. She seemed upset and said, "But everytime I get back up, I get knocked down. It's hard to see anything but failure."

"Oh, Andy was right, Chris. You aren't failing. You've been defying the doctors for years, since you were eleven." She kept her eyes down and nodded. God, what a paltry consolation. She didn't want to be defying doctors, outwitting fate. I wouldn't either. Who wants to be a goddamn heroine? All she wanted was her health—a chance to live—a long, normal life—predictable, ordinary, an everyday treasure.

She touched her lips, patting them carefully, and said, "Drat! I knew it. I feel them coming. Cold sores!"

I was about to ask what she felt, thinking she wanted to change the subject, when she said, "Sometimes I curse God for making me sick, but, other times, I'm on my knees thanking him for giving me so much time." I didn't say anything. "It's getting harder to fight back though, Mom. I'm so *tired* all the time. I don't know how much longer I can go on." She said it so simply, as if she was giving a weather forecast. "What if I reach the point where my life isn't worth fighting for anymore?" That she even raised the thought made me wonder if she was already there. Her voice was steady, but mine wavered.

"Life . . . is worth living, Chris, even just to observe, and watch nature, and know you're loved." She looked at the IV in her wrist, patting down the edge of the curling tape. Her voice was soft.

"I can't appreciate it when I can't breathe. When I have these fevers, I melt away like the witch in *The Wizard of Oz*. I don't even have the strength to stand up and go to the bathroom."

I felt like a naive fool. "I'm sorry, Chris . . . I can't know what it's like for you. I've tried to put myself in your shoes, so many times, and I can't. I'm stupid and sentimental but I love you very much." When she looked over at me, she wasn't smiling, but her eyes were warm and forgave me.

"You're not stupid," she said, "you're just not sick." She closed her eyes and we both stopped talking. I held her hand but it wasn't enough. It never was.

I brought her home on Christmas Eve. The oxygen tanks were ready, a large tank for the bedroom, a portable unit for downstairs. Jenny came running out the back door and hugged her sister.

"Hi Chris, I missed you so much. Are you feeling okay?"

"Yes, much better."

"I need you to help me wrap my Christmas presents." Chris smiled, remembering the fun they'd had last Christmas, and Jenny went on, "and we've been waiting for you, to trim the tree." Jenny pulled her in to see the pristine Scotch pine resting in its stand.

"I'm so glad you waited for me, Jen." When Jim carried Chris upstairs to her sunroom, Jenny came over to me, her eyes enormous and troubled.

"Mommy, is Chris all right? Why is Jim carrying her?"

"She still has pneumonia, Jenny. She's going back into the hospital in a few days for more medicine. It's a very bad pneumonia . . . the worst she's ever had."

Jenny looked up the stairs. "Can I go in her room?"

"Of course. Chris will love it."

"Oh good." Her face relaxed. "We can wrap presents in her room." She started up the stairs. "But Mommy, you can't come in, okay?"

When Jim came down, there were tears in his eyes and he hugged me a long time—very tight. We made trips to the wood-pile, bringing in logs for all the fireplaces. I brought some up to Christine's sunroom and we lit a fire. She said a burning fire was like a heartbeat in her room. Later in the afternoon, I moved the fire screen aside and we roasted marshmallows while Chris sat on the sofa wrapped in her comforter. She wasn't using oxygen.

Jenny ate her marshmallows and then she ate mine and said, "I'm going to roast some for you, Chris." We watched her inciner-ate them. Chris snuggled deeper into the corner of the sofa.

"I'm so glad I'm home."

"Me too," Jenny said. "Don't you hope it snows?"

"Oh, yes."

We sat in silence watching Jenny play with the fire, poking it with her marshmallow stick till the sparks flew. Jim came in with some more logs and sat down to smoke his pipe. Chris asked, "Can you blow smoke rings with a pipe?" Jim gave a wise nod and started releasing smoke rings like Gandolf in *The Hobbit*. He loved being the center of our magic circle.

We whiled away the afternoon, watching the fire glow and the day fade, making it last. I wanted her life to be worth it. A few snowflakes fell—not even enough to dust the ground, just enough to tease and get our hopes up. Chris called her father and asked him to spend Christmas Day with us. She was too sick to travel to the city.

She was home for three days and I hardly took my eyes off her. I watched for signs of her failing and pondered her fragile beauty, memorizing the sound of her voice and her face. She was too pretty to be so sick. There was no melodrama, no pain, no blood, just weakening, slipping away and sleeping, fainting with fever, and trying to breathe. When her cough was violent, her lips turned blue. She never wanted to be alone and she never was.

On Christmas Eve Jim carried her downstairs, and she wrapped herself in her comforter again.

When Cindy and Ted came over to help trim the tree, Chris was asleep again. I felt her cheek and she was burning up—her fever spiking. The fevers were so violent. We'd devised a Tylenol blitz plan, two Tylenols every two hours. But still the fever crowded in over the Tylenol and she slumped over the arm of the living room sofa, almost hidden under her comforter. I woke her to give her two more and a salt pill. She didn't seem to know where she was, shivered, and without a word succumbed to the fever again. Jenny was busy trimming and didn't see this, but I was frightened and went into the kitchen to call Celia.

"Celia, is it possible Chris is too sick to be home? I'm afraid something terrible will happen." There was a long pause.

She inquired gently, "Is it too much for you to have her home?"

"Of course not. I just need to know what to do." How could she ask?

She spoke so slowly. "There's nothing to do. She should stay home and enjoy these three days with all of you. When she comes back in on Monday, she won't be home again."

I was shocked and said, my voice low, "Are you sure? Is it that bad?" I'd just called to say how bad it was, but still it couldn't be that bad. I had to strain to hear her answer.

"Yes. She cannot get through this pneumonia with her lungs." I couldn't believe it. Celia said she'd be home all weekend if I needed her.

When Chris woke she watched us trim the tree and we played *Amahl.* It was skipping in two places now.

On Christmas Day her fever was down. Jenny's father picked her up at eleven, so she missed Christmas dinner. Cindy and Ted and Lysa came, and my sister Vanessa arrived with Jerry from the city. Jim's children had never met Jerry and to them he was a star. He brought Chris an electric guitar and amplifier and he played some songs after he hooked it up. He didn't say much at first, but no one let him stay quiet for long. There were questions about "Saturday Night Live," and "The Muppet Show" and "Seasame Street." He did his many voices on request, Chris added her own, and they laughed and winked as if they shared some special magic. They were quite a pair. The warmth of his visit and his love for Chris touched us all and pushed aside the melancholy shadow.

Back in the hospital I feared for her life. With the lift of Christmas gone, her strength ebbed still further. She didn't leave her hospital bed and she seemed like a thin white shell, barely alive, breathing in the shallows. I talked to Celia.

"I think maybe she's given up, Celia. I don't blame her. She's too exhausted to go on."

"Oh no she hasn't. She's putting up the battle of her life. You just can't see it. She's stopped sliding and she's holding on. If she can keep on she may turn it around."

"But you said . . ."

"I know . . . I should have known better. This girl won't give up. She wants to live." And two weeks later, on January 14th, Chris came home.

25 ⋆ Pressure Point

When Christine returned home after Christmas, we lost control over the illness. The winning combination of Chris and Celia was not enough. Like some stealthy probing thing with tentacles clutching, the disease extended into parts of her life that before had been free.

She said, "Mom, I have such a heavy feeling in my chest—pushing me down. There's something tightening, like a rubber band around my lungs, and this full feeling, like I've drunk too much beer." She couldn't get up the stairs without stopping to rest and breathe several times.

One night, she came into my room with a pad. She'd written the word *disease*. Then she wrote it again, *dis-ease,* and said, "Mom, I never thought about this word, but I feel just this way. There is no 'ease' in my life anymore. I'm living in a state of dis-ease."

Familiar symptoms, nuisance factors before, became relentless ordeals, squeezing the strength out of her and draining her emotional reserves, crowding out the joy she always found in life. She went from having no appetite, but knowing how to make herself eat, to having continuous nausea, and now she couldn't force herself to eat.

She felt useless and worthless and said, "I think I should get a job. I need something to connect with." So we looked into it. I'd seen a help wanted sign at the Greenwich Cinema and hesitantly suggested she apply. "It isn't much, Mom, but there's not a lot I can do and I can't work full time. I'll feel more useful if I'm working and maybe I'll meet someone. Do you think they'd hire me with this hair?"

"Sure. It looks nice on you." And they did. She worked three nights a week, taking tickets and selling popcorn. She was a long way from her dreams, but the customers enjoyed her purple hair and she liked talking with the ushers after the movie started. She wasn't well enough to drive, park, and walk to the theater on cold February nights, so I dropped her off and picked her up. When I did, and she waved good-bye to someone through the glass doors and walked to the car alone, I understood why she didn't say much about her job. She was embarrassed. I wanted to say, "Chris, everyone knows this isn't your life's work—it's just a way station," but a deeper instinct told me to keep still.

Things weren't going well. She had been released from her Christmastime admission after six weeks, but she was home only five weeks before returning to Harkness on February 24th with bad bleeding. She was eighty-nine pounds. All of her symptoms were worsening. Overpowering her. She railed, "Mom, I've lost eleven pounds. Do you know how much that is? You know what a pound of butter looks like? Picture eleven of them."

I looked at her. "I never thought of it that way."

"I know. No one does but me." And because she couldn't eat, they fed her. Under anesthesia, they opened up her arm again and reinserted the broviac catheter so that the quarts of liquid nutrition could be pumped in.

I met with Dr. Ores and she said, "Christine can go home in a few days, but I'd like to leave the broviac catheter in her arm. Do you think you can learn how to do it at home?"

"Hyperalimentation at home? Oh, Celia, Chris will hate that."

"I know," she said slowly, "but she can't go on without it. Her weight is critically low. She needs something besides medicine to fight. She needs energy and she'll only get that from food."

Christine was furious. She fought Dr. Ores on this, a desperate fight.

"I'll eat!" she argued. "I'll drink Vivonex all day. I'll force myself! Don't leave this *thing* in my arm. I won't have it!" She pleaded, she argued, she cried—and as days went by she gave Dr. Ores nothing but icy silence.

It wasn't just that the catheter would be taped to the inside of her arm, and the dressing changed every other day, but she was going to be connected to a machine every night—a blue computer the size of a shoebox called a Cutter pump—while the nutrition ran into her arm.

I tried to reason with her but reason had nothing to do with it. She was fighting for her independence, struggling to get free of the machine that would pin her down. I talked quietly with her one afternoon in the hospital. She was full of spunk. There were pink highlights in her hair and some rouge on her cheeks. Her lunch tray was untouched and I slid it out of the way and sat down, kissing her cheek.

"Hi, dear, how's everything?"

"Okay."

"Have you seen Dr. Ores today?"

She scowled and turned away. "Yes."

"What's the matter?"

"You know," she muttered.

I sat and tried to think of what to say. "Did you have an argument with her?"

"Oh, not exactly, but I'm not going home with this *thing* in my arm."

"Did you tell Dr. Ores that?"

"Not in those exact words."

I understood. That was what she had wanted to say. I went on. "Chris, when you feel nauseous, you *can't* eat. No one could. You've been trying for weeks. It isn't working."

She pulled herself up and looked at me in anger. Her lips knit together, turning down the way they did when she was a little girl. She grabbed a pillow, started to cough, and buried her face. Then she slumped back and threw the pillow to the floor. "Oh Mom, why can't I ever win?"

I didn't know what to say. I felt the same way.

"You know, Mom, I always used to feel like I was one of the

lucky ones. I mean, lucky to be as normal as I am. But now"—she stopped for a split second—"but now, I feel like them, like Kendall, and Sarah and Cory. They weren't lucky and they gave up, and they're all dead, just dead."

I didn't like the way she said it, flat and practical, like she was trying to get used to it. I waited.

"Dr. Ores told me that Kendall died because she gave up. I haven't given up, but I . . . I don't feel special anymore. I'm not one of the lucky ones." I moved quickly to the head of the bed above her, sat, and leaned against her back lightly. She extended her arms in front of her like a sleepwalker. "Look at my hands. They tremble all the time. What is it?" I'd noticed it too.

"Have you asked Dr. Ores?" She shook her head and leaned back against me.

"I'm so ashamed of my body. It's so thin and misshapen. How is anyone ever going to love me?"

This I could answer. "You'll be loved, and you *are* loved, because you're a lovable girl. I've drawn the human figure in life class and a lot of people would give anything to be slim and graceful like you."

"But men like curves and I don't have any."

"You will again. I know you hate the catheter, but it may help you to get back your curves." She looked up at me in annoyance. "No one will even see the catheter, Chris, it's so small and on the inside of your arm."

"But how can I have any life of my own—tethered to this machine? What if I want to spend the night out?"

"Well, just skip it for a night. You'll run your life, not the machine."

She sat thinking and I waited.

"If I did, you wouldn't give me a hard time?"

I shook my head. I could feel her exhaustion. We were both so broken. "You're already having a hard time, Chris. I'm on your side, remember?" Her words hurt. It had been a while since I had given her a hard time about anything.

She must have read my thoughts. She said sweetly, "I know, Mom, it's just that I feel like you and Dr. Ores are ganging up on me." She relaxed for the first time and the tightness across her eyes and forehead disappeared as she leaned back and turned up the sound on "General Hospital."

Accepting the catheter was a turning point for Christine.

In March, she wrote a letter to Jamie, her friend from Rye Country Day, but she never mailed it.

> *As for me, well, it's too depressing to go into without sounding like a Greek tragedy. In a nutshell, I just haven't been well lately. It seems everytime I get back on my feet, I'm knocked back down quicker than before. I've been in the hospital 3 times since this fall (I just got out 2 days ago).*
>
> *Over Christmas it was the worst, and I just wasn't sure I'd manage thru it. I haven't given up yet, but at times I do wish it would just end. I'm so tired of struggling and suffering.*
>
> *It's not that I want to die. I just don't want to live like this. The last 6 months I've been doing nothing. I haven't been able to do anything.*
>
> *Since I'm not going to school (I'm applying to NYU in the fall) I have no friends to hang around with.*
>
> *To top it off (this sounds like a comedy routine on Saturday Night Live), my pet rabbit Godzilla and my dear cat I.V. of eight years died while I was in the hospital. I.V. had feline leukemia and had to be put to sleep. I never got to hug and kiss her good-bye. My Mom was so upset she was afraid to tell me until I got home.*
>
> *I've seen a psychiatrist, but she can't really help me. I'm beginning to feel like Job. Everynight I pray and I know people are praying for me. But it hasn't seemed to help.*
>
> *Why I don't know.*
>
> *Oh well, I don't want to dump nothing but miserables on you, so . . . hmmm, having a little trouble thinking of something good.*
>
> *Well, if I can stay healthier and out of the hospital, just*

a little more, things will brighten up for sure. I think what
I really need is to fall in love. It's always the cure-all.

Take care and love, Christine

I brought Chris home on March 6th with all the hyperalimentation stuff and a feeling of dread that I didn't want to admit. It wasn't so terrible what I had to do, but I was so afraid. The procedure was exacting and sterile and, in my view, a mistake could be fatal.

What I hadn't expected was the volcano of rage that erupted between us. Neither of us could handle the intrusion of this horror into her life and the resulting hysteria lasted for two weeks, until slowly, slowly I learned.

Each night, close to midnight, I worked to set up the infusion procedure so it would be safe, sterile, and trouble free. From a six-foot IV pole, I hung a two-quart bag of clear golden lipids, like honey in a transparent plastic sac that looked like a cow's udder. A tube flowed down into the catheter the surgeon had implanted into her arm, passing first through a chamber in the computerized pump, the Cutter pump, that would regulate the lipid's flow.

We never got used to it but the first two weeks were bad and the first three days the worst. It went something like this: I'd fiddle with the directions for fifteen minutes. Then I'd break open the sterile rubber gloves and stand there, thinking, picking up tubes and clamps and putting them down on a sterile sheet.

Chris would start, "Could you please try and hurry up."

Minutes would pass, then—"Moooommmmm . . . come on."

"Could you try and be patient?"

"I *am*. You're just so slow," she insisted.

"I'm reading the directions."

"You've read them four times already."

"I know, but after each step I look at the next step before I do it to be sure I understand it."

She rolled her eyes and said, "How many steps are there?"

"Twenty."

"What step are you on?"

"Five."

"Give it to me, I'll read it off to you." I'd hand it to her and she'd snatch it rudely, saying, "God, I know it by heart just from watching you learn in the hospital."

"I'm not used to it yet." I pushed a sharp connection piece into the bottom of the lipid bag and then released a clamp on the tubing that hung down from it.

"No Mom, *not* like that! GIVE it to me. God you're as bad as the nurses on the floor. Am I going to have to teach you everything, too?"

"I'm not a nurse and it's hard."

"Hard! It's not hard, it's simple."

"Well, not for me, and I'm afraid of not keeping everything sterile."

"Don't worry about that!" she scoffed. "The *nurses* never do."

"Of course they do."

"Of course they don't! I ought to know, I watch them everyday. Some of them touch the needles with their fingers."

"Don't be so critical," I said.

"Don't be so dense!"

"You're so damn rude. I ought to walk out of here and leave you stranded."

"Oh, that's great, Mom."

Thank goodness Jenny never heard us. Our words bounced off the walls loud and sharp like the ricochet of a misfired bullet. And the insults glanced off—and in an hour we were over it. I'd apologize and then she'd apologize. I always went first. And the next night we'd go through it again.

Another time, she put a tape in the VCR and ran it on fast forward to get by the opening copyright warnings. I was standing in confusion, looking at the lipids, flicking the tube, wiping everything with alcohol swabs over and over, afraid I'd infect her and she'd die of blood poisoning, and she watched me with growing scorn.

"God, Mom, don't ever decide to be a nurse!"

"Don't worry. I wouldn't spend two years of training to be a doctor's maid."

"I don't think Miss Goobler would be too happy about that remark." I glared at her and she snapped, "Would you just hurry up!"

"Why, Christine, are you *going* somewhere?"

"No, but you're making me nervous, hovering and standing and fiddling." She was so intolerant.

"Well," I said, "if you're nervous, it's because I am."

She scoffed, "You're not getting ready for *surgery* you know."

"Oh really? Well, maybe I can find a surgical clamp to put on your mouth."

And then it would be quiet while I worked. She wanted it done so I could watch the movie with her but I was slow. She'd start in again.

"C'mon, Mom, that clamp has to be shut before you start the pump. Hurry up."

"I can't hurry. If I don't take my time, I'll make a mistake and have to start over."

"Boy, you'd never know you went to Bryn Mawr."

"Who the hell do you think you're talking to?"

"Here, give it to me. Can't you remember anything? You have to close the clamp or the lipids will get all over you. Remember what happened yesterday?"

"Oh, right." Then she looked up and pointed to something.

"Could you try and fix that?"

"What?"

"*That* thing." She pointed again.

"*What* thing?"

"*God!* The thing that looks like a cylinder. The top is on wrong and it's going to pop off later."

"Oh."

I slowly learned to do things more quickly and then I'd panic just before starting the pump. And my ineptitude would set her off.

"Chris, I'm afraid to start the machine." She groaned, and rolled her eyes.

"Start it!"

"Well, let's see. Push this, set that and that, and push start?"

"Yes," she sighed impatiently. "You did it in the hospital. Can't you remember?"

"I'm not sure."

She rattled it off. "Set the rate of infusion, set the amount of time and the amount of fluid, and push start. I wish you could hear yourself. You sound like a retard. They wouldn't have let you do this, if they didn't think you could manage it."

"I know, I know, I'm just not good with machines."

And then a couple of times I got mixed up and touched something with the sterile gloves. That then made them unsterile, and I had to start all over, saying, "Wait, what does this tube go into?" I picked up the book and studied the directions again. I read and nothing went in, as if a wall inside my head were keeping the different parts of my brain from connecting. My lips moved, my eyes read, but I understood nothing. This was stupid. I didn't want to do it. I was blocking.

Jim overheard our fights a couple of times and he said to me later, "What's going on with you two? You never fight like this."

"I just can't handle this new machine and I hate it and resent it and so does Chris and we take it out on each other. It doesn't mean anything."

"Well, I hope not. It sounds like holy hell in there."

"Don't worry, it's getting better."

"Oh, I couldn't tell."

As bad as I was at the machine part, I was terrific with the dressing changes. Chris never had a word to say when I changed the dressings, but it was okay. I didn't need compliments. I'd always been a whiz with a paintbrush or my sewing and inept with machines.

Before long, I could set up the infusion process without thinking. I did make a terrible blunder one night, though, and I think I could have killed Chris if she hadn't caught it.

The catheter in her arm had a plastic cap for the daytime and I always removed it immediately before twisting the infusion tubing into the catheter opening for the night. I'd been doing it for almost two months and, without thinking, I unscrewed and removed the catheter cap before I was ready to put the tubing in. I was standing, clearing the last of the air bubbles out of the tube that hung down, my mind elsewhere, and suddenly Chris looked at her arm and screamed, "Mom . . . the catheter . . . it's open!"

I stared blankly. What was she talking about? I was still staring at the catheter with the cap off when she put her finger over the top and said, "Mom! I'm breathing. Air's coming in! God, how long has the cap been off? I'm taking in air through my arm!"

I woke up. "Oh, God," and I swabbed the tip of the tubing and the catheter top and inserted the tubing as fast as I could. We stared at each other, our eyes locked together and I said, "It was off about forty seconds. What do you think? Will it be okay?" Forty seconds she'd been breathing, taking air in through the open cap in her arm.

"I don't know," she said, "I just don't know." I was thinking to myself, Her lungs are so inefficient, maybe the shallowness of her breathing will save her.

"We'll know in a few minutes," she said, and when she said it, I knew she was going to be all right, and so did she. I relaxed and sat down next to her, on the bed. She shook her head slowly. After all her abuse in the beginning, she said nothing now.

"Chris, of all the mistakes I worry about, I never even thought of this one."

She said quietly, "Close call."

The Cutter pump never stopped driving us crazy, though, because the alarm bell would go off in the middle of the night, and I'd have to come in and stand flicking the lines till whatever had set it off was cleared. When Christine was in the hospital in May, for Mother's Day, she drew a funny picture of herself with the pump and wrote a poem.

> Pimentos are red
> Cutter pumps are blue
> You're such a great mom
> I'd be lost without you.

I didn't know whether to laugh or cry.

Journal Entry: March 1982—Harkness

It's lonely and I've nothing much to say. Except that life is Hell. When I die I won't go to Hell—I've already been there.

My dreams seem so far away now, so distant. Life these days is a constant limbo, neither here nor there.

Sporadic bursts of activity and happiness are much too few and far between. I am alone in this effort to live although my family is always there.

I love them and need them greatly. There are times when I feel hope and that a great sack has been lifted from my head (but not many).

Sometimes I frighten myself because I almost feel comfort at being in the hospital. It's an excuse for sitting around (at home I have no excuse).

But then I think of how often I'd like to strangle everyone here (no matter how nice they are) and I realize that I don't want to be here.

I definitely want to take more acting lessons.

Some people's lives are so easy . . . with nothing more than the expected and usual ups and downs:

failed relationships,
losing jobs,
death of someone near,
loneliness.

While I have (or will eventually have) all that and more (or less).

The rest of the pages were blank.

26 · Three Penny Opera

The good thing that happened when she came home that March 6th with the hyperalimentation setup was that she began to take acting lessons with a teacher from New York, who gave a class in Stamford. It was method acting and she loved it. She couldn't stay out of the hospital long enough to have a career on the stage, but maybe movies. She talked about her dreams again, waiting for me to say, "Chris, you're fooling yourself, be realistic," but I didn't say it. In show business, anything was possible. I said, "Chris, you have something that makes people watch you and I don't mean your purple hair. With your father's help and some luck, you could make it."

She accepted everything except the part about luck. She didn't believe there was such a thing as luck for her, and when she said, "But how?" I said, "Because a director could shoot around you if you got sick, or reshoot if you had a coughing spasm, which you never would."

She'd say, "Maybe you're right," or "Fat chance," depending on her mood. And I reminded her, "You've never missed a rehearsal or a performance in any of the plays at school and you've never coughed on stage or singing with the band."

And the theater called her back. John Egan asked her if she wanted to be in the chorus of *Three Penny Opera,* at the Westchester Community College, where he was a drama major. He was playing the role of Mr. Meachum, and Chris said yes.

She was so sick. Where would she get the voice? She had no lungs. Where would she get the strength? She couldn't eat and she could hardly breathe. Unable to walk a level block without gasping, she was eighty-seven pounds. Nothing stopped her, either, but a week after rehearsals began on March 25th, she had to go back into the hospital. Boy, was she mad—she'd been home three weeks—*three* measly weeks. She wouldn't give up the part, though, and refused to miss a rehearsal. You would have thought she had the lead, but the theater was her life's work and now the play was her whole life.

She talked to Celia. "Dr. Ores, you've *got* to let me out for rehearsals, no matter what. I won't miss even one."

Dr. Ores looked at Chris with surprise and pleasure. "What do you mean, Christine? You just got here a few days ago, blue in the face—you couldn't move and you couldn't breathe."

"But that was *last* week!"

"Turning the world upside down would be easier than getting you out for rehearsals, you know. This isn't a hotel."

But Chris knew that Dr. Ores understood and she pleaded, "Couldn't you try? I know how creative you are—"

"I'll look into it." And she arranged for Chris to leave and be readmitted officially at one in the morning. To this day I don't know who at the hospital knew what was going on. Sometimes if you push against the system, it gives.

But what Chris went through. She had to have her IVs pulled, and her veins were so scarred and collapsed that getting the needle back in was an ordeal for her and the doctor. And she wouldn't let just anyone do it, only doctors who had gifted hands. Never again had she let anyone stick her over and over, looking for a vein, missing it or going too deep and piercing through it.

On the first night of rehearsal, I gave Jenny and Jim an early supper, went back to the hospital with Chris's clothes, and we drove to Westchester Community College in Valhalla. I sat in the back of the theater and watched Chris enjoy new friends. She sat and talked with John, joked, laughed, sang in the chorus. John scooped her up in his arms as though she were his favorite teddy bear and walked around with her in his arms. She wore an over-size red cotton jumpsuit with long sleeves to hide her thin arms and the catheter. She had bright yellow sneakers. No one seemed to notice her hospital ID bracelet.

When rehearsal was over, I waited in the back, invisible and unknown to everyone except John, while she lingered and talked. Then we drove back to the hospital and Chris talked happily about the play, wishing she didn't have to go back. We got there at 1 A.M. and headed for the only open door at night, the emergency entrance.

But we had a problem. Somehow, the permission slips had gone astray and no one knew who we were or what we were talking about when we returned. The tenth floor of Harkness is remote from the emergency room of Columbia Presbyterian—a labyrinth of corridors, elevators, ramps, double doors, and tunnels going from one building to the next. Chris stopped abruptly in the emergency room and looked around slowly, shocked to see so many people, black and Hispanic, old and poor and helpless, injured and sick, drugged and beaten up, moaning, crying, sleeping, and staring into space, some with children, all from the streets of Harlem and Washington Heights.

A nurse was sitting at a desk and I went up to her and explained that Chris was a patient returning to the tenth floor of Harkness and was expected. The nurse looked at me blankly and said, "That's impossible." I glanced at Chris and she gave me an I-knew-it-was-too-good-to-be-true look. I was too tired to cajole and convince the nurse, and my temper flared.

"The fact that *you* don't know about this and *you* don't understand and you don't see a permission slip is your problem, not mine. My daughter is a patient on the tenth floor and we're going back up to the floor so she can go to bed." Noticing how good it felt to be rude and imperious, I turned abruptly, took Christine's arm, and headed for the elevator with her.

Chris muttered, "Yay Mom, you told *her,*" surprising me with her approval. Usually she was embarrassed if I made a fuss about anything.

I muttered in return, "Don't look at her. So far she hasn't opened her mouth and I don't want to get stopped now. It's a good thing I know the way through this maze."

The nurse recovered and called after us to stop, but after years and years of experience with the ever-changing rules and the bureaucratic screwups at Columbia Presbyterian, I wasn't afraid of anything or anyone. I said to Chris, as the elevator door closed, silencing the nurse's voice, "What can they do—arrest us?"

She was coughing hard from our hasty exit and could only shake her head in disbelief, her eyes sparkling. I suspect the nurse called the floor and confirmed our story, which is all I'd suggested she do in the first place. As we rode up, Chris breathed easier and said, "I don't remember emergency admitting *ever* looking like that when I was little. What happened?"

"We used to walk through during the day, remember? The night is different . . . it's always like that. Everytime I come. There are more injuries, more violence, more suffering . . . more everything at night."

"It looks as if there's been a battle in the streets. We live in another world, don't we?"

I thought back to the years when she was a clinic patient. "Yes, we do. We're very lucky." The elevator stopped. The night nurse wasn't at the desk and we walked slowly now, down the silent dim hallway to her room, tucking our small victory away, a bittersweet adventure we'd enjoy later, when the play was over.

I drove back to Greenwich and crawled into bed and Jim, who always worried when I went to the hospital late at night, woke up mumbling, "How was rehearsal?" and I said, "Fine, she had a wonderful time." Within a week she had a crush on the boy playing Mack the Knife. I asked John on the phone one night if the others knew about the hospital.

"Mrs. Gordon," John replied, "they don't know a thing, except for Monica, and she knew who Chris was from my talking about her so much. She didn't know Chris was in the hospital till she noticed her hospital ID bracelet. She pulled me aside and said, 'Is Chris in the hospital now?' and I said, 'Yes,' and she just stared. She couldn't believe it. But no one else knows, not even the director."

Chris stood out in the chorus, although of course she wasn't supposed to. The director had asked them to create a life for themselves, to work out "bits of business" in the crowd scenes, and she put her heart into creating her role—one of a poor flower girl who worked the streets of London. I drove all over Westchester, going to thrift shops, to find the right raggy old clothes and accessories to add to her costume—a shawl with fringe, black gloves with the fingers cut off, pointy shoes, a little pouch bag to hang from her waist. She did her own makeup, capturing the haunted look both Brecht and she desired.

John told me after the play, "No one believes how serious she is. The director told me Chris is very professional and he wished the others were like her."

Chris got out of Harkness in two weeks this time, thank God— in time for the run of the play. We went to two performances. Dr. Ores was going to go, but then was on call and couldn't make it. Chris was disappointed. Although flash pictures weren't allowed, I loaded my Nikon with combat film, as Chris called it, a special high-speed recording film used, I heard, by the CIA for photographing in the dark. My camera setting was ASA 4000. Two people in the audience tapped me on the shoulder to whisper my flash wasn't going off, and I felt like a photojournalist telling them I was using special high speed film, while I prayed it was working. The next day, when I held the negatives up to the light, the pictures were there—a magical and wonderful surprise.

So she took one more step toward her dream of making it in the performing arts. She believed she could be a star, if only. And for a brief moment, her star flashed across an obscure stage.

One night in April, I went to her room later than usual to see if she wanted me to hook her up. She was on her knees, leaning on the bed, saying her prayers. I stopped and almost stepped back out, but she got up slowly and sat on the edge. I felt awkward. "I didn't know you said your prayers kneeling."

"I usually don't." She sounded so tired. "Maybe God will hear me better."

I sat next to her. "Do you think God listens?"

She shrugged. I'd noticed her Bible in different places in her room so I knew she was reading. "Sometimes I think he does," she said.

"Me too, sometimes."

"Most of the time, I think whoever God is, or Christ was, he doesn't have time to listen—to individuals."

Our conversation was like a halting fugue with out-of-place pauses. She put her hands over her eyes, pressing pain out of her temples and said, "If he didn't listen to the prayers of six million of his own people, I don't see how he can hear one small voice."

How odd, I thought. She abhorred references to the Holocaust, and I said, "Two small voices." She looked at me and closed her eyes, pulling back the covers to get into bed. "Oh Chris, what I wouldn't give. If I thought it would work, I'd give you one of my lungs."

"I know, Mom." She did, too. For a while, we'd clutched at the possibility of a lung transplant, since the exocrine glands that cause the thick mucus are in the lungs. But Dr. Ores had said it couldn't be me and it would have to be a heart *and* lung transplant. At that time no one had ever tried such a dual transplant; it would be impossible for a patient as ill as Chris.

By the end of April, Christine's weight was critically low. The only thing keeping her going was the hyperalimentation every night. It was hard to understand why her low weight was so dangerous, but Celia explained that she had no reserve. Every pound she lost now was a loss of strength, not just weight. She was cachexic. Her muscles would start consuming themselves and she'd go into heart failure. Celia was steady when she told Christine, "You need to come in tomorrow."

I went to pack her bags, but I'd never unpacked them. The Three Penny Opera had just closed. She was only home for twenty-two days.

Celia was going on vacation and things were difficult at the hospital when she wasn't there, so I was uneasy. Chris was admitted at noon and by three it was clear the hyperalimentation wasn't going to arrive in time for that night. She'd lose another pound. I had to move quickly.

Finding a phone, I began to make calls. When I got Dr. Levy's office, the doctor who followed Christine's nutrition, his secretary told me he'd gone for the day but gave me the number for the hospital pharmacy that made up the bags of solutions. But the pharmacy said there was a waiting list and Chris wouldn't get the "hyperal" today or tomorrow. They couldn't say when. When the covering doctor for Celia told me he couldn't control the pharmacy, I called them back and had a fight with the pharmacist. He said they only had the staff to supply ten patients at a time. I offered to pay the overtime if they added to their staff. He told me it was impossible and I said, "That's absurd. Nothing's impossible. What are you telling me? That Columbia Presbyterian is going to let a patient die because they can't afford to add someone to their staff? I don't believe you."

"That's the way it is."

"Well, I won't tolerate it. I'll go over your head."

"It won't change things. She'll have to wait."

"We'll see." I hung up.

I spent the night in Christine's room and made a few more calls while Christine sat and listened to me twisting and turning through the bureaucratic maze—lost. She slept fitfully and awoke in the morning ghostly white. She tried to eat some Cream of Wheat but she was too nauseous to swallow.

Dr. Levy came in. He was sympathetic and disgusted with the system, but nothing changed. The pharmacist was implacable. When Dr. Levy left, I said to Chris, "That's all I need. I'm going to try to get to the president of the hospital."

"Good," she muttered. "Serve the pharmacist right if he lost his job."

Celia's office gave me the president's name and number, a Dr. DiMartini. Calm now and calculating, I dialed the extension and asked for him. Of course his secretary said he wasn't available and asked if she could help. I just asked politely, "Is this the proper number to reach Dr. DiMartini?"

"Yes, this is his office."

"Thank you. I'll call tomorrow."

Okay. I knew the number was right. Now, how to get past the secretary? I thought out loud to Chris.

"He's the president, so he won't leave the office at five o'clock like normal people. Executives work late. I'll call at six." We studied each other and then both shook our heads slowly as we thought more and I said, "No, executive secretaries work late too, because their bosses do."

"But maybe not *as* late." She smiled and twirled an imaginary mustache, then dropped her hand on the covers as if it were too heavy.

"Right. *She'd* probably leave at six." Chris nodded shrewdly as I said, "I'll call at 6:45. He'll think it's his wife calling and pick up the phone. That's what Jim does."

We both sat back and Chris closed her eyes. I noticed her hands again. Something was funny about them. Not her fingers, something else. They looked larger than before. Was it because her arms were thinner? She said, "Mom, what about tonight? The hyperal—I need it."

"I'll bring it from home. The machine, the pump, everything."

"You can *do* that?"

"No, of course not. Medicine from home? No hospital allows it. But I'll do it anyway." Christine smiled and we sat quietly.

"What about Jenny?" she asked. Jim was away and children weren't allowed on the floor even for visits, let alone overnight.

"I'll bring her too. Might as well break all the rules."

She propped herself up on the sagging pillows and stared out at the darkening sky. She clicked on the TV and before the sound came up, she said, "I love it. We'll show them."

So I drove home to get Jenny and the machine and the solutions. Like an old friend, a former ally, my anger returned and I knew what to do. The plan was to call Dr. DiMartini from home at 6:45 and return to the hospital after the night staff was in place—about nine o'clock. Harkness had no guards. Instead they locked all the doors, but I'd recently discovered a small door, the private nurses' entrance. You could hardly see the door from the street. I'd go in there with Jenny. If all went well, the elevators wouldn't be busy and we'd zip right up. At 6:30, I got ready to call the president, jotting down the things I'd say. I had to be calm and coherent. He wouldn't like this call. Following my plan, I watched the minute hand, waiting for 6:45. Then I dialed his number. It rang once and someone picked up the phone.

"Hello."

"Dr. DiMartini?"

"Yes." My heart jumped.

"Dr. Di Martini, I'm sorry to call you so late, but it's important. My name is Mrs. Gordon. My daughter is a cystic fibrosis patient followed by Dr. Celia Ores and she was admitted the day before yesterday to the tenth floor of the Harkness Pavilion."

"Why not Babies Hospital?"

"She's twenty."

"Oh, I see."

I explained about the hyperalimentation and Dr. Ores being away and the problem with the pharmacy. I took my time, but he listened. Then he asked, "Was it an emergency admission?"

"Yes, but it wasn't labeled as such." I knew what he was thinking, that it wasn't really an emergency, but it was, and I said, "One of the things that makes this a great hospital is its ability to respond. I can't accept the pharmacist's statement. And as a mother, I won't let my daughter's life be jeopardized because of a policy that isn't working and could be changed. I've a good mind to come into the hospital with the equipment from home and just give her the hyperal myself."

There was a pause and he said, "Well, of course, if you were to do that, there's no way that I could stop you." Now I paused.

"I beg your pardon. Are you saying it's all right for me to . . ." I didn't finish.

"Well, no. I'm certainly not saying that it's all right or giving permission, just that there's no way I can stop you."

"Mmmmm. I see. Well, let me not keep you on the phone any longer. I do hope you can call the pharmacy and suggest that they add to their staff so all the patients who need this can be helped."

"I'll see what I can do."

"Thank you, Dr. DiMartini. Good-night."

I hung up and dropped my head back, sighing and laughing as if I'd just won a marathon. I'd kept my cool. He'd as much as said, "Do it if you have to."

It was 7:15. I'd been on the phone for half an hour. It seemed like five minutes. I called Chris. The phone rang a long time before she said hello.

"Chris? I just got off the phone with the president of the hospital." She answered slowly.

"It worked? You got through?" Her voice was faint like it was coming through an oxygen mask.

"Yes. I'm coming in with Jenny. I'll explain when I get there."

My panic was coming back. It took me half an hour to organize the machine, the solutions, and the sterile tubes so they fit into one sailbag. I could hardly lift it. I went up to get Jenny. I'd have to carry the poles separately.

"Jenny, I'm taking you with me to the hospital tonight. You and I are going to spend the night with Christine."

"We are?" Her face lit up in disbelief. "Oh, Mommy, I thought I was too little."

"You are. But it's an emergency." I knelt down in front of her and held onto her arms as she listened to the story. She didn't fidget and then ran to get her sleeping bag. Driving in, I explained the rest.

"Dear, what we're doing isn't bad or wrong, but it *is* against the rules. We may be stopped. We may get to the room and be told to leave. But we won't go. They may get angry and call the police but, even if they do, Jenny, I'm not afraid. Nothing is going to keep me from helping Christine. If they try to stop us, we'll call 'Eyewitness News' so fast they won't know what hit them."

"We will?"

"Yes. Because the hospital won't want it on television that they refused the medication a child needed and tried to stop the mother from giving it. That would look very bad for the hospital."

"Oh."

"It's a mother's instinct to protect her children, Jenny, just like a mother lion that fights to the death if she has to protect her cubs. I feel a little like a mother lion."

"Boy, this is exciting."

When we got there, no one saw us struggle in the side door with the clumsy bag and the elevators were standing open. The night nurse on ten was nowhere to be seen and I took one more long breath as we walked quickly down the quiet hall to Christine's room. I dumped the heavy bag with relief. Chris was wide awake, waiting for us with a big smile and a welcoming hug for Jenny. The oxygen was still on but no sign of the mask. I set up the cot behind the screen.

Chris rang for the nurse and when she came in, Chris said, "Martha, this is Jenny. She's going to sleep behind the screen.

Mom brought the hyperal in from home." The nurse started to say
something, but Christine put her finger to her lips.

"Please don't tell. Pretend you don't see her, okay?" And she
tipped her head to the side like a puppy.

Martha looked at Jenny. Letting a child on the floor could get
her in real trouble, but she said, "I don't see her. She's not here.
I do see the hyperal, but I won't say anything. You know I can't
even touch it, though."

"Why not?" I asked, trying to distract her from Jenny.

"Against regulations. It may not be sterile." Chris started to
laugh but I gave her a look. The nurse was on our side.

And so we did it. I kept the hyperal going for the next four
nights and kept arguing with the pharmacist to provide it. And
Chris told all the nurses that we had the number for "Eyewitness
News" and we weren't afraid to use it. Jim came back from Cali-
fornia the next day so I didn't have to bring Jenny in again and
it was just as well. The second night, I went in the same side door
with my clandestine bag of solutions, rounded the corner to the
elevators, and there, in a navy uniform, for the first time ever, was
a hospital security guard.

"Can I help you, ma'am?"

"I'm going up to ten to spend the night."

"You need a pass. Here, sign this."

I took the pass and went up, amazed. Was he there because
of me? Or maybe because of Jenny? No, impossible. The hospital
could never put guards in place that fast. Still, it was an odd
coincidence.

To this day, they have a twenty-four-hour guard by the Harkness elevator. And on the fifth day, the pharmacy began sending
up the hyperalimentation. I called Dr. DiMartini to thank him,
but never managed to get through again.

27 · Closing Down

She was in for a month, got out May 28th, and went back in on June 17th. She was spending more time in the hospital than she was at home. Jerry was in Canada taping the new cable series, "Fraggle Rock," with the Muppets. Chris was supposed to come with us to Lake Winnipesaukee in New Hampshire. We'd rented a big house on the lake for a month so she could invite her friends. But now she couldn't come. I was going to cancel the vacation, but Chris wouldn't hear of it and, when I talked it over with Celia, she said Chris was better off remaining behind without us, than having us all stay home on her account. I didn't want to leave. She wouldn't even tell her friends she was back in the hospital.

"Chris, then you won't have any visitors. You can't cut yourself off like that."

"Well, I am." I'd been thinking about hiring private nurses and she'd given me the perfect reason.

"Okay, then, but I'm not letting you sit in this room alone for days on end. I think it's time to hire private nurses."

She looked at me in surprise. "Oh, I'd love that." Now I was surprised.

"But you never said anything."

"I know." Maybe I should have hired them years ago.

Before we left for New Hampshire, I rented a VCR for Christine's hospital room and set up a mailing system with our local video store. But I knew what would happen. I couldn't leave her. I'd be back and forth and back and forth. I was always torn. I'd be home, hurrying to get things done so I could go in to see Chris, and then, after I was there awhile, I'd start thinking about getting home for Jenny and Jim. It was hard to keep my balance.

Driving to Lake Winnipesaukee on Thursday I said to Jim, "I'm going back on Monday, Jim. I can't leave her alone. Try to understand. I'll spend a couple of days in the hospital and then fly back up."

"Go," he said with a hug, "she needs you. We'll be okay." I couldn't wait to see her.

Chris and I had a wonderful two days and two nights. I didn't have to go anywhere or do anything—no pressure, just us. We stayed up half the night and talked. Pulling over the wing chair, I leaned on the bed close to her and we watched David Letterman and VCR movies, and Uncle Floyd, although we never seemed just to watch TV. We'd always be partly involved in a second diversion, like reading Bogue and Vazaar (as Chris called *Vogue* and *Bazaar*) or *Mad* or *National Lampoon* or *Cream*, or analyzing Janet Maslin's or Pauline Kael's movie reviews, or even just criticizing the overblown drivel that passed for fashion copy in the retail ads of the *Times*. She thought the Saks copy was the silliest. Two more opinionated people you wouldn't find, and we either loved or hated everything—there was no in between. The new Esprit catalogue arrived and we ordered fall clothes for her. I saw Prince for the first time on TV at 3 A.M., performing in what looked like his underwear. Chris had said, "Mom, you've got to stay up and see this new singer. Last time I saw him he had a bra on his head. He's Puerto Rican, I think."

He wasn't, but we thought so at the time. I watched him sing—seducing the audience with his hips, his lips pouting like Marilyn Monroe.

"He's very sexy, Chris, but I'd like him better if he didn't try so hard. He's a little like the Saks ads."

She laughed. "I know, but he's so great."

The private nurses we hired were young, one a beautiful black girl, Barbara, with long red nails, who devoted herself to Chris, and the other a soft-spoken young woman, Norma, with her hair in a bun. She too warmed to Christine and I was touched by their response. With everything done for her, it wasn't easy to see how weak she was. We never talked about death or dying. I wondered why. Maybe she needed to keep our time together away from the terror. Maybe the terror was hidden in our need for closeness.

I flew back to Lake Winnipesaukee on Wednesday morning and swam and fished around the island with Jenny and Jim. Everyday at dusk, a great blue heron flew over our house on the way to his nest, his great head nestled back into his body as he flew. But I had to fly back to Chris. It was the same thing again—such a wonderful time. I told her stories about New Hampshire, fishing in the rain and the blue heron.

"And Jim sank our canoe," I said.

"He what? Jim? He messed up?" It was unheard of.

"Yes. He had an outboard motor on the back and it was too heavy and, before he even had it started, it pulled the back of the canoe under. I was just coming down the driveway in the car with Jenny and we saw him sink about a hundred feet from shore. It was so funny. At first he didn't seem to realize he was sinking, until he saw the front of the canoe rising up out of the water, and then the back of the canoe started to disappear. When he stood up the whole thing slid out of sight. We went running down the dock laughing and screaming." It was wonderful to see Chris laughing.

I went to our video store in Greenwich to exchange movies and that night we watched *Ragtime* and *It's a Wonderful Life.* We tried playing backgammon but we couldn't concentrate on the game, talking and forgetting who had the next move. I got pretzels—salty ones.

Norma Simmons, the night nurse, leaned against the bathroom door watching us with a madonna-like smile. When she was outside getting linens, I asked her, "What do you find so interesting? You watch so quietly."

"I've been wanting to meet you. Chris talks about you all the time. I hope you don't mind." I felt awkward.

"No, but I feel like we're leaving you out."

"Oh please. I've never seen her so cheerful. She's such a fountain of information and ideas." She stopped and added, "She needs you very much."

Those words again, meaning, "because she's dying." She needed a lot more than me and I'd seen her a lot more cheerful. It made me feel guilty—that I was glad she needed me—because I wanted so much more for her. I said to Norma, "What do you mean?"

"Just that. As soon as she knew you were coming back, her outlook changed. Her energy was different. She must have said, 'When my mom comes' ten times yesterday."

"It shouldn't be me," I said. "It should be her friends or a young man."

"Does she have friends at home?"

"Oh, yes."

"I wondered, because no one calls and she won't call anyone."

"She forbid my telling her friends she was in the hospital this time because she just got out three weeks ago. She made me swear."

Norma shook her head and said, "What a terrible promise to have to keep."

This time when I flew back to the lake, I wasn't ready. Time was so precious. Dr. Ores called.

"Jacquie, I wonder if you might think about cutting your vacation short."

"Of course."

"Do you think it will be all right with Mr. Gordon?"

"Yes, we've had two weeks. It's not fun without Chris and Jim knows I'm only half here. We'll come home."

"I think it would be best."

None of us minded going back, not even Jenny. The lake was beautiful, but we'd never love it the way we loved Martha's Vineyard and we all missed Chris. In spite of the worry that kept me awake at night, I felt such peace those days when I went down to visit her. Nothing was tugging at me to leave. Time poured slowly for us both—an undiluted concentrate of time. I remember those few days with the same clarity as the day she was born and the day she died.

She came home on August 6th under troubling circumstances. Despite pneumonia, she was discharged by Dr. Neu because there was nothing more he could do for her. His arsenal of antibiotics was depleted and her lungs were resistant even to experimental drugs. She was sliding now. The morning we left, she was so shaky she couldn't walk and asked for a wheelchair.

I went to ask Miss Goobler, and saw Dr. Ores walking down the hall. I knew she was looking for me. Chris was her only patient in Harkness and she said, "Do you have time to talk?"

We sat in the sunroom and she said, "I went to look at Christine's new X rays this morning. I've been putting it off. I just didn't want to see what I already know. Her lungs are terrible, just terrible. There's lung disease everywhere."

This was the third time I'd seen Dr. Ores choked up when she talked about Christine. I said, "Worse than before?"

"Worse than before. We can't make a dent in this infection." She swallowed and tears appeared. I didn't say anything. What could I say? My eyes were full of tears as well.

Celia went on. "We'll just have to see how she does on her own for a while. I don't know what's keeping her going."

I felt tight and scared inside and said, "I don't know if I'd call it 'keeping going.' The only place she goes is to the hospital. Have any of your patients with cystic fibrosis ever been as sick as Chris is and fought back, got well enough to have a life worth living?"

She didn't answer right away. What was going through her mind? Was she trying to think of a patient who had? Was she debating whether or not to tell me? I was expecting the worst so her answer surprised me.

"Yes. Two of my patients. Kevin and Rolf. They worked out with weights, they built up their strength, they did a great deal of postural drainage, and they did make it."

But I wasn't encouraged in the least. "Do you think Chris can do it? She seems like an invalid now. She can't breathe enough for normal activity—let alone exercise."

"She's done it before, but she's exhausted and she's terrified. With lungs like hers, I just don't know. I'm sending her home with Lasix to eliminate the hyperal fluids which were contributing to the heart failure and Digoxin to regulate her heartbeat."

How could there be any hope but still I hoped. The orderly came pushing the wheelchair down the hall and I went to help Chris. She usually breezed out of the hospital, laughing and hugging her favorite nurses, clowning and blowing them kisses. Not today. She waited by the elevator, shrank into herself, and watched the dial move silently toward number ten. Karen and Mary, two of her nurses, came over. Karen was not much older than Chris and she hugged her tenderly saying, "See you soon." Mary had a twenty-year-old daughter and was very fond of Chris. She bent over, brushed her hair back, and looked at her. "Take care, Chris. You'll do okay. I know you will."

The elevator door opened and Chris said, "Bye, Mary."

I tried to put myself in her shoes. How must she feel going home like this? I wanted to scream no, no, and I realized that her silence wasn't only fear, she was ashamed and embarrassed. I whispered, "I love the way the nurses love you. I'm so proud of you." She said nothing.

On the way home she was quiet, fiddling with the FM, looking for WLIR, her New Wave station. We were almost at the Greenwich toll when she said, "Mom, you know in the last five years, I haven't been home *once* to see the apple blossoms and the dogwoods. I've missed the leaves turning in October too. I'm always in the hospital then."

I knew and I remembered what I'd said at Christmas about life being worth it and observing nature. I pushed the memory away. Maybe it wasn't worth it.

In the spring I'd fill her room with branches of dogwood and magnolia, lilacs and apple blossoms clipped from our trees. She used to tease me and say, "Mom, do you come to see me or to landscape my room?" But she loved the flowers from her friends and her father and the Muppets. Sometimes I was cross with her because she was so terrible about writing thank-you notes. She'd say, "I'll do it tomorrow, I'll do it tomorrow." And she hardly ever did. I never did understand why she was so bad about that when she was so thoughtful in other ways. And my scoldings did no good.

I watched the white lines on the road fly beneath us. We left the parkway at exit 28 and turned up the hill to our house on Round Hill Road. A few hydrangeas were spilling over the stone wall as we turned in the drive . . . no apple blossoms or dogwoods, no lilacs or magnolias. They were long gone.

28 ⋆ Single Threads

Coming home was a fragile feeling this time, but happy just the same. Home was home and it was always too quiet without her. I brought her things upstairs in several trips while she made her way up the stairs slowly, climbing three or four steps and then sitting down to rest, resigned and smiling.

She tried so hard. We did everything. She rested and slept and coughed violently and had thumps and took her masks and pills and Vivonex and hyperalimentation. Bruce came over and spent time with her. They were writing songs. John and Mark came too. Claudia lived in Washington, D.C., now and Chris missed her a lot. I went to the video store every day as she caught up on all the movies she'd missed. Her father brought her books.

On her birthday we took her to see *Private Lives,* a revival of a Noel Coward play on Broadway with George C. Scott. She was twenty-one.

We had dinner first at Les Pyrenees, a small French restaurant near the theater, and after we ordered Chris asked Jim to teach her about wine, saying, "Most wines come from two regions don't they? Burgundy and one other—I forget."

Jim smiled and said, "More than *one.* There's Beaune, Beaujolais, the Loire Valley."

"That's the other one I know."

"There's Bordeaux, the Côte De Rhone, the Côte Rotie . . ."

Chris looked at her glass. "What's this?"

"A Beaujolais." Chris took a tiny sip.

"Not bad. Côte Rotie—what's that mean?" she said sweetly.

"Côte means side or hillside. Rotie means roasted. These wines come from the Rhone River Valley where the grapes are in the sun all day."

"On a roasted hillside," she translated, looking at me in surprise. "Doesn't that sound weird? A Frenchman says, 'I'll have a roasted wine, please.'" She laughed.

Jim smiled and said, "Then there's my favorite region—Champagne." She was getting interested.

"Is cognac a region?"

"Yes, but of course it's not a wine."

"Oh, right."

"Do you want to learn more?"

She pretended to be indignant. "Of course! I don't want to be a helpless girl who doesn't know what to order. I want to *know.*" She meant it. Jim warmed to the task as she asked more questions. I wondered if she'd asked him to teach her about wine so she wouldn't have to talk. Talking took her breath away.

Jim picked up the Beaujolais. "See how the bottle has sloping shoulders? This shape bottle is always a burgundy."

"Gee, are you sure? I've seen white bottles like that."

"Those are white burgundies."

Chris turned to me and muttered, "I didn't even know there *were* white burgundies."

The restaurant was full with soft light and low voices, the sounds of diners all around us. Everyone was going to the theater. She loved it, her eyes moving from Jim to the people, to me, and back to Jim again. When she stood up, a careful observer would think she had a stomachache or some internal pain she moved so economically. Only a doctor would notice the skin on her neck being drawn in deeply between her collar bones.

Jim said, "Wine has legs, you know." She looked up.

"Legs? What do you mean?"

"There's glycerine in it. Watch." He swirled the wine in the glass and held it to the light to show her how the wine stuck to the side of the glass as it ran back down. "See the little rivulets? Those are called legs." Chris copied him and, leaning her elbow on the table, held the glass to the light—looking. Jim and I watched her.

"I don't think this wine has such great legs," she said. "Am I right?"

Jim swirled again and looked. "Right. Great tits and ass though." She laughed, and Jim blushed with pleasure.

What fun we had that night. We almost forgot she was sick. Some things crystallize in your memory and stay forever. That dinner was one.

She drank deeply and laughed with Jim and me, and this was what she found with her friends—life, not sickness. No wonder she took such risks.

Walking slowly across the street to the theater, I took her arm for a minute, walking ahead of Jim and said, "What have I done to deserve such an amazing girl? I adore you."

She smiled and groaned. "You're just saying that because it's my birthday," but her voice was full. She knew I loved her. The play was a riot and she laughed herself into coughing spasms, but the laughter around us was so loud no one noticed.

With the end of another summer at hand, the prospect of a lonely winter was on her mind. Her friends were leaving again. She felt tired and lost. "Mom, I can't seem to find a direction this fall. I just don't know what to do."

I suggested she go back to school part time, but she said no. She didn't have enough voice now to take singing lessons. She was quiet and morose, almost as if she was in mourning. Late at night, when I thought of it, I cried and cried, until I could shut the thought from my mind—too awful to think of. I still biked ten miles every morning while Chris was asleep and the unwelcome thought would come back and the wind would blow the tears to the side of my face.

I spent more time with her. I'd go to bed early with Jim, wait till he was asleep, then get up and tiptoe out of the room. Some nights she was out with friends, even now, but she was coming home early, so usually I'd find her watching a movie on the VCR, in the den.

We'd spend the next few hours together and I'd hook her up to the hyperal machine when she was ready. If I missed the beginning of a movie, she'd rewind it and we'd start from the beginning. There was no sense of hurry . . . the night spread out before us.

Sometimes we listened to her music. She was buying more and more records and tapes. I suspect a look at her record collection would serve as an anthology of New Wave rock music of the early eighties, excluding heavy metal which she didn't like. I made a list once—sixty-one groups. She was listening to new classical music too. She filled her time with music, books, and films because she had no other choice and I stayed up later and later with her, finding it easy to slip into my old habits.

One night she came into our room and curled up on Jim's side of the bed, squishing his pillows under her. She was working on the lyrics of a new song she was writing and was tired of working alone.

"When I finish this, I want you to read it, okay Mom?"

"Sure." I thought her lyrics were quite good.

Jim appeared in his robe, glanced at Chris sitting on his side of the bed, and said, unpleasantly, "Chris, do you mind?" He said it so cold and hard I shot a look at him. How could he talk to her like that? Chris picked up her writing things and left the room. I saw a tightness in her chin as she mumbled, "Sorry."

"Jim, what's the *matter* with you? Is it going to hurt your precious side of the bed if Christine sits there? The bed is big enough for all of us. How could you say that to her?"

He was defensive and said, "What do you mean? All I did was ask her to move." Sometimes his possessiveness made me furious. He always said words weren't important but I thought words could kill.

"That's not what I heard," I said. "Your tone of voice said, 'Could you get out of my place and don't sit there again—I don't want you here.' You could have been gentle or charming and said, 'Could you make room for another?' or something like that."

He heaved a sigh. "I'm sorry, I didn't realize."

"You never realize."

I was so mad, I didn't want to be in the same room with him and I went downstairs to cool off. He was usually so wonderful to Chris. She was so lonely now, so in need of closeness.

Fifteen minutes must have passed as I wandered downstairs in the dark, still fuming. Then I went up to her room. She was sitting on the arm of her sofa, her back to me, staring past the dark windows. She didn't move and I walked over and sat behind her. Silence. I pulled myself up onto the sofa back and leaned around to look at her. Tears were streaming down her cheeks. And my own tears came—changing my anger.

"Oh Chris, I'm so sorry." I hugged her and she cried and cried and so did I. "Chris, he didn't mean it. You know how he is. He can't understand it when anyone touches his things. He's funny like that. He adores you. He's told me so many times."

Choking on her crying, she said, "I know, Mom, but it still hurts, the way he said it. Like I was contaminated or something."

"I know, I know, please forgive him." Why now, I thought. She doesn't need any more hurt, not even a drop. I thought my heart was going to choke me with the pain. Death was calling her name, and though I wouldn't listen and barely heard and only in the dark and very late, soon I'd have to release her hand and let her go. Maybe that's why we held on so tightly now.

"Chris, have you been sitting here the whole time?" She nodded and wiped her nose on her sleeve as she'd told Jenny a hundred times not to do. Who cares? I thought to myself, and found myself giggling all of a sudden. She turned to me and I wiped my nose on my sleeve too, exaggerating and making slurpy noises with my mouth, the way Jim did to make us laugh. She giggled and handed me a Kleenex.

"That's *so* disgusting, Mom."

We weren't over it, but at least we'd stopped crying. Such a minor slight. Funny how it gripped us both so hard—like a dam breaking. There's just so much a heart can hold in silence. We sat for a while, each with our own thoughts.

"Chris, Jim's going to bed. Do you want me to get up later and watch a movie with you?"

"Yes. I'm going to watch *Dressed to Kill*."

"Oh, good." We'd stay up late, cozy and quiet.

When I went back into our room, Jim said, "Maybe I should go in and apologize." I wasn't angry anymore.

"That would be nice." He left the room and came back five minutes later with tears in his eyes, and hugged me. He didn't say a word and I didn't ask. The image of Chris sitting alone, pushed aside, has never left me.

We didn't talk about the future. I found a list she'd written of possible plans. She rested and harbored her strength during the day, sleeping till noon so she could go out in the evening. She didn't drive her car. The little brown Datsun, still showing her RCDS parking sticker, sat in the driveway. She'd scraped off the handicapped sticker from Manhattanville.

She was so dear about her beloved music. She said one day, "Here Mom, two tapes to listen to in the car, Lene Lovich and Pig Bag."

"Pig Bag?"

"Mmmmm, they sound sort of like bad Latin band music. You know like at half time?"

"I don't even like good Latin band music."

She shrugged. "You may like it bad." I laughed.

"Chris, are you not feeling up to driving?"

"The stick shift is hard for me."

"If you want to use my car, you can." She looked shocked.

"You'd let me drive the Mercedes?"

"Yes, you're a good driver."

"Oh, that would be so good. Can I take it tonight to Drea's house? It's her birthday and she's having a party before everyone goes back to school."

"Fine."

"They're gonna tease me. Oh well."

And Tuesday night, on August 24th, she went to Drea's party alone. John had offered to pick her up, but she did want to drive that Mercedes. Drea was touched when Chris extended a small gift-wrapped box to her and said, "Happy Birthday, I'm sorry it's late."

Several of her friends thought she looked tired. At moments

of rest when she was listening or not thinking about how she held herself, they saw something hard to define in her posture—an exhaustion, a stillness, maybe depression. Amy noticed it and Phebe. Mark noticed it too. They were surprised she didn't want to play Charades and they finally got her to do the last round. She left early and Mark walked her to the car.

"Your mom needs the car at twelve o'clock?"

Chris joked, "She likes the car in early. It's still young."

Mark smiled. He knew she was tired. "The car suits you. Night." It was a lonely drive home and she cried.

Wednesday Bruce came over and they went to the movies. Before she went to sleep, she said, "Tomorrow night John and Mark and I are going out one more time before Mark goes back to Amherst."

She'd been so sick all day, throwing up and running a high fever, I thought it was crazy to plan going out on Thursday, but I didn't say anything.

She went to bed at midnight but didn't get much sleep. The stupid Cutter pump kept going off all night, waking her up with the ping-ping warning that there was air in the line. The machine would keep pinging until it was cleared or shut off. She flicked the lines and reset it five times, knowing there was no air in the line, but it kept going off again. She finally called until she woke me and together we redid the whole thing and it stopped waking her up with false alarms.

She woke at noon drugged with pain from a crushing headache. She'd used oxygen all night. But her lungs were so congested they couldn't release all the carbon dioxide in her blood and it was building up in her system, giving her pounding headaches. It also acted like a narcotic, making her groggy. Eventually, with enough, she'd lose consciousness. A machine helped her to breathe, a machine fed her. She ate nothing solid.

She was so weak, going to the bathroom was a planned event and I'd been helping her down the hall every morning, pushing the IV pole along the shag rug as I walked behind her.

Thursday morning, I stood outside the bathroom door and shut my eyes tight, praying Please God, don't let her throw up this morning, not today.

She called breathlessly, "Mom, I'm going to throw up." I hurried in, put my arms on her shoulders, and handed her Kleenex while she threw up in the sink. There was nothing to throw up, just waves of dry heaves. She was gasping and choking, trying to get her breath. She whispered, "Oh God. Oh God."

I gave her some water to sip. I was helpless and heartsick. Why was her throwing up so violent? Dr. Ores told me in all her years, she'd never seen anything like it. Why couldn't it be me? By now, I knew God never let you take your children's suffering, but even so, I kept asking. I bent my head next to her in silence, leaning against the sink, the porcelain cold on my legs, her forehead hot against my cheek. Her fever must be spiking again. She leaned on me, her shallow quick breathing less labored.

"Oh Mom," she said softly.

"Oh Chris," I whispered.

The breeze that blew all summer along the top of Round Hill Road slipped in the bathroom window, a soft pleasant breeze. It made her shiver.

"Want to go back to bed, dear?" What a stupid question I thought to myself. Was there any choice?

She said, "I think it's over."

We made our way back down the hall and I cursed God for letting her suffer so.

"Mom, when I throw up like that, my head feels as if bombs are exploding in my brain. I can't stand it anymore, these PLO headaches." I held her close. How could she joke at a time like this?

"Do you think you could keep some Tylenol down? It will help the fever and probably the headache."

"I'll try."

I helped her back into bed, and gave her the Tylenol. She reminded me that she was going to see *Poltergeist* that night with John and Mark. But she was worried. She felt so weak.

Impossible I thought and suggested that she wait and see how she felt later.

"Okay," she said. "Mom, do you have time to sit with me for a while?"

I felt my throat constricting again and I said, "Sure." I slid across her pink satin comforter and leaned back against the wall on the inside of her bed. I squeezed her toes through the comforter.

"Aren't you hot with the comforter on?"

"No," she said, smiling. Her father had bought it for her sixteenth birthday and her canopy bed. She'd told me once that Mark loved it. It was more than a comforter, it was memories.

I asked, "Chris, don't you think maybe John would be just as happy coming over here and watching a movie? I could go pick up *Cat People*. You haven't seen it, have you?"

"Oh no, Mom. You're forgetting. John and I are taking Mark." She was taking a breath every three or four words. "Mark's never been to a horror movie. John and I, think it's high time, he was initiated." She rested. "We're going to drive over to his house, after supper and not tell him, which movie we're going to see, until we get there, I think I can do it, if I rest all day, and save my strength."

"I'm sure you can, dear. It sounds like fun, for you and John at least. Just be sure you have Tylenol in case your fever spikes."

We sat quietly. A week before she was laughing at the theater with us. Now she could hardly walk.

"Chris, these last few days—I'm nervous. I don't think we have it under control anymore, do you?"

"No, I don't know what it is, but I'm getting worse again so fast." No antibiotics, I thought, and she said, "Maybe you should call Dr. Ores and see about a bed for me on Monday." I worried all day. Had her life hung on such a slender thread all these years? Without the antibiotics, would she have been dead in two months?

She spent the afternoon listening to music. Karen Virga did her thumps at four. She lived in Danbury now, but she drove the forty-five minutes everyday to treat Chris. Karen stayed and talked with her, as always. She was worried. The day before, they'd been talking about funerals and Chris had said she wanted there to be laughter at hers. Karen couldn't get it out of her mind. As she left, Chris got up and gave her a long hug. She'd never done it before. Karen was touched and hugged her back warmly.

A little later Chris asked me if I had time to pick up some new tapes for her. The new Split Enz, *Time and Tide,* and the Marshall Crenshaw album. She asked me to stay first and listen to a song from her new Kate Bush album, *Lionheart.* I asked, "Is Kate Bush popular? I don't know her at all."

She thought a minute. "She's English. She has a small cult following here, but she's better known in England."

I studied the back of the album cover while I listened. All the lyrics were there, but Kate Bush had written out the lyrics to this song in her own longhand. I read along as I listened to her haunting soprano.

> Oh England, My Lionheart
> I'm in your garden fading fast in your arms.
> The soldiers soften, the war is over
> The air-raid shelters are blooming clover,
> Flapping umbrellas fill the lanes
> My London bridge in rain again.
>
> Oh England, My Lionheart,
> Oh England, My Lionheart,
>
> Dropped from my black spitfire to my funeral barge
> Give me one kiss in appleblossom,
> Give me one wish and I'd be wassailing
> in the orchard, my English rose,
> Or with my shepherd who'll bring me home.
>
> Oh England, My Lionheart,
> Oh England, My Lionheart,
>
> I don't want to go.

My face was still but my mind grabbed at the words and life tore apart inside me. Was she telling me at last? I had been waiting for her to speak. She had, but with such delicacy, I wasn't sure.

"It's a beautiful song. I love the way she sighs the chorus, 'Oh England.' Could you play it again?"

"Okay."

"Chris, do you remember when you were little I used to call you Christine the Lionhearted?"

"Yes." She sat on the sofa close to me as we listened again.

There was no mistake. There were those words—"the war is over
. . . my funeral barge, give me one kiss . . . give me one wish
. . . my shepherd who'll bring me home . . . I don't want to go."

I was numb and wordless. I had no answer, no poetry of my
own. Years of pain felt no different from this moment of pain. It
was all the same. I couldn't imagine what she must feel. I was
hollow and an empty wind blew through me.

At seven o'clock, John Egan called to say he was on the way.
Chris was still upstairs when he rang the bell and I answered the
door quickly so I could talk to him before she came down.

"John, Chris isn't doing well. She shouldn't be out. She can't
breathe. Promise me you'll drop her off right in front of the movie
before you park the car and then do the same thing when you
leave. If there are any stairs at the movie, take them very slowly."

He said in his usual cheery manner, "Oh sure, Mrs. Gordon,
no problem at all. I always do that, anyway. Maybe, I'll just carry
her. I often do, just for fun." And up the stairs he went to spend
some time before they left to pick up Mark. John reminded me
of Bruce sometimes. They were always so cheerful. Did they have
no inkling of how ill she was? Perhaps not. Even now she rarely
mentioned her struggles to her friends.

When she came downstairs, I could see why they had no clue.
She was wearing her baggy Esprit pants, with a white T-shirt and
an oversize tan linen blazer with the sleeves rolled up. Anyone
else would have been roasting. She had her Davis Park fireman's
badge on the breast pocket and the antique amethyst brooch her
father had bought her. She often wore a tie, a narrow straight one,
with her sweatshirts—a black one tonight—and bright turquoise
Seven Star sneakers showed yellow socks with little colored stars
all over them. No one would think she was ill so well did she
distract them from the trembling in her hands and her weary
posture. She moved cautiously, as if she were walking on thin
ice, afraid she might slip in her sneakers. She left with a "Bye,
Mom."

Mark noticed Chris was her witty self but didn't clown around
as much as usual. They held hands in the movie and as they left
the theater, Chris held up her hand, white and trembling.

"Look Mark, you've squeezed all the blood out of my hand. My fingertips are blue!"

Mark laughed. "Well, this was your idea, not mine," and John said, "It was a great idea. You should see it again Mark. I liked it much better not having to wonder what was coming next."

They sat on the ledge of the recessed display window and John went to get the car. Mark didn't know why they weren't walking with John, but he didn't ask. Then they all drove back to Mark's house listening to Christine's new Marshall Crenshaw tape.

They sat and talked to Mark's parents and when John and Chris got up to leave, Mark gave Chris his long affectionate good-bye hug. He was surprised at an unwelcome thought that tumbled into his mind. He wondered as his arms were wrapped around her if he'd ever see her again. After Chris and John left, Mark's mother commented that she'd never seen Christine looking so tired. Somehow she had found the strength to spend that warm Thursday evening with Mark and John, two young men who loved her.

29 · *Lionheart*

When I heard the front door open and close, I knew Christine was home. She wouldn't come up right away. She'd get a Coke and rest before trying the stairs. It was a warm, sticky night and sleep was the last thing on my mind. I went downstairs.

She stood near the door watching out the narrow hall window as John's car pulled away. I sat down on the bottom step and asked her how the evening had been. She didn't answer right away.

"It was fine," she finally said and sat down beside me.

Usually I got a detailed synopsis of the movie whether I wanted it or not, but not tonight.

"Did your fever come back?"

"I didn't give it a chance. I took Tylenol."

Still sitting, she backed up three steps and then stopped on the fifth step, resting.

"Are you tired?"

"Yes."

"Would it help if you leaned on me to go upstairs one step at a time?"

"Yes. I'd like to lie down before you hook me up, though. I'm too tired for the VCR." I put my arm around her waist and helped her up the stairs.

Her hair smelled sweet like the perfume in her shampoo. Her new cat, Max, a luxurious black Persian, was sitting at the top, waiting for her and watching our ascent with interest. She felt too warm, but it was August and the air was warm.

She lay down on the bed, sliding her hand under the pillow for the tiny tubing that led to the oxygen tank at the foot of the bed. She asked me to turn on the oxygen. At night, she fixed the narrow tubing so that it encircled her head, but when she was awake, she just held the tube up to her mouth as she needed it. She closed her eyes, holding the nozzles to her mouth. Max studied Chris from the floor and jumped up, pushing, pawing, and purring as he curled up next to her head. Max could never get close enough and she loved it. Sometimes I'd come in her room and find her on the bed reading, sitting like an Indian, her elbows on her knees, her hands supporting her head. Max would be asleep around her neck.

She whispered, "Hi Max," reached up to pet him, and asked me if I'd get her a Coke. I went to the kitchen and fixed one and prepared the bags of hyperal fluids for infusion later. When I was back upstairs, I climbed onto the bed and she asked, "Is Jim asleep?"

"Yes, dear. He gets up so early," I reminded her. He took the 6:29 train to New York everyday.

"I know, I just thought he might still be up." She paused. "Mom, do you think Jim knows that I love him?"

I studied her profile. I just loved her nose. "I don't know, have you ever told him?"

"I don't think so, not in so many words. He's a good man."

"I know. I'm glad you feel that way."

"Would you tell him I love him?"

I said nothing for a moment, just wondering, and then I agreed. "Yes, I will if you want me to."

Chris looked over at me and nodded—a quick little nod. She had some sort of pale gold dust on her eyelashes that I hadn't seen earlier. I wondered if Mark or John had noticed it. She asked, "What's the oxygen set at—two and a half?"

I crawled off the end of the bed, as if I were checking the dial on the oxygen tank. I knew very well the level I'd set was 3. There were ten settings and Celia had suggested it remain at 2 or 3.

"It's on three. Should I turn it up to three and a half?"

"Well, I think maybe up to five for the moment."

"Okay," I said. I felt a jolt of alarm but numb and dreamlike my hand touched the dial and turned it up to five. I watched my hand and it didn't seem like my hand. Dr. Ores's words the first time we'd used oxygen came back to me. When I'd asked what to look for at Christmas she'd said, "You will know if she is going to live, she will go on without oxygen. And if she isn't, she'll ask for more and more." I had said, "What do you mean?" And she explained that it wasn't something Chris would do on purpose, but because her lungs would be less and less able to exchange the blood gases, the more oxygen she took in, with so many of the passageways blocked, the more carbon dioxide would be trapped in her blood with every breath.

I stared at the knob pointing to level 5. Still dressed, Chris was curled up on her side, her eyes closed. I sat on the edge of the bed again.

"Chris, I worry that you need this much oxygen. I think we should go into the hospital tomorrow, not wait till Monday. This isn't good."

"I think so too."

Earlier in the day she had been playing her new albums, explaining to me how the Australian groups were coming into their own. She'd been making out a list of possible plans for the fall, talking about acting classes and dyeing her hair again, maybe green. She had showed me the bright green Crazy Color, but wasn't sure she had the guts to dye it green. She was going to bring the green and fuschia dyes to the hospital on Monday in case she had the energy to do it.

I didn't think she would. The Christine I knew had almost disappeared from view, as if she were lost in the shadow of a solar eclipse.

After a while, she got up, put aside the oxygen, and put on her pajamas. She seemed more than tired. She seemed drugged. I arranged her pillows and said hesitantly, "Chris, are you moving in slow motion so that you won't get out of breath?"

"Yes, I'm really congested. I can't get enough air."

She lay back down and I sat next to her for a few moments longer, and then said, "Good-night."

She squeezed my hand as she whispered, " 'Night, Mom." I went to bed saying my prayers, filled with a sense of dread.

I woke her up the next morning at 11:30. Her therapist, Priscilla, had come and gone. Chris felt less nauseous than usual but she hadn't turned down the oxygen during the night and she had a blinding headache, the worst she'd ever had.

"If I move, it feels like my brain is slamming against the inside of my head, like ship's ballast reeling in a storm." I gave her a Fiorinal. Before long, the headache eased.

I unhooked the catheter and as she stood, she held on to the bed to steady herself.

"Mom, I don't think I can get down to the bathroom without the oxygen."

"Wait, I'll go down and get the portable unit." It looked like a torpedo on a dolly with wheels. My steps were even and steady, but my mind was racing. She seemed so calm and matter-of-fact, but everything she said and did was alarming. Maybe she just didn't have the energy to show her fear. But she had never had to use the portable oxygen to go to the bathroom. What was happening?

I dragged the strolling tank up the stairs. It thumped noisily, heavier than I expected. I switched the tubing from the regular unit, and walked down the hall with her, one step at a time, wheeling the torpedo tank next to her. I said, "As soon as you get dressed we'll go to the hospital."

Dr. Ores didn't even know we were coming that Friday afternoon instead of Monday. I hurried downstairs and called David Gainza, who handled the major medical red tape. He'd admitted Chris so many times, he had suggested several months earlier that if I ever needed to bypass the usual billing interview, which was time consuming, I could call him directly, and he would arrange a quick, nonemergency admission to the tenth floor.

"David. It's Mrs. Gordon, Christine's mother. She was supposed to come on Monday—is that what your records indicate?"

"Yes, Mrs. Gordon, it's all set."

"David, she's not doing well at all. She used oxygen all night and she can't breathe. We're coming in right away. I haven't even had a chance to reach Dr. Ores yet. But could you do something for me? Would you have a wheelchair down by the Harkness emergency entrance so that I can get her into it as soon as she gets out of the car?"

He said, "Yes, Mrs. Gordon, I can do that. Do you need oxygen too?"

"No, just the wheelchair."

He added, "Mrs. Gordon, if you can just ask Dr. Ores to call me on my extension, I can set this up quickly. She won't have to come over from Babies."

I thanked him and called Dr. Ores's hospital office and left word. She was on her way to her other office in Englewood. I went back upstairs and helped Chris get dressed. I stuffed her pillows into the floppy duffel bag and she reached over and picked up two small books.

"Here, pack these too." I glanced at them, one black hardback with no writing on it and a dog-earred pocket book of Russian short stories. I stuffed them in.

"Chris, will you be able to get downstairs and into the car without oxygen?"

"No Mom, I don't think so." She stood next to her bed, holding on to the headboard.

"You can't?" I asked. Her lips were blue.

"I can't breathe." I sat down on her bed, examining our choices. She couldn't walk downstairs without help from me but how could I help? The torpedo unit wasn't really portable. I needed both hands to move it.

I said "I'll call Med-X and ask them to send over a Lindy Walker. I'll explain it's an emergency." Med-X was the company that supplied oxygen units for home use. A "Lindy Walker" was an over-the-shoulder unit in a small leather case like something that a stewardess would carry. It was truly portable with a two-hour supply of oxygen.

But Med-X couldn't come. All the drivers were out. I'd have to pick it up myself. I was horrified. How could I leave Christine alone? I went back to talk it over with her.

She said she'd be fine for a half hour. I was scared, thinking back to that terrible spring day when I had left her alone and she'd bled. And yet, I trusted my own resources and God more than I trusted a private ambulance service. Chris felt the same.

So I drove to Stamford praying that she wouldn't bleed or die of heart failure while I was gone. Watching the roads to my right and left, I drove through red lights and stop signs. When I got to Med-X, the low cement building looked like a deserted bunker. A small sign saying Med-X was the only marking.

I didn't have to get out of the car. The manager was waiting for me. He opened the back door of my car, set the unit on the floor quickly, and said, "Drive carefully, Mrs. Gordon." I drove fast. My thoughts were jumbled. If the Med-X man had heard the urgency in my voice, had Chris? People could be so nice, so helpful, if they knew you were okay. Like him, and David Gainza at the hospital, and Rose and Miss Goobler . . . all these people who knew the rules, and took a chance to help you, breaking or bending the rules. These were the kinds of people that made institutions, bureaucracies like Columbia Presbyterian, human. I wondered if the hospital appreciated them. Would the police understand when I ran a red light? I heard a horn blowing behind me. I kept going.

I didn't care if I was stopped, because I thought the Greenwich police would probably put on their sirens and escort me back, if they knew why I was speeding. At least, that was my fantasy as I drove. I could still hear the effort of her breathing.

When I got back, I stopped in the kitchen to calm my pounding heart before I went upstairs. Chris was okay, lying helpless on her bed. I hooked up the oxygen to the little Lindy Walker, slung the carrying case over my shoulder, and we started our slow descent, weaving, jolting down the back stairs, one step at a time. Christine was behind and one step above me, her arms over my shoulders, shaky and unsteady, leaning hard on me for support.

At the bottom of the stairs, I stopped and then we walked slowly across the kitchen and out onto the back porch to the car. It took so long. I felt like a nurse helping an old and feeble patient. We were terrified but the only way to get through this was to stay absolutely calm and not waste a move, so that's what we did. She didn't have the strength to panic. Gingerly, I helped her into the front seat and she held the Lindy Walker in her lap. I went to get the torpedo unit, dragging it down the stairs and lifting it onto the car floor in front of her. I didn't dare rely on the Lindy Walker, in case we ran into traffic or had an accident. It might run out of oxygen.

I drove the thirty miles in twenty-five minutes. As we pulled up to the emergency door, the wheelchair was on the sidewalk. God bless David. Chris got herself into the wheelchair without my help, saying, "Mom, you can leave the oxygen in the car. I think I feel a little better."

I said, "Okay," and wheeled her inside.

Miss Goobler was expecting us. David had told her. I saw her take in Christine's color and demeanor, and see that she was all right at the moment. She said cheerfully, "Your room is ready for you—room 104." I had never noticed her check Chris like this before. Was I hypersensitized or was she?

After Christine was settled onto the bed, she seemed almost herself again. She joked with the nurses about her brief stay at home, saying to Mary, "I just missed the great food here." She didn't pick up the oxygen tubes. She felt safer here and she sat cross-legged on the bed. Her economy of movement was evident. She was taking time to think before moving—judging how much air she would need, and if it would be there. But it was an amazing recovery, nevertheless.

I opened the wide window overlooking the Hudson. One of the things Christine liked about Harkness was that its windows really opened. The windows in the new Babies Hospital were sealed shut and she found it to be stifling, even with air conditioning. She thought people who were sick needed the emotional lift of fresh air coming into their room, no matter what the season.

Tugboats and barges moved noiselessly on the wide river below, seeming to inch their way in and out of view through the clear spaces between new high-rise dormitories. Though obstructed by the recent additions to the hospital complex, the view of the river was timeless and majestic. The steady tugboats were distant, small, unreal shapes on the river . . . another world. The vision of Christine moving at the same eerie unnatural pace as the tugboats slid past.

Someone came into the room and introduced himself to Christine, the attending resident, but I kept looking out the window. I could still see our struggle down the stairs.

A cooling breeze wafted in, lifting the beige casement curtains. The resident got up, introduced himself to me, and hurried out of the room. His name was Dr. Greenman. He was tall and handsome in his rumpled blue oxford shirt.

Chris gave me a devilish look. "God, where's my makeup? Could you look for it? Woooof! He's gorgeous. Just my luck . . . the first good-looking resident in two years and I look like this."

"You're feeling better." I smiled.

"For the moment. He said he was moving to another floor tomorrow. Damn!"

More staff people came in and out—nurses, the nutritionist, a waitress, an intern, and a cardiologist. Dr. Greenman came back and said that he'd be staying on Christine's case after all. I suspect he asked someone if he could make a change in the rotation. Everyone who came in had questions and Chris was tired. She gave me quick looks and I answered for her. I moved from the window to the bed to the chair, to the desk, trying to stay out of the way.

I found the cosmetic bag and handed it to her as she popped up the mirror on the bed tray, and fussed with her hair. There was a welcome pause, the room empty of personnel. I kept quiet and sat in the blue leather Windsor chair. Chris leaned back and pushed the tray aside.

"No use, I've got to wash my hair."

"Oh Chris . . ." I sighed.

"I know," she said, closing her eyes.

"Mom, I must tell you . . . when—at home—when we were going down the stairs . . . I . . . I really thought . . . 'this is it.' I thought I was dying. I barely had strength to stand."

Tears spilled down my cheeks and I felt my heart stumble and fall.

"Christine, I have to tell you how I felt too. I was almost as afraid as you. But, oh God, I . . . I'm not ready for you to go yet. I'm never going to be ready." My throat started to close, choking off my words, and her eyes filled with tears. Breathing with difficulty, I struggled on. "Oh Christine, I've been trying to prepare myself all my life . . . I . . . I don't want you leave. You've got to hang on." She listened, watching me try not to cry, her face breaking in anguish.

"I know, Mom, I'm not ready to go yet either," and she started to cry silently, "I never will be."

I sat next to her and hugged her, knowing we were both living in the same fog, pretending it wasn't happening, trying to be strong for each other and strong for ourselves, and succeeding. But it *was* happening and we had to let each other know that when the fog lifted, we saw clearly and our hearts were breaking together. Nothing changed, nor was it any easier or more real to face it openly for that moment.

I still couldn't imagine life without Christine any more than I could imagine Christine without life. Nor could I begin to understand how she must have felt—being the one who finally had to face it. Soon I would have to let go of her hand and let her go alone. I was losing her, but she was losing everything.

But then—she defied the doctors for eight years . . . what if? Someone came to draw blood and I got up, stepping away from the bed. Chris looked annoyed.

"What are you drawing blood for? Someone came for bloods half an hour ago."

The aide looked at his chart. "I was told to come and get blood before three."

Christine said curtly, "Well, it's been done, just tell them I refused."

The aide looked at me.

"She's right. Sorry."

The aide shrugged and left the room.

I stayed for the afternoon, telling Chris I'd keep trying to reach Jerry up at the Cape. She was supposed to be there with him. We talked a little. She didn't have any magazines, so I went

to the news store on Broadway, buying all the rock 'n' roll magazines I could find.

Chris asked the nurses to find a cot for me. They had ordered
one for Monday, not today. Her despair and fear were put aside
and she was cheerful when I left and a little wistful, as she always
was if no other visitor was going to take my place.

30 ⋆ Waiting

I came back that night and the IVs were started. We waited. We knew what to look for; we'd been through it so many times. We understood that most of the airways would never be unclogged again, that a huge amount of her lungs was inoperative. But she just needed enough to live on. I didn't ask myself what kind of a life she'd be able to live.

In the morning I dashed home, and came back in the afternoon. The lobby was busy as it always was on Saturday. There was a line of people waiting to get their visitor's passes. The new security system was still in effect. The hospital often started new regulations only to change or discard them several weeks later. Dr. Ores said it was because of the high rate of drug thefts in the hospital. Besides looking for the best possible system, they kept it moving so it was difficult to figure out.

The new guards were young, tough, and skeptical. I never tried to cut into the line even though they knew me by now. But today, I skipped the line completely and kept walking—eyeing the guard to see what would happen. The guard picked up a pink cardboard pass and held it out to me without a word as I walked past him to the elevator. I didn't like the way it felt good. I'd rather be a stranger. I went up, pushing back the need I always felt to rush down the hall to her room, and opened the door to her faint but cheery, "Hi Mom." The room was oddly quiet. I was surprised. She always had the TV on, even when she wasn't watching. She didn't like the quiet she always said. It was too lonely.

She smiled like a little girl with a secret and watched me plop magazines and pretzels on the bed. I wondered what had cheered her up. Moving under the IV tubes, I bent over and kissed her, resting my cheek on her cheek. "Ummm, you smell good."

"The nurse washed my hair," she said.

"Maybe that's it, but you always smell good."

She looked up at me. "Do I?"

"Uh huh, you do."

"I had a talk with Dr. Greenman," she offered.

"Is he the cute one?"

"Yes, he's *sooo* nice," she said.

I settled into the blue wing chair and put my feet up on the footrest. She leaned back. "Mom, I hope you don't mind if I sleep for a while. I'm tired today."

"I don't mind, I'll sit and watch you," but her cheerful smile of a moment before was gone. She had wanted to be cheerful for me but she couldn't keep it up, she was too frightened. I helped her rearrange her pillows, squishing them this way and that to let her sleep sitting up.

She pushed her head hard back onto the top pillow.

"I love you," she said.

"I love you, too," I said and she closed her eyes, still sitting up. It was unusual for her to sleep in the afternoon. Her eyes popped open. "Did you reach Dad?"

"No dear, but I left a message at the cafe. I gave them this number. They said he was singing tonight." Jerry performed nightly in a cafe in Provincetown when he was on vacation.

"Good," she whispered and slept.

And so the mornings and the afternoons and the nights passed and she waited for the drugs to work. She was so still all the time. She ate nothing. The hyperalimentation ran twenty-four hours a day. She made no phone calls and forbid me to tell her friends where she was.

Dr. Ores had told me the hospital had small apartments that parents of sick children could rent to be nearby and I made an appointment to see them. Her father got back from the Cape on Monday, the third day. When he'd gotten the message, he'd called Christine's room. Chris had been too tired and short of breath to talk on the phone and when he asked, "Chris . . . are you okay?" her voice was so faint he had to cover his other ear to hear her say, "Dad, I'm not doing so great. I'm scared . . . could you come home?" He caught the first plane back to New York and we took turns staying with her.

We were afraid but we didn't talk about it. It was easy to keep the fear hidden inside and I wondered why. We acted normal. There was no reason to wonder. We'd been doing it for years, but now it seemed out of place.

I was numb with worry and barely functioning at home. It was good that Jenny was on the Vineyard with her father, so I didn't have to. The idea of going home and fixing dinner was unthinkable.

Dr. Ores adjusted the antibiotics; took new sputum cultures to grow in the lab, looking for the first sign of the infection weakening. She monitored her heart and kidneys and regulated the oxygen levels. Chris was using more and more and her headaches were getting worse from the carbon dioxide. She pleaded with me when the nurses were out of the room.

"Mom, please, could you bring me some Fiorinal and Tylenol? I can't stand these headaches. The nurses make me wait too long."

So I did. On her own, she'd take a Fiorinal between the hospital doses of Extra-Strength Tylenol, not always, but when the headache was unbearable.

Her meal trays went back untouched. When the maids brought her meals, they would look at me. Had they seen this sitting up dying before? I'd say nothing but nod a silent greeting and they'd quietly leave the tray. Chris heard them come in. She'd say, "What's that, Mom, dinner?" and I'd say, "No, Chris, it's lunch."

The only time I cried was driving back and forth to the hospital. Sometimes I had to pull off the road. She was getting weaker, sitting in the same two positions day after day, night after night. The rhythm of life was gone, the going to sleep and waking up. She didn't know what time it was. She couldn't lie down because it was harder to breathe. None of life's comforts was left, not even sleep, and I watched her endless sitting, one leg folded up Indian style, the other dangling over the side. At times she rested her head in her arms on the bed tray, but most of the time she sat unsupported, pale and swanlike, her head resting back, her chin high, her throat arched gently out. Her shoulders slumped forward, like wings folding in to rest from the strain of a long flight and a dark tunnel of time closed around her. When I thought about it, I couldn't get a deep enough breath. What was on her mind in these motionless hours? I couldn't understand and as the days passed, I wondered how she remained that way for so long. But she did, wrapping herself in a cocoon of graceful silence.

Rosemarie and Kay, our two private nurses, rubbed her back when she was exhausted from coughing, held their hands in a tight band of pressure around her temples when the headaches were bad, and let Chris lean on them for comfort or sleep.

Each day, she'd perk up for a little while but I never knew when this would be. Sometimes I'd catch it and sometimes I wouldn't.

There was one thing Christine still focused on and that was Jenny. Jenny's birthday was Thursday, September 2nd, and I'd promised Chris I'd bring Jenny in on that day. I hadn't told her yet that Jenny wouldn't be home for her birthday as promised, and I wasn't sure when her father would bring her home. I'd canceled her birthday party at the last minute.

Thursday, Jenny's birthday, I arrived after supper. Jerry was leaving and kissed Chris good-bye. We talked in the hall a minute and Jerry said, "She's been asking about Jenny."

"I know."

"She seems a little better today," he said and left quietly.

Chris was awake and more alert than she had been for several days. Maybe the antibiotics were starting to work, or maybe it was for Jenny. I leaned over to hug her, and her cheek was cool, like white silk. No fever. She looked at the open door behind me. "No Jenny?"

"No, I'm sorry. I should have told you. Maybe tomorrow." Chris looked puzzled and disappointed.

"She didn't get home for her birthday? Drat." I waited, saying nothing. "Nine is an important birthday. I wish she was here right now, that little squirt. I—" She stopped, stared at her fingers, lost in thought.

"Chris, what?"

She didn't look up. "Nothing . . . nothing." She reached down and picked up the pale green oxygen mask and put it on over the tubing she already had around her head. Two oxygens.

She fell asleep and I sat down and watched her. A dusty gold light filled the room and faded softly as the sun sank, but Chris didn't see it. I went to the window. A beautiful sunset was fading. Low clouds in the west over New Jersey darkened to navy blue and the raggedy bottoms glowed with fiery red-gold light. Below, the cars on the West Side Highway were lost in the dark except for red tail-lights streaming silently along. I sat back down and slipped my hand into hers. Her sleep was coma-like and the hours passed.

Christine had been so sweet with Jenny the morning she left for a month on Martha's Vineyard with her father. Chris had said to me the night before, "Mom, *promise* to wake me up and send Jenny in to say good-bye—just before she leaves," and I'd promised.

That morning Jenny's father had arrived at ten and I'd woken Chris up and said, "Jenny's about to leave, dear, do you still want her to come in? Are you enough awake?"

Chris woke up with a start saying, "Oh yes, where is she?"

She was right behind me. "Bye, Chris. I'll miss you."

Chris said, "Jenny, come here," and she hugged Jenny with one arm, leaning on the other. "Jenny," she said, very serious now. Jenny focused on her sister and so did I. Christine held up her trembling forefinger that looked just like E.T.'s finger in the movie, and imitated, in a perfect E.T. croak, "Be-e-e Goo-o-d." Jenny had seen the movie four times and her eyes got bigger as Chris lowered her hand and slowly walked her E.T. fingers across the covers and up her pajamas, pointing to her own heart. She said, again just like E.T., "OUUCCHHHH." Then watching Jenny's rapt face, Chris raised her finger up in the air once more and letting it tremble, she moved it through the air ever so slowly toward Jenny, bringing it to rest lightly on Jenny's forehead. Quoting the little E.T., she croaked, "I'll . . . beee . . . right . . . here."

It was the farewell scene between Eliot, his little sister, Gertie, and E.T.—to perfection. Jenny's eyes were huge and unblinking as she stood with her mouth open, mesmerized by Christine's magic. Chris lay back down, smiling at Jenny, and said no more. I waited, feeling the magic too, letting it linger, then I extended my hand to Jenny.

"Come on, Jen, your dad's waiting."

Jenny said, "Bye, Chris," and took my hand as we hurried down the stairs. "Mommy, she sounded just like E.T.!"

"I know. Chris is amazing the way she can do that."

"Boy, she sure is," Jenny said as she turned to hug me. "Bye, Mommy." And she'd run down the brick walk to her father's waiting car.

I must have dozed in the chair. Awake, the only sound was the private nurse flicking the IV lines. My hand was warm, still nestled in Christine's. She hadn't moved. It was twelve o'clock. I leaned forward, listening to her labored breathing, when she squeezed my hand. Startled, I looked up. "Chris?"

"What?" She was still, her eyes closed.

"Oh nothing. I thought you were asleep."

"No."

I knew she couldn't talk. My arm was numb from reaching to rest my hand in hers. I said no more and wondered why I felt more separate than before.

31 · Indelible
Heartbeat

Jenny finally got home late the next day, her birthday past, and I told her Chris was sick in the hospital again. She looked up at me, disappointed, but she was used to it.

I was in the front hall downstairs, getting ready to visit Chris on Saturday afternoon.

"Oh, Mom, please," Jenny begged. "Can't I come and sleep in her room like last time. It was so fun. I haven't seen her in so long . . ."

I was torn, and tried to think of a way to manage it. We stood in the hall and I looked down at her and brushed strands of hair out of her face, glad Jenny thought it was fun, spending the night in the hospital with her sister. But I knew I could never get her past the guard at night—not anymore.

"I know we did it before Jenny, and it was a real adventure. But that was special. It was an emergency. They have guards posted at the door now, twenty-four hours a day."

She wouldn't give up. She held on to my arm. "Oh please, Mommy, let's try. I didn't see Chris on my birthday and I didn't see her on her birthday either. I bought her presents in Martha's Vineyard. Please."

I sat down on the stairs. Maybe I could get permission . . . but on Labor Day weekend . . . no way. I wouldn't be able to find anyone.

"Jenny, I know. It isn't fair, is it? You and I know you're grown up enough to come with me, but the hospital doesn't know and they won't let me bring you." She was crushed and I tried to

332

distract her. "Can I see what you got her for her birthday?" She took me upstairs to her room and pulled a thin brown paper bag from a pile of unpacked things in the corner of her room. She held up a new T-shirt, watching me closely. The T-shirt had a huge pair of luscious red lips printed across the front—like the ones in the opening credits of *The Rocky Horror Picture Show.*

"Oooooo neat," I said, approving.

Then she unfolded a narrow silver lamé men's tie, saying as she handed me the tie to examine more closely, "I think it's very punk . . . don't you?"

"Oh yes, Jenny," I said, stifling a laugh. "Chris will love it."

"I know," she said. I hugged her, the kind of long crushing hug that Jenny loved.

I left for the hospital and Jenny stood on the back porch and watched me go. My thoughts stayed with Jenny a long time as I drove. She was used to seeing Chris reappear and never thought about death, but even Jenny would know at first glance that something was different. Would I find a way to help her understand what I couldn't understand myself, that she was going to lose the big sister she adored, who helped her get through her night fears, who played Barbie dolls with her and liked it, who understood how hard it was to be around her father when he had a temper tantrum. I clung to my threadbare hope that once again Chris would rally.

This Labor Day was a sultry summer afternoon. It had rained almost every weekend in July and August that year and now that the summer was over, it was glorious. The lobby of Harkness was empty and my footsteps clattered on the marble floor. All three elevators were standing open and the guard handed me a pass.

I said hi to Miss Goobler, surprised to see her still on duty, and walked down the hall to Christine's room. The door was closed, the usual sign tacked onto it: DANGER No Smoking—Oxygen in Use.

I stopped just inside the door, not moving or saying a word, waiting to hear some familiar sound signifying Chris's presence. Only the sound of the summer wind whispering through the window and one of the curtain cords tapping restlessly on the glass window guard could be heard. I looked up at the dark television screen.

Chris was sitting in the same position as when I'd left but reversed. I walked around the bed and sat on it. She was ashen, her lips lavender blue, her short blond hair pushed every which way. She felt the bed move and leaned back against me.

"Hi Chris," I said.

She didn't answer. The nurse wasn't in the room and through the open window, a shaft of sunlight pierced the air, the hot square of light hitting the floor and angling across the room. The oxygen was off. Not a sound came from the street below. Christine shifted her weight carefully, still leaning on me and said softly, "Mom. I think . . . I'm going to die."

Her whispered words hung in the still air, but didn't penetrate. My eyes closed and my head slumped forward, too heavy to support. I put my arm around her waist from behind and pressed against her back carefully, whispering, "Oh Christine," and we sat like that for a long time just breathing together.

Kay came in. "Hello Mrs. Gordon."

"Hello, Kay." Chris stayed motionless as I got up and sat slowly in the wing chair. Kay turned on the oxygen. With her eyes closed, Chris adjusted the tubes under her nose.

For a while I tried to read the front page of the *Times*, but by the time I got to the second paragraph, I'd forgotten what I'd read in the first.

I looked at Chris, comatose, perched like a mute swan again. The skin at the base of her throat formed deep gouges between her collarbones as it strained in and out and a familiar distant sadness came closer, creeping into the room, filling it. I could see it in the curtains, listlessly moving as currents of air slid in the window and stopped. I could hear it in the dull bubbling of the oxygen and I could feel it in my stomach, a hollow, swollen, hot feeling pressing outward. If death was in the room, this time he'd come in friendship.

I thought back to the winter. Her suffering at Christmas had so frightened me, I'd begun thinking about how to say to her, it was all right if her courage ran out and she let herself be taken.

Was it fair to ask her to keep on fighting when her life was so out of balance? If I did, would it speed her to her death? What made me think I had any say in the matter? She was suffering, not me, but still, I let her know it was all right. Up till then, I'd never thought she might give up.

At the time, she was taking piano lessons and guitar lessons and learning to read music. She was sitting at the piano practicing J. Thompson's first-year piano pieces. Sunlight curled warmly around her back and I listened to her play the piece. She finished and sighed.

"It's fun, but it's so hard and takes so long."

"Chris, there's something I want to say. It seems your hospital admissions . . ." I stopped, groping carefully, speaking gently. "Well, you seem to have less and less time when you're free of suffering. I don't want you to feel you have to keep on fighting for me. I don't want you to give up . . . but don't do it for me." I paused a minute and looked at her face. She was okay. I went on.

"I mean, you know how I always say life is worth living? It's easy to say when you have your health. Maybe there's a time when it isn't worth it. I don't know, but please know, Chris, I love you. If it's ever too terrible to go on, don't do it for me."

She was looking down at the keys, her hands in her lap, and I was hardly breathing. She looked up and our eyes met. She looked down again.

"I know, Mom." I don't think she knew what else to say and neither did I. I groped again.

"I wasn't sure . . . we've been fighting so long."

We sat in silence for a minute and then she said, "Thanks," and bit her lip and started to play again.

If ever there was a time to hug her, that was it, but I didn't. I was afraid to move. She stopped and turned to a piece in the back, a harder one.

"Want to play the bottom part for me?" I nodded and slid over next to her and together, with no mistakes, we played the duet she liked. We never spoke about it again.

Now I sat watching and remembering, thinking of anything but the future. I went to the cafeteria for coffee. It was deserted except for the cashier who looked up from the paperback she was reading to take my forty cents, and an old woman sitting at a table, her head slumped in sleep. I brought the coffee back up and poured it from the Styrofoam cup into the unused china cup on Christine's dinner tray. I drank it slowly and watched her some more. She opened her eyes.

"Mom, is Jenny coming?"

"Yes dear, in the morning," I said.

"Oh good," she said, closing her eyes again with a trace of a smile.

How I loved her and how lucky I was to have her. Friends and acquaintances thought Christine must be a burden and would ask me carefully, with sympathy and maybe admiration, how I managed. They meant well. But they didn't understand. It was never that way at all. Christine made my life wonderful. There was a grace and beauty in her that touched everything she did, and it touched me.

Even now, filled with unspoken fear . . . death tugging at her sleeve . . . she was uncomplaining, unbegging. She couldn't breathe anymore and I said to myself, "She can't fight if she can't breathe" and I didn't ask her to.

Giving her oxygen didn't help now. She was running out of lungs not oxygen. She sat so still. She had to. If she exerted herself in the least, she'd start to suffocate because there was no place left in her lungs to get extra oxygen. I imagined the reason she sat so straight was that there was just a little clear space left at the top of her lungs and if she leaned over, that little space would fill with fluid.

Would this be where it happened, on the tenth floor of Harkness with the doctors, the nurses, the IVs? She waited on her hated battlefield—a thin tracing of herself. What a paltry prize for death who would claim her now when there was nothing left to claim. She'd given all of herself to us—another victory.

The afternoon slipped into evening and suddenly it was nine o'clock. I went down the hall and called Jim. I started to cry. He said, "It's not good, is it?"

"No, Jerry thought she was better, but it must have been her good time. She's worse if anything. Can you come tomorrow morning with Jenny? Chris is asking for her. I promised Jenny I'd come home and get her but I don't want to leave."

He said he would and I went back to the room. At midnight, Kay left and Rosemarie came. Rosemarie got Chris up gently and sat her in the wing chair. She changed the bed and helped Chris back into it. When Chris said to Rosemarie, "I can't get enough air," Rosemarie insisted they do thumps. Chris didn't want to but Rosemarie helped her carefully into a lying position just the same.

It was awful, as she choked and gasped, but then it was a little easier to breath as they went on.

"Rosemarie," Chris said, "you're being like Hannah . . ."

I smiled. Hannah was a daytime staff nurse, very efficient and very German with a strong accent. She was a little too bossy at times and Chris had thrown an empty barf pan against the wall once, when Hannah had said, "You *must* eat. This von't do!" Now, as Chris lay with her back to me, ready for more thumping, I heard her say softly, in Hannah's German accent,

"You must eat, Christine . . . zat is a *rool* here and dis von't do."

Rosemarie started to giggle. "Miss Goobler told me you could imitate *anyone.*"

"My voices are legend," said Chris.

While Rosemarie was pounding on her chest, I looked at Christine's left ankle. It was swollen and huge—bigger than her knee. Her foot looked like an oversized clubfoot dangling off the edge of the bed. When Rosemarie was finished, I looked at her anxiously and mouthed the words. "What's that . . . her ankle?"

Rosemarie signaled for me to go outside the room with her. Standing in the hall, I asked, "What's wrong with her ankle? I've never seen that before . . ."

"I'm not sure, Mrs. Gordon, but I think it's renal failure."

"What's renal failure?"

"Her kidneys are failing . . . the fluids in her body accumulate and flow to the lowest point and pool there."

"Oh Rosemarie." My voice was full of horror, "I think Chris is dying . . . Dr. Ores does too." She seemed unsure of how much

to tell me but she nodded in agreement. "Rosemarie, Chris hasn't
seen her sister Jenny. She was supposed to be here on her birthday but she didn't make it." She nodded. She knew all about it.
"I was going to bring her tomorrow . . . but . . . well . . . how long
does Christine have . . . I mean . . . just based on your experience
of course."

Rosemarie considered a moment before saying, "I think she'll
be like this for two or three days."

"Do you think it's safe for me to go home and bring Jenny back
at eight tomorrow morning? Mr. Gordon was going to bring her
in . . . but maybe I can . . ."

Rosemarie answered, "I think you could go home to get her.
There's time."

I wasn't sure what to do. We both went back into the room and
I started making up the cot. I decided to stay. Then I changed my
mind again. Christine didn't seem to know I was there. Rosemarie
was standing by the bed watching her.

"Rosemarie," I said, "it's after midnight now—I think I'll go
back to Greenwich at one . . . and come back at seven in the
morning with Jenny and Jim."

Chris sat forward slightly and opened her eyes, looking over
at me. She seemed dazed.

"You're leaving? Oh, please don't go, Mom . . . please stay
. . . oh, please stay."

I looked at Chris in relief and dismay and went to her saying,
"Oh Chris, of course I'll stay. I didn't know if you knew I was here
. . . I don't have to go at all."

She let her head fall back against me and closed her eyes,
saying in one breath, "Oh, thank you for staying, thank you for
staying . . ."

I bent over, touching my cheek to her forehead, and felt my
heart finally break . . . the pain so strange, so familiar.

"There's just no question dear . . . of course I'll stay. Jim will
bring Jenny," and I sat down on her bed, nestling close to her like
a fallen leaf curling around a twig. It was still night.

I got up and walked to the window, the door, the hall, to the
little cot—overwhelmed, trying to stop my throat from closing,

trying to push away the strange dense pressure growing in my chest. I tried to sleep a little, but I heard every sound. Rosemarie administered to Christine, giving her a long back rub, doing a few gentle thumps, helping her to the commode, which had been moved into the room, next to the bed.

I lay thinking and trying not to think, and Christine sat without moving. Rosemarie left the room and Chris didn't stir. I listened and watched alone. I studied the shadows in the room and heard a shuffling. Getting up nervously, I turned on the desk lamp. I didn't want shadows in the room. I lay back down on the cot. Maybe I slept. Rosemarie came briskly in and startled me up. I was all nerve endings. Innocent noises sounded ominous. I wanted the night to be over, I didn't want the night to end. Everything was all wrong.

At four o'clock Rosemarie adjusted the IV and Chris woke up with a start, taking Rosemarie's hand and saying, "Jenny . . . Jenny?" But her eyes remained closed and I heard Rosemarie say, "No, Chris, it's me, Rosemarie . . . Jenny's coming in the morning." She shook with a violent coughing spasm and Rosemarie pressed her hands against Christine's forehead so the pounding in her head wouldn't be so bad. I was awake, lying on the cot, getting up and lying back down again. At 5:30, Rosemarie was sitting, awake and alert, near Christine's bed.

I watched the shadows retreat from the room, as dawn crept in, spreading astringent blue light. The rooms on the east side of the hall must have been filled with the first warm light of the sun, but the sky to the west was cold and pale, hesitant, unwelcoming—still night. This day did not seem to want to arrive.

Christine started to cough again, a low, wet cough. I sat up fast—I knew the cough. It was the blood cough. Rosemarie handed her a cup and Chris spit blood into it. She looked in the cup and moaned, "Oh, my God . . ." and her cough kept on coming, low and insistent. Her shoulders and back fell forward with each cough.

I was at her side and held her hand. Rosemarie hadn't seen this before.

"Rosemarie, we need a cough suppressant, right away."

"We'll have to get a doctor's order. Dr. Ores is off call . . ."

"No," I interrupted her, "call Celia—she told me it was okay."

Chris was leaning back almost off the edge of the bed and I put my arms around her waist from behind her as she coughed against me. I had to hold her with both arms to keep her from falling off the bed. She clenched the covers with one hand. She was struggling and struggling to breathe . . . to get air through the fluid . . . it was terrible.

Rosemarie moved quickly, grabbing the phone by the bed. She woke Dr. Ores and the codeine was ordered immediately. Rosemarie went to the nurses' station to get a syringe and gave Chris the shot, then I went to get the night nurse while Rosemarie held on to Chris, supporting her as she coughed. There wasn't a lot of blood, but she couldn't stop coughing. She was suffocating.

I ran down the hall and asked the night nurse to come quickly with suction equipment—the thin soft tubing that clears an obstructed bronchial tube—and then ran back to the room and stood at the door looking at Christine with panic, holding the door partly open. Once again, I heard the sound a straw makes as it draws from the bottom of a glass, but louder than ever before, in and out—in and out. She struggled to get air. I couldn't go in the room. I was frozen . . . terrified.

How can I be such a coward, I thought, and I went in, my heart pounding. Then I went back to the door again looking for the night nurse. Where *was* she? The door to the room across the hall was open. I saw the woman patient appear at the door in her robe. For a moment our eyes met, and then she closed the door. I wish I hadn't seen it, that door closing. The night nurse came down the hall with the suction equipment. I couldn't believe how slowly she was walking and I urged, "Hurry up!" I wasn't polite.

I stepped into the room again and held Christine, still helping her stay upright, while Rosemarie called the head resident and kept saying to Chris, "It's all right, Christine . . . it's all right . . . the resident is coming . . . the doctor's on the way. He'll be here in a minute . . . hang on . . . hang on . . . it's all right."

I heard Christine whisper, "Daddy . . . Daddy . . ." The night nurse was setting up the suction equipment. Christine was in my arms and my head was bent low, close over her shoulder, and I heard her whisper as she gasped for breath, "What can the doctor do . . . what can the doctor do . . ."

I looked down at her face as she leaned back heavily against me, the merciless cough continuing, and I said, "Oh my God, Rosemarie—she's turning blue. Oh no . . . she's turning blue!" As I said it, Christine went limp in my arms—her head dropped forward, she stopped breathing, she was unconscious. Rosemarie looked at her watch. I looked at my watch too—6:30 in the morning.

We moved her quickly, sitting her back against the pillows. Her head fell back—her chin up—and it was easy to guide the soft tubing down her throat, and apply the gentle suction that would clear the passageway and let her breathe. The suction worked right away and she started to breathe again, but remained unconscious.

I called Jerry from her bedside. He wasn't home and I left an urgent message with his friend Steve, who shared the apartment at times.

Christine remained in a coma for seven hours. The nurses cleared her bronchial tube every five minutes—the secretions accumulated so quickly. In a coma, there is no cough reflex, and the bleeding stopped.

She looked the same—as if she were asleep sitting up, except that her hands rested at her sides with the palms turned upward, as I'd seen them only once before, three years ago, when I'd come back from getting her schoolbooks and she'd had the terrible bleed at home alone.

Dr. Silverman, who was covering for Dr. Ores that weekend, came in and stood at the foot of the bed. He was subdued, leaning his hands against the footboard.

"Mrs. Gordon, do you know what's happening?"

"Yes," I said.

"Do you understand there's nothing we can do now?"

"Yes, I know," I said flatly. "You don't have to explain anything."

When Dr. Silverman left the room, I walked to the window as

I had a hundred times, and stared out. Why hadn't she just slipped into a coma peacefully—as Celia had said she would, from the carbon dioxide her lungs were retaining. Why had God done this—let her suffer for an hour with terror and suffocation and drowning, knowing there was no way out. It seemed like one last kick out the door. My best friend, Nancy, said to me later, when I expressed my bitter feelings, "Jacquie, you know Christine wouldn't go peacefully—she was too much of a fighter."

But she would have gone peacefully. She was ready. She was waiting for death to find her on that wrinkled hospital bed. She wasn't fighting anymore. Helpless before the end, her body betrayed her one last time. She would have accepted this, too, with her usual grace, thinking, I'm sure, things just never go my way. But I couldn't. God wasn't to blame but I blamed him anyway.

I turned and sat back down next to Christine. There were tears streaming down her face. I looked at Rosemarie. "What's that?" I whispered. "It looks like tears. Could she be crying . . . in a coma?"

Rosemarie studied Chris, uncertain, and shook her head slowly, saying, "I don't know . . . I've never seen it before."

I took a Kleenex, the kind Chris liked, and gently wiped the tears away.

Her father arrived at 7:30. Steve must have reached him immediately. As soon as he arrived I went down the hall to telephone Jim, saying, "Jim, please wake Jenny and come in as quickly as possible. Christine is in a coma . . . but she may come out of it."

"I'll be there within the hour," he said.

"Jim, don't tell Jenny . . . about the coma . . . I'll explain to her what's happening when you get here."

After I hung up I sat in the dark of the phone booth and sobbed and sobbed. Chris had been saving strength for Jenny and would have said good-bye if Jenny had only been there. I still wonder what words she would have left with her sister.

I should have brought Jenny with me the day she begged to come, a second chance and I'd passed it by. What had I been thinking of?

I opened the door of the phone booth and walked back to the

room, not bothering to dry my eyes, and sat down, explaining to Jerry what had happened.

Rosemarie was finished at eight. She wanted to stay and care for Chris but she had a little boy at home and she couldn't stay past nine. I called the nurses registry at 7:45 and, on a holiday weekend, they found yet another good nurse very quickly. She arrived at 8:30, crisp, slim, looking more like a resident than a nurse. Her name was Nina and she'd grown up in Greenwich. She had the quick, sure, confident demeanor of a doctor. Chris would have liked her.

A little after nine o'clock, the guard called up from the lobby. Jim, Jenny, and Cindy and Ted were downstairs. I explained to the guard that my daughter was in a coma and this was her family and he let everyone up together.

I was at the elevator door when it opened and the first thing I saw were Jenny's eyes—dark and clear—looking up at me, probing past my numbness, puzzled to be up so early on Sunday but happy to be there, with her presents for Christine in her hand. I gave Jim and Jenny a kiss and took Jenny's hand with a squeeze.

"Jenny, let's sit and talk for a little."

She followed me into the sunroom. I sat on the rattan sofa, holding Jenny close to me as she stood listening. My voice was thick with emotion. There was no euphemism that would make any sense to a nine-year-old.

"Jenny, Christine is sick. She's very sick this time. She just can't get better any more. Chris is going to die." Jenny looked at me and then looked quickly away, her face a blank. She was still there, but she'd disappeared. I let her handle the news her own way for the moment, hugging her close. I wasn't doing much better myself.

"Dear, do you want to see Chris?" She nodded. "She can't see you, dear—and she can't talk. She's in a sleep she can't wake up from. It's called a coma. But I think she can hear you." I didn't think any such thing, but I said it for Jenny. What I didn't know was that it might have been true. People who've recovered from comas have said they heard what went on. How I wish I'd known. I would have spoken to Chris—a lifetime.

I walked down to her room with Jenny, saying at the door,

"Wait a minute, Jenny," and I went in first. Christine was the same, sitting back against her pillows, but I didn't want Jenny to see the suction tube being put down her throat. Then I brought Jenny in.

Jerry said sweetly, "Hello, Jenny," and she didn't answer, just put her birthday presents at the foot of the bed. She walked up and slipped her hand carefully into Christine's and stood by the bed holding her hand for a while. She looked up at me, a little uncertain, and I nodded to let her know that what she was doing was just fine. Jenny didn't speak and didn't cry, but stood like a statue, looking at Chris, and I knew I'd have to help her unlock her tears later. Then I brought her down to the sunroom to sit with Cindy and Ted, her presents for Chris in her hands again.

Jerry stood at the top of the bed as the hours passed, and blotted the dewy perspiration on Christine's forehead. Twice more, tears rolled down her cheeks and Jerry caught them with a tissue. We looked at each other, wondering about the tears— knowing they were real. I sat on the bed next to her and held her hand. Cindy and Ted and Jenny and Jim came in from time to time, asking politely if it was all right. Cindy's face was wet with tears, and so was mine, and I saw Jenny watching, trying to understand.

Twice during the morning, residents came to do arterial blood gas tests, which meant drawing blood from her groin. I remembered how Chris always said the worst tests were the blood gases, and I turned them away. The second time, I was gruff and snapped, "Don't you dare touch her with that needle. She's suffered enough." Maybe Chris heard me. Jerry looked at me in grateful agreement.

Christine's breathing grew shallower and shorter as the hours passed, as if the fluids were filling the little space she had left. Her heart struggled on, trying to force the oxygen-poor blood through. Nina made minute-by-minute checks of Christine's heart rate. Once she said softly, almost to herself, "What a heart she has. It should've stopped hours ago."

For the last hour, Chris had been breathing six quick little breaths every sixty seconds with a ten-second wait between each one. For a while I matched my breathing to hers, to know what it felt like, even if she couldn't feel it. It wasn't enough to sustain life for much longer. Jerry stood, holding her right hand. I sat on the bed, holding her left hand, and Jim sat in the wing chair. It was almost two o'clock.

Jerry said to Christine, his wonderful voice husky and breaking, "Look for the light, Christine—open the door and walk through, toward the light."

One more door. The tears ran down my cheeks as if they'd never stop as I counted the seconds between each breath—10, 11, 12, 13, 14, 15 . . . I looked up at Jim, he'd noticed the long interval too . . . 17, 18, 19 I counted to myself. Her next breath hadn't come. Jerry looked down at Christine . . . 22, 23, 24, 25 . . . and he moved aside as the nurse came close and put her stethoscope to Christine's chest. Lowering her head in concentration she said, "Her heart's still beating."

She stood back for a few seconds and put the stethoscope on Christine's wrist listening for more long seconds. Then she bent quickly over, listening to her heart once more. Almost 60 seconds had passed. Nina looked at her watch and said quietly, "There is no heartbeat."

She was gone.

Postlude

★
★ ★

In the moments after Christine died, when time started to move again, I went to her bed again and again, looking at her—lying inert and silent, etching the vision of her death in my mind and on my heart, carving the image deep, because I knew her death would be unreal and I'd have to return to this image to understand that she was gone.

About a month later, Jenny and I were out doing errands. The image I had carved so deep was with me everyday. But I hadn't begun to accept her death. It was baffling to me, this empty silence. Where Chris used to be there was a hole in the air. Nothing. Chris would have taken out a pad and written no-thing, to help me understand. Driving by the large cemetery on Ridge Street in Rye, Jenny asked a question I'd been wondering when she would ask.

"Mommy, is Christine in a grave somewhere?"

"No dear," I said.

"Where is she?"

"Christine was cremated."

"What's that?"

"It's one of the things that people do with a person's body after the spirit has left it. When people are cremated, their bodies are burned and their ashes are put into a vase. Then sometimes they are scattered in the wind."

Jenny looked at me in stunned shock, saying nothing for a moment. Overwhelmed, she lowered her head, saying quietly, "I think I prefer the other way."

"You mean burial?" Almost imperceptibly, she nodded. I continued, "It was a very difficult thing to decide, Jenny. At first, I thought I would rather bury Christine, too. But, you know, Christine was always cold. And . . . it seemed so awful to me to think of her all alone and cold in the ground. I just couldn't."

"But Mommy—at least you're safe in the ground in a nice box," she said.

"Yes, but in time the box rots away, and then so does the person's body. You know, there is a saying in the Bible about all living things—plants and animals and people. That we all come from the dust and we all return to the dust when we die. The words are "ashes to ashes, dust to dust" and I believe it's true. When people believe in that, they choose cremation—returning their body into dust quickly. In many countries, they burn their dead. We sometimes scatter the ashes and dust over the land most loved by the person or in the waves or in the wind—and the person's soul goes back to God."

I paused waiting for some response, but Jenny just stared straight ahead. "It's terrible to think of, isn't it? But to me, it's terrible to even think of Christine dead . . . of her gone . . . forever. All of it is terrible."

We drove for a while in silence and were almost home from our errands when Jenny asked me, "Mommy, do you believe there's a heaven?"

"Well, Jenny, I believe there is a much larger life after death. I don't actually believe that heaven is a place that has a gate that you go through to get there. But I do believe that the spirit lives on. I don't really understand how, but it keeps on living." She was quiet—thinking.

"Do you think there's hell?" she asked.

"No, Jenny, there is no hell. Christine used to say to me, 'Mom, I know I'm going to heaven when I die, because I've already been to hell.' "

Jenny turned to me. "What did she mean?"

"Well, Jenny, sometimes, not all the time, but when Christine was very ill, she felt as if her life was hell. She was trapped—always sick—and she had no rest from her sickness." Mark had said "she spent her life rejoicing," but he didn't see the suffering and neither did Jenny.

Suddenly she said, "Like when I woke up from having my tonsils out and it hurt so much and I was so scared?"

"Well, yes, but worse. You were frightened but you knew you'd get better. Christine knew she'd never get better . . . only sicker. She was more than frightened. She was terrified. Sometimes her hands trembled from fear." Celia had told me the trembling was not from lack of oxygen. I looked at Jenny as we pulled into our driveway. Her eyes were somber, dark and hard with thinking, and she said, "She *knew?*"

I nodded. "She knew," and shut off the motor and we sat in the car. I went back to the cremation to see if I could undo any of the horror. "It's a holy fire, Jenny. Some people call it a sacred fire when a person is cremated. Many, many people do it. But it's hard to think about it, isn't it?" There was a tight little nod. "Don't think about it, Jenny."

The subject didn't come up again for several weeks. In November, a week or so before Thanksgiving, I was tucking Jenny into bed on a school night. She always took her time, enjoying her bedtime rituals. We were fussing with the covers while she sat under them, getting ready to lie down. She liked the covers on her bed loose and untucked, and she pulled and tugged to free them on the far side. I was making a jelly roll of her comforter at the foot of the bed so she could pull it up easily in the middle of the night. She finished arranging her covers, flopped down, and turned on her side, thoughtful and quiet.

"All set?" I asked.

She looked at me, not answering. Lying on her side—with the covers pulled up over her head to help her forget her night fears—only her eyes and one hand holding the covers away from her mouth could be seen.

"What is it, Jenny?"

"I was just thinking about Christine's dust." I sat down on the edge of the bed.

"What were you thinking?"

"About . . . how can she go to heaven if she's only dust?"

"It's hard to explain, Jenny. It's Christine's spirit, her soul, that's in heaven."

"Is it . . . in the sky?"

"Yes, it's there, and it's everywhere . . . all around us. When people die and go to heaven, they don't take their bodies with them. It would be too crowded. Only their spirit goes. That's why we bury, or cremate, people's bodies. Do you know what I mean by spirit?" She nodded.

"What do I mean?"

She thought a minute. "A ghost," she said.

I smiled. "No dear, not a ghost. There are no ghosts. Your spirit is what you are inside . . . your mind, your love, your energy, your heart and your soul . . .*you.* You can feel a spirit . . . but you can't see it or touch it." She was listening carefully and I was choosing my words just as carefully.

"Jenny, when I say that Christine is dust, I don't mean the dust you find in the house."

"Oh," she said.

"It's a different dust." I searched for the right words.

"What kind of dust?" She pushed the covers down a little. I thought some more and she waited patiently.

"Special dust . . . stardust."

"Stardust?" she echoed, her eyes widening. I nodded and waited for her. Then she smiled, a knowing smile that told me she understood that not everyone who died was stardust . . . but Christine had been a star.

"Yes . . . Christine is stardust," I said, aching and remembering that silver stars flipped out of her hair when she danced. I hugged Jenny, a long, not-wanting-to-let-go hug, and kissed her good-night. She pulled the covers back over her head and turned out the light.